ARCHITECTURE AND POWER IN AFRICA

Nnamdi Elleh

With Forewords by
David Van Zanten
and
Jane I. Guyer

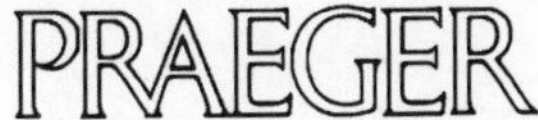

Westport, Connecticut
London

Library of Congress Cataloging-in-Publication Data

Elleh, Nnamdi.
Architecture and power in Africa / Nnamdi Elleh.
p. cm.
Includes bibliographical references and index.
ISBN 0-275-97679-3 (alk. paper)
1. Architecture—Africa. 2. Architecture and state—Africa. 3. Masjid al-Hasan al-Thānī (Casablanca, Morocco) 4. Basilique Notre-Dame de la Paix (Yamoussoukro, Côte-d'Ivoire) I. Title.
NA1580.E443 2002
720'.96—dc21 2002028763

British Library Cataloguing in Publication Data is available.

Library of Congress Catalog Card Number: 2002028763
ISBN: 0-275-97679-3

First published in 2002

Praeger Publishers, 88 Post Road West, Westport, CT 06881
An imprint of Greenwood Publishing Group, Inc.
www.praeger.com

Printed in the United States of America

The paper used in this book complies with the Permanent Paper Standard issued by the National Information Standards Organization (Z39.48-1984).

10 9 8 7 6 5 4 3 2 1

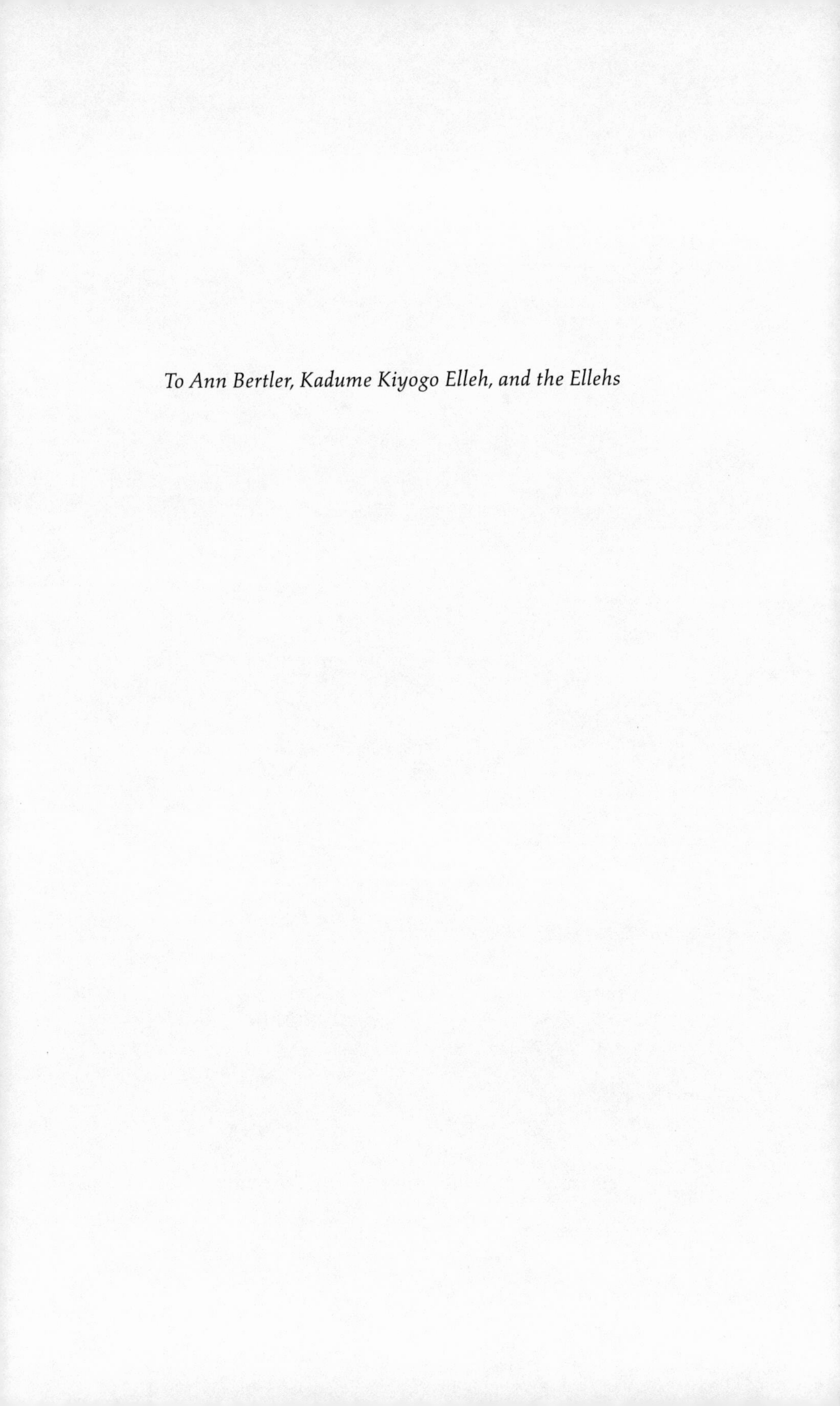

To Ann Bertler, Kadume Kiyogo Elleh, and the Ellehs

Contents

Illustrations

Foreword

David Van Zanten
Professor of Architecture History,
Department of Art History, Northwestern University

In this text Nnamdi Elleh traces the theater and spectacle of the production of two immense religious buildings in West Africa in the very recent past: the Hassan II Mosque in Casablanca, Morocco, and the Our Lady of Peace Basilica at Yamoussoukro, Côte d'Ivoire.

Theirs is a complex, puzzling story, and he follows it across its many dimensions. There is something eerily impressive, to my North Atlantic mind, in the emergence of such structures quickly and almost unobserved at what once was the end of the earth. It inspires a number of reflections.

First, a worldly shrug: In our rapidly homogenizing world, why should not projects of the size of these be possible anywhere? Billion-dollar oil rigs, airports capable of receiving 747s, harbors equipped to fill guzzling supertankers, four-lane highways extending forever across the jungle or desert seem possible anywhere—isn't that what Bouygues, Bechtel, Halliburton are for? The desert sands are ground into concrete, then shaped. Why not into a mosque or a church, oil-rig scale? All that is needed is the command.

Second, nonetheless, surprise: Among all these constructions, these two are points of symbolism, and not ones of political or corporate power—palaces and office towers—but ones of religious force. Such monuments of passion and faith are little theorized in our new world industrial landscape. What might their meaning be? We have coined the word "postcolonial" well before we have had a firm meaning for it—are these buildings a hint?

Third, discomforture: Monumental, symbolic architecture has always been something made by hand, over a long period of years, with difficulty. We remember that "Rome was not built in a day"; that the quality in the medieval cathedrals we have been made to notice is the small differences in their details indicating construction in small increments over long periods; that Hitler and Speer imagined the monuments of the Third Reich as ruins to come; that Cecil B. DeMille imagined for us armies of slaves constructing the pyramids to the sonorous crack of Hollywood whips. How could architecture so expansive come into existence at Casablanca and Yamoussoukro so fast and quietly?

I write this in the aftermath of the tragic evaporation of the World Trade Center towers in New York. Architecture at the turn of the millennium in giving itself to spectacle seems to have taken on a reciprocal flimsiness. So, fourth, horror: because this is the environment in which humankind must live and find continuity, shelter, and safety. Is our built world providing such anymore? What happens when someone gets in the way of such architectural theater? Clearly it is possible in our market-controlled world that we throw the buildings away, but what happens to people?

At the end of World War I a German utopian designer, Bruno Taut, tried to balance his experience of man's ability to produce staggering technological works for destruction and his own sympathy for the fragility of human life, to fantasize in watercolors that, were a free humankind given the means to build hugely with steel, glass, and electricity—and had also the right to play—our earth might slowly burgeon into a vast sparkling colored flowerbed of imaginative lighted constructions, sparkling in the heavens when seen from other planets. Might such works as those at Casablanca and Yamoussoukro be glimmerings of such projections? As the tools of European domination are passed to the dominated, might they come to be manipulated to produce things not yet imagined? If so, what is fascinating to me is to wait and see what might follow.

Foreword

Jane I. Guyer
Professor of Anthropology,
Northwestern University

African monumental buildings are rare in both number and style. They dominate their surroundings by aesthetic difference as well as looming size. The pyramids, the slave castles, the rock churches of Ethiopia, Great Zimbabwe: They stand out not only in scale but also in form, in almost every way different from the buildings of the people who have turned to them in fear and admiration, or simply woven daily life in and out of their shadow. In Africa, permanence and power, their merging in ideology and artistic expression, and their penetration into the lived realities of ordinary people seem to have been plausible only very intermittently. The grandiosity and materiality of monumental representations flourished better in worlds where power thought of itself as categorical and eternal, and where it instilled exacting disciplines to achieve conformity of act and imagination in its subordinates. There, the expressive gradient from mundane to monument was long. The life of the lowly was more imprinted by the powers that controlled them. Specialist artisans worked for clients across a wide spectrum of wealth, playing back and forth across the great divides of social distinction, making small allusions to national icons in parochial places and writing into large public arenas elaborated versions of the small pragmatics of everyday life. The monument stood at the extreme end of a range of allusions to the permanence of power and value.

By contrast, in most of historic Africa, political and spiritual power on earth was not conceptualized as permanent, and the permanence of an imposing structure did not ensure its rulers continuing power over people's life and thought. Most African architecture-for-living was free to respond spontaneously and sensitively to life as lived. Like people's own houses, the palaces added and subtracted chambers and building complexes, cleared new spaces and filled them with functional structures, opened and closed pathways to the outside. The decorative arts were lavished on doors and wall paintings, veranda-posts and shrines, most of which were ultimately movable or replaceable. Indeed, there was a positive value to replacement. The magnificent goldwork of the Akan smiths was often melted down to make new articles as new political stars rose in the pantheon of state. The geographical centers of power could be shifted and communities refounded. Shrines rose and fell in popularity. Some of the greatest and longest-lasting powers over life and death, such as the Ibinukpabi oracle in eastern Nigeria, were not buildings at all but natural sites of wondrous qualities. Maintaining power in Africa has required persisting in action. A single act of construction has rarely offered any key to, or symbol of, persisting influence into the future. In brief, power over people was not obviously realizable or representable in monumental form.

So the new monumental buildings of independent Africa are a departure, an innovation, an invention. The question this deeply informed book asks is a classic one for social history: Where are the "people" in these new expressions and exercises of political power? The answers are fascinating because the creation of the Hassan II Mosque in Casablanca and the Our Lady of Peace Basilica in Yamoussoukro is presented in such detail, as an unfolding process. The reader can trace out all the mediations and ruptures that would create, over time, a new gradient of aesthetic and political linkage between the monumental and the mundane, the political center and its constituencies. By recounting all the artistic, material, economic, and political steps in the realization of these massive projects, Elleh recapitulates the misgivings, oppositions, arguments, economies, and determinations that construct not just the physical monument but an architecture of commitment. He sees the buildings as now complete only in the physical sense. The story of their connection to the people is not yet written. The contentions and participations remain and ferment even now that the projects are completed. The varied sources of rejection—such as the fundamentalist rededication to their own mosques in Morocco and the passive nonattendance of the population, even on Christmas Eve, in Côte d'Ivoire—have not yet played out. And in the longer run, all monuments simply demand attention: not just the gaze of awe but the sweep of the cleaner, the budget allocation of the accountant, and the devotion of the regular user. Elleh asks whether the artistic power of these monuments is sufficient to last beyond the waning of the personal political power that built them. As he points out, some attempts at monumentalism are simply eroded or destroyed when the popular or factional political will turns in other directions. Monuments everywhere are vulnerable to a neglect, which can escalate as the ravages of the elements rapidly reveal any tawdriness of materials or shortcuts and afterthoughts in the design.

Elleh himself is inclined to judge both the mosque and the basilica harshly by these standards. They are misplaced in their artistic and political environments. He sees them—particularly the basilica—as anomalies, outdated utopianisms indexing to a colonial era long gone, and therefore particularly vulnerable to neglect or outright rejection. By the time African leaders had the resources to devote to monumental architecture, their aesthetic visions had reverted to a prenationalist—or postclassic/traditional—repertoire. All the vigor of the populist modernism of the 1960s and 1970s was already considered vulgar or inapposite for greatness in a classic style. Elleh clearly regrets this, in the present work and in his study of the urban planning and architecture of Abuja. The new Nigerian capital city, conceived and built during the oil boom years, was intended not only as a monument but as a way of buffering politics from the teeming masses of popular life in Lagos. His work therefore stands as a plea for a larger artistic space for a nationalist imagination that already carries within it the links to popular life that these foreign structures have yet to create.

Elleh's agenda will be a struggle to achieve. But stating it so clearly and in such detail invites much greater attention to the everyday political and artistic response of modern African populations to their built environment, complete with its anomalies, posttraditionalisms, and legacies of colonialism and populist yearnings. The vision that created these two religious monuments also created many secular buildings that are equally anomalous: the huge lobbies of office buildings and hotels, complete with fountains and chandeliers; the "palace of culture" spaces from which crowds are excluded; the new markets, either far from the central urban beaten paths, or so densely modernist in spatial efficiency that there is insufficient light, storage space, refuse disposal, delivery access, and even room to move. How are they all actually used? maintained? referred to in daily speech and artistic performance? Perhaps people already look back at some selected parts of the real colonial architecture—the tree-shaded boulevards, open verandas, gardens of tropical trees and flowers (all labeled), thatch roofing to soften the sound of rain—as a familiar and even comfortable architecture of public space, in spite of its reminder of history. Popular assimilation of all the various modern public architectures to life-as-lived—through commentary, allusion, and routine use—is the next step to explore, since people do create a modern public life

Here we may see the shrewdness of the builders of these particular monuments. Although Hassan also built palaces, his mosque went far beyond the architectural ambitions of, for example, Mobutu, whose personal palatial homes lie in ruins comparable to the fate of his power and reputation. Both Hassan and Houphouët-Boigny died within a few years of finishing their monuments, but both probably trusted that a devout people would eventually find *some* way of living with, or at least not desecrating, a sacred space. They invited popular participation even if their architectural styles may be alienating. As Elleh writes, popular use will be the proof of their prescience and their ambition.

The space Elleh opens up for study therefore offers many possibilities for new research devoted to the larger canvases and longer-term unfolding of modernity in Africa. This book takes a wholly original topic, treats it with classic punctiliousness, and therefore challenges new work to take the modern forms and expressions of power in Africa seriously as an ongoing, complex, and passionate engagement.

Preface

Architecture and Power in Africa was conceived nearly seven years ago during three separate incidents. I was completing the galley proof for my first book, *African Architecture: Evolution and Transformation,* when the idea for this book began to evolve. I consulted my mentor, Professor Udo Kultermann, several times during the last stages of the premier work. In many of our conversations, he reminded me that *African Architecture: Evolution and Transformation* is a preamble to the work that remains to be done. My next work, he emphasized, should focus primarily on how indigenous African architects, indigenous construction companies, and African urban policy makers and leaders are shaping the urbanscapes of the continent. Kultermann also reminded me that many African architects have been trained since independence, but their works have been overlooked in favor of the works of the more established European firms who have dominated the continent's building design and construction industry since the colonial times.

That fall, 1995, I began my graduate studies in the Department of Art History at Northwestern University. My first seminar, a class of eight graduate freshmen, was about the Bolshevik revolution of 1917 and its impact on the arts of the then Soviet Union. The first slide on the board was the towering Boris Iofan design for the Palace of the Soviets. Otto Karl Werckmeister gave the pointing stick to each student around the table to stand up, go to the board, and speak about the object. Whenever the pointer was handed to another student, he prompted the student to make new points that had not been said or to contradict what the previous student had said. By charging the class so polemically by means of the towering image of Lenin on top of the building that Iofan had proposed, Werckmeister focused the interest of the students on the Soviet revolution and its arts. Also, the first draft of the book on which he is still working, *Political Confrontations in the Arts: From the Great Depression to the Second World War 1929–1939*, was one of our primary readings in the class.

But there is another strand to the polemical stage that Werckmeister had created in our class. To the shock of my seven colleagues and me, he unilaterally promoted me to be the "expert" on "Art and Politics in Africa." From that moment, whenever he went around the class asking questions about the events surrounding the Bolshevik revolution and the arts that were produced during that era, he also required me to tell the class how art and politics have influenced the production of monumental objects on the African continent since the postindependence years. Thus, he got me thinking about art and architecture in a different framework. Also, my thoughts went to Ethiopia, the Mengistu Haile Mariam's regime, and the socialist moments that were produced in that era; to Alexandria, Egypt, where a new national library that promised many things to the Egyptian people had been completed; and to Abuja, the new federal capital of Nigeria, a project that I pursued for my dissertation and about which I released a monograph that explores where the city fits within the schema of twentieth-century architecture and urbanism.

Architecture and Power in Africa, a book that focuses on the basilica at Yamoussoukro and the mosque at Casablanca, represents one strand in the gamut of the discourse that took place in Werckmeister's class. I held independent sessions with Professor Werckmeister throughout the year to explore various aspects of art and politics in Africa. In addition, I was holding seminars with David Van Zanten, where our discourse focused on in-depth analyses of my thesis project on Abuja and the many politically-inspired capital cities and urban design projects in Africa. The socialist-inspired city of Dodoma, Tanzania, initiated by President Julius Nyerere; Lilongwe, Malawi; Nouakchott, Mauritania; Gaborone, Botswana; and Yamoussoukro, Côte d'Ivoire, were also on our list.

The third incident encapsulates the questions that I pursued in the book, but it came later. In 1997, I gave a presentation at the institute—the Program of African Studies at Northwestern University—on Abuja, Our Lady of Peace Basilica, and the Hassan II Mosque. Jane Guyer, the director of the institute, asked: Where are the people in these projects? What is the people's share in the cost of these projects? Thus, the roles of the patrons, the architects, the people, and the monuments in the respective societies where the two religious urban design projects were built became my focus.

My inquiries into the relationships between the patrons, the architects, the people, and the monuments were further reinforced by the events of 11 September 2001. I arrived in Washington, D.C., on 2 September 2001 to complete the last year of my Samuel Ittleson Fellowship at the Center for Advanced Study in the Visual Arts (CASVA), National Gallery of Art. I was putting finishing touches on this manuscript when the incident happened. Following 11 September, I was forced to pull back and contemplate the unspeakable crime that was perpetrated upon the people of the United States of America when the buildings were attacked. Following the debates of pundits from all disciplines and the media closely, I realized that the terrorists chose the most sacred symbols of the United States for their targets.

The terrorists knew that buildings do not stand alone. Whether it is a home, a bank, a church, a mosque, an office building, a capitol building, or a memorial building, a building generally stands on the aspirations, beliefs, cultures, hopes, capabilities, and the achievements of the societies who built the edifice. Architecture and civil engineering are technical vehicles for weaving these beliefs into physical forms. Thus, when the terrorists attacked the World Trade Center, they attacked the shrines that encapsulate some of the most sacred beliefs and achievements of the United States. However, before one can understand these sacred beliefs, one has to dig beyond the spheres of architecture into the cultural, economic, political, and technological contexts that brought the buildings into reality.

These factors have been explored on a broad spectrum as the fundamental instruments that define modern architecture in all its propriety. The styles of architecture engendered by these factors in the twentieth century can be seen as summaries of the ideological forces that shaped the architectural practices of the era. In this regard, exploring the Our Lady of Peace Basilica and the Hassan II Mosque in the sociopolitical context in which they were conceived, planned, and realized implies that we are dealing with one of the fundamental subjects of modern architecture, urbanism, and urbanization of the twentieth century. This is in light of the fact that the buildings were accomplished in architectural styles that are far from what we consider "modern architecture."

The study of modern architecture, urbanism, and urbanization in Africa has one dimension that cannot be ignored: the impact of late-nineteenth-century and twentieth-century colonialism. When a pioneer like Udo Kultermann discussed *New Architecture in Africa* (1963) and *New Directions in African Architecture* (1969), he paved the way for the study of modern and traditional architecture in Africa on multiple levels. Kultermann's work has been followed by: Frantz Fanon (1963), Janet Abu-Lughod (1980), Susan Denyer (1970), Labelle Prussin (1969, 1986, and 1995), Gwendolyn Wright (1991), Zeynep Çelik (1997), Suzanne Preston Blier (1998), V. Y. Mudimbe (1994), and many others. *Architecture and Power in Africa* would have been impossible without the work of these pioneers of African art and architecture. Some of the works that focus on twentieth-century urbanism in Africa raised serious questions regarding colonial urban practices on the continent. And rightfully, they exposed how vile the colonialists were in their vicious architectural and urban design practices.

After nearly half a century since many African nations obtained their independence and began to reconstruct the cities of the continent from the oppressive and endemic psychic ruins of colonialism, *Architecture and Power in Africa* brings one major question to the table: Is it possible to evaluate the urban aspirations of Africa's postcolonial leaders employing the same paradigms and standards with which we evaluate the urban aspirations of the colonialist conquistadors? That is, can we take off the veil of "race" and see the leaders of postcolonial Africa simply through the results of their deeds just as we have explored the deeds of the European conquistadors? What remains when we take off the veil of race?

Perhaps, we will be left with humanity, a complex entity, whose behaviors can be selfishly motivated by economics and aspirations for sociopolitical actualization and self-survival. It does not matter whether you are European, Asian, African, Native American, or whatever you profess to be. Your deeds will speak for themselves whether or not, in the pursuit of the realization of your aspirations, you have considered the possible impacts of your efforts on the human beings around you. These are the questions I have pursued in *Architecture and Power in Africa* on multiple levels and in different scenarios: What was the nature of the relationship between President Houphouët-Boigny and King Hassan II with the populations that they were ruling when they were building the sacred objects for the worship of God? How did the architects translate the visions of the two leaders into physical realities? What do these two monuments mean for the populations in which they were realized?

The setting is a complete cycle of human experience and global confrontations in the twentieth century. The two projects originated in the 1960s, the era of independent moments in Africa and intense ideological conflicts between the

Soviet-led "Eastern Bloc" and the United States–led "Western Bloc." The two projects were realized in the 1990s, the era of the collapse of the Eastern Bloc. The end of the cold war was marked by intense poverty in Morocco and the Côte d'Ivoire, and the adverse economic conditions in both countries were exacerbated by the austerity measures that were imposed on them by the International Monetary Fund (IMF) and the World Bank. That being the case, I explore why the two leaders were determined to celebrate their reigns of power by building the monuments in their respective countries regardless of the fact that many people in Morocco and the Côte d'Ivoire were facing severe economic hardship. This question should be addressed beyond the boarders of Morocco and the Côte d'Ivoire, particularly in light of post 11 September 2001. Hence, it is not out of reach to ask: Why did we celebrate so quickly that we have won the world war, when in reality, poverty and political disenfranchisement of the masses, the root causes of the ideological origins of the cold war, have not been defeated? In Morocco and in the Côte d'Ivoire, Our Lady of Peace Basilica and the Hassan II Mosque, two African "icons of crisis," are alarms crying out that, as long as there is abundant poverty (poverty of education, poverty of mutual respect, poverty of familiarity with the other, poverty of understanding) and political disenfranchisement, the spheres of political discourse will continuously be contested bitterly. Ironically, the builders of the icons of crisis did not envision that the edifices which they had built would function as contested public spheres.

I must confess: I am the first to be guilty of selfishness, one of the faults of which I am accusing the builders of Africa's most ambitious twentieth-century icons of crisis. During a train ride from Fez to Rabat, Morocco, I encountered a man with two young children. I'll call him Idriss. As the ride continued, we maintained eye contact. He was on a different seat. Later, I moved closer and greeted him. There was silence after we exchanged greetings, but I could tell that he wanted to say something to me. Finally, he broke his silence and asked: "What have you come to do here? You rich foreigners come here with your fancy bags and clothes, ride in luxury air-conditioned buses, which those of us standing on the outside could hardly see through. You have your fun, and you go back to your countries without caring about those of us who live here," he concluded.

"No, I am not here for fun. I am here to do research on the magnificent mosque which your country has realized in Casablanca." The expression on his face changed after my comment. He looked away, maintaining silence, but he was not disinterested. "I will speak to you about this mosque," he replied. "I have to make sure that you are not an agent." Looking around his shoulders, and cautiously, he debated whether or not to talk about the mosque. Later, he did. "I was imprisoned for not contributing one hundred dollars for that mosque. It was a rich neighbor who paid for me. Truly, with five children and a wife, I did not have the money, and because of an accident, I can no longer work to earn money as I used to." Idriss cannot walk without the aid of crutches under his armpits. Even then, it was a serious struggle. Our long conversation touched me, but I reduced it to research material. I was a scholar looking for the stories about the mosque, and I had found one among many other stories. This selfish attitude came to a climax at Yamoussoukro as I walked from the bus station to the shrine.

At the terminus of the unpaved boulevard, the edge of the lake, as I looked forward and saw the primary object of my mission in the distance, with great enthusiasm I took the first photo of the object, trying to accommodate the foreground into my lens. When the camera snapped, the sound of the click made someone who was lying down, face up, to roll over, facing downward and hiding himself from being snapped (Fig. 14). But I was too enchanted by the view of my research mission to care about what I had seen. In fact, seeing the "figure" turning over so slowly, as if he was taking his last breath, and about to die, did not register at all in my consciousness at that moment. I was blinded by my own selfishness to research the basilica and write about it. I did not even ask: What is wrong with the man? Instead, I headed toward the object of my mission, overlooking the most important thing along the way, my fellow human being.

It was not until weeks had passed, and the slides had been returned from their processors, that I realized what I had seen. As I stared at the image, I realized that Yamoussoukro was only a moment and a place. It could have been Lagos or any other city on earth. Truly, at Lagos, underneath the endless maze of the overhead bridges, which acrobatically somersault and terminate in multiple directions, shelters where people live can be seen by passing vehicles throughout the year. The under-bridges are homes—which are made of cardboard, rejected plywood, and all sorts of aluminum panels and plastic papers. I also realized that by his turning around, the "figure" was not just a figure. He was a human being with a name, he had dignity, and he did not want to be seen in that condition. How many great moments of human need have I selfishly overlooked, maintained silence before, or removed myself from for one selfishly motivated reason or another?

This text cannot compensate for the moments by which I was tested, but in which I have failed woefully. However, I hope that it serves as a reminder that the built form is not just a thing; it is a sacred ground upon which we all write the stories of our everyday experiences and make meaning out of our existence, hopes, aspirations, and beliefs.

Acknowledgments

I am thankful to the scholars who have provided the road map for me to explore these complex avenues of architecture, urbanism, and urbanization. Many thanks to Professor Udo Kultermann, Dean Robert Greenstreet, and Wendy K. Lochner for their invaluable suggestions during the course of this project. I thank Dean Elizabeth Cropper, Therese O'Malley, Ruth Fine, Bette Talvacchia, Shreve Simpson, Helen Tangires, Elizabeth Kielpinski, Casey Benson, Kim Rodeffer, Peter Lukehart, Richard Ormond, Nicholas Penny, Casey Blake, and Larry Silver for providing a supportive and kind environment while I was completing this book at the Center for Advanced Study in the Visual Arts (CASVA), National Gallery of Art, Washington, D.C. I appreciate the contributions and support of my colleagues at CASVA: Carla Keyvanian, Kara Cooney, Alona Nitzan-Shiftan, Mary Pixley, Barbara Christen, Hajieme Nakatani, Eike Schmidt, and Stephen Pinson.

Many thanks to Penny Livermore, Jane Guyer, David Van Zanten, Gwendolyn Wright, Robert Bruegmann, Mark Henchman, Michael Stone-Richards, Ikem Okoye, Otto Karl Werckmeister, Janet Hess, and Nihal Perera for contributing to this document in different ways. I thank the chair of my department at Northwestern University, Professor Hollis Clayson, and my colleagues for their support. I thank Dr. Patricia Ogedengbe, David Easterbrook, Russell Clement, and Russell Maylone, the librarians at Deering and at the Africana Library, Northwestern University, who went out of their way to see to it that I had all the materials I needed for this project. I am likewise thankful to the associate director of the Program of African Studies, Dr. Akbir Virmani, for his encouragement.

Each project has its own inconveniences, and often, it is closest friends and immediate family who bear the brunt of the inconveniences. As such, I thank Bill and Carole Becwar; Keith Brown; Jack Shepherd; Martin and Lucy Reinheimer; Aaron Vinegar; Ronald Loeffler; Bob and Judy Heise; Tom and Rachel Glennon; David, Mark, Dan, and Leila Bertler; Anne de Luengas; Annette Lott; Nurudeen Amusa; Patricia and Lenny Ochogu; Nwana and Hjani Elleh; and all the Ellehs for their understanding and support while I was working on this project.

Finally, my thanks go to my editor, James Lance, who provided logistical and inspirational support and was instrumental in helping this project come to fruition.

Introduction

ICONS OF CRISIS

> Some men raise temples in the desert. Others raise cathedrals in the jungle. King Hassan's Mosque rises from the sea, inspired by a verse from the Koran. "And the throne of God was on the water." (Leslie Plommer, 1993)

In 1985, President Félix Houphouët-Boigny of Côte d'Ivoire commissioned a Renaissance building that derives from Greco-Roman style to be built following several architectural precedents from St. Peter's Basilica in Rome. In the same year, King Hassan II of Morocco commissioned a colossal mosque in Casablanca, styling its most conspicuous structure, the minaret, after two twelfth-century mosques—the Mosque of Hassan in Rabat, and the Almohad Mosque, the Kutubiyya in Marrakech. Our Lady of Peace Basilica, Yamoussoukro, Côte d'Ivoire (Fig. 1), was completed in 1990, closely followed by the Hassan II Mosque (Fig. 2.) in 1993. Being, perhaps, the two most ambitious religious monuments of the twentieth century, they provide the focus for this book.

The construction of Our Lady of Peace Basilica and the Hassan II Mosque are examples of how two African leaders, Houphouët-Boigny and King Hassan II, changed the foci of their national Departments of Public Works into religious missions in order to exempt themselves from political accountability, cover up mismanagement of public finances, and disrupt the freedom of religious and po-

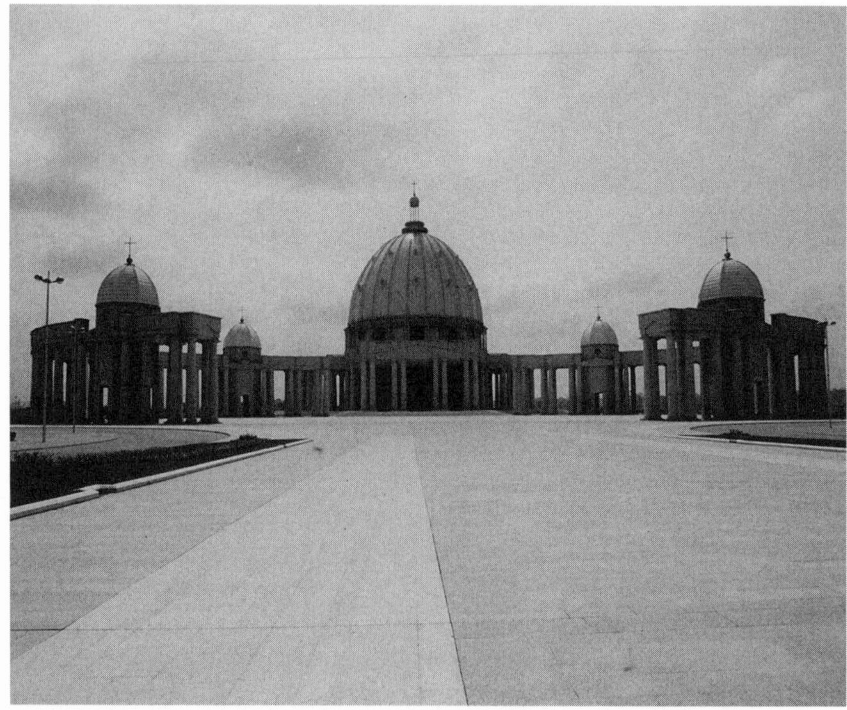

Fig. 1. Northern façade showing the parvis. Photo by Nnamdi Elleh, 1998.

litical associations. By redirecting the goals of their national Departments of Public Works during the construction of the monuments, the leaders also blurred the lines between loyalty to the political leadership, political patronage and punishment, conflicts between national and personal commercial interests, employment, unemployment, and religious devotion. Houphouët-Boigny and King Hassan II are not the only leaders who have exploited public works for political gains on the African continent. Such practices are common. However, the extent to which the two leaders and their followers went to disseminate information masking the political intentions of the projects sets them apart from all other public works on the African continent.

The casual reader might get the impression from writings about the monuments that the two edifices, located three thousand miles apart in two different countries, are totally unrelated and are distinctively separated by religious differences. But looking at the strong parallels between the biographical profiles of

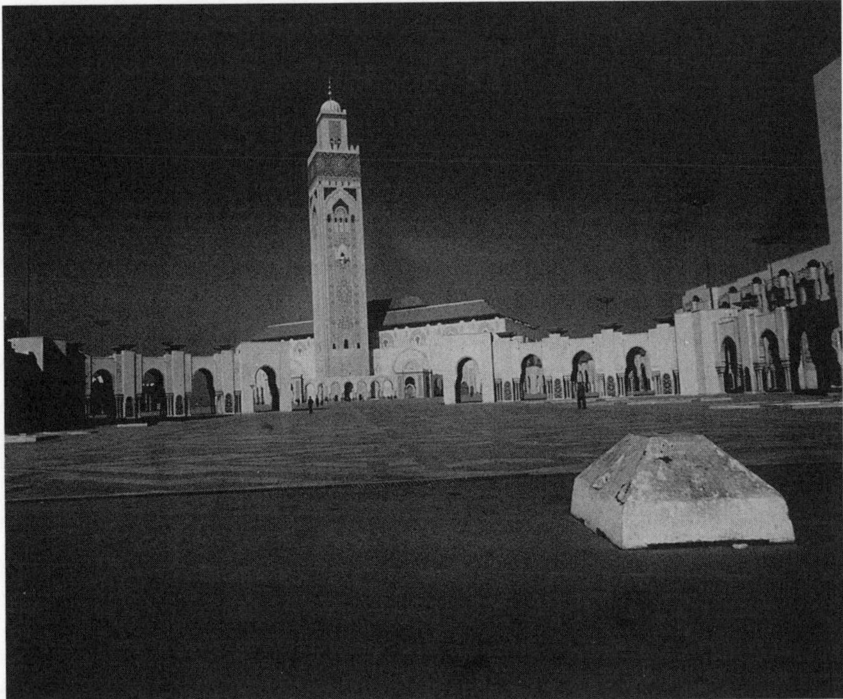

Fig. 2. The entrance to the Hassan II Mosque from Rue de Tiznit, flanked by the library and museum. Photo by Nnamdi Elleh, 1998.

the leaders, one cannot help but wonder whether they were discussing their ambitious monuments with each other. Or perhaps they were competing with each other without communicating, believing that actions speak louder than words, and that the world would be awed by their monumental achievements. Both leaders ruled their respective countries with an iron fist, and both presided over countries that were once French colonies. Both leaders went through the French educational system during the colonial times. They both came from aristocratic backgrounds, enjoyed wearing business suits to disguise their aristocratic heritage, and were immensely wealthy. It was also symptomatic that the two leaders would choose to undertake such monumental projects in a time when many other world leaders were building high-rise structures to project the commercial and industrial successes of their countries.

It is unsettling that the architects who designed the edifices, and the people in the innermost circles of the leaders' governments, dubbed their leaders "The

Great Builders." They vigorously defended the ideological reasons for building the projects as if the leaders who commissioned them were complying with specific destinies imposed on them by God. Their writings often implied that God intended to recall their leaders to the world beyond only after these destinies had been fulfilled. The advocates passionately believed not only that the projects were divine mandates but also that it was necessary to fulfill these mandates according to specific architectural dictums from antiquity. At Yamoussoukro, this meant the replication of a Renaissance building that derives from Greco-Roman architectural artifacts, while in Casablanca it was the replication of architectural artifacts from twelfth-century Islamic monuments.[1] These artifacts are often connected in one way or another with earlier ones as is Our Lady of Peace Basilica with St. Peter's Basilica in Rome, and the Hassan II Mosque is with two twelfth-century mosques in Rabat and in Marrakech.

As outlandish and bombastic as the claims of the leaders and their agents might seem, we need to take them seriously, considering that the edifices have actually been realized. The claims raise issues pertaining to architecture and power, and how these two nebulous concepts can infringe upon the daily lives of the masses in the communities where such edifices are built. They also raise questions pertaining to temporality, political succession, and the roles of monuments in consolidating collective national memories. Most important, these two projects are the epitome of how many leaders of African countries exploit the departments of public works in their countries and public funds for the advancement of their political interests.

We cannot ignore the fact that the projects were commissioned during the most tumultuous years of more than three decades of governance by the two leaders in their respective countries. In 1985, when the basilica was commissioned in Côte d'Ivoire, Félix Houphouët-Boigny, who had been president for nearly three decades, had become an uncontested national icon popularly identified as "Le Père de L'Etat" (The Father of the Nation).[2] In Morocco, economic fluctuations and internal unrest, coupled with the long-standing war in the western Sahara, brought the country to the point of national cataclysm. To make matters worse, a rising interest in political participation by Islamic groups was already shaking the confidence of the innermost circles of the governments of most of the nations of Moslem Africa, particularly in North Africa. Morocco was highly vulnerable to the upsurge of religious movements. As in the Côte d'Ivoire, in the year the mosque was commissioned, the king had been the only indisputable political icon of his country since he ascended the throne in 1961.

I call these two derived monuments *icons of crisis* because of their aim to communicate specific ancient architectural styles and ornamentation, and because of the tumultuous economic, political, and social settings in which the monuments were produced, appropriated, and perceived in the Côte d'Ivoire and in Morocco.

On the basis of my research of archival documents, government publications, journal articles, newspaper and magazine articles, oral interviews, and site visits, this book explores the ideologies that inspired the replications of a Renaissance-inspired Greco-Roman style of architecture and ornamentation at Yamoussoukro, and the replication of several twelfth-century Islamic architectural precedents in the Hassan II Mosque. Côte d'Ivoire and Morocco are not the first countries to employ architectural ideologies for resolving social conflicts. Many countries have done it before, and each case has its own particular justifications. Ideologies arise in certain situations such as those in postcolonial Côte d'Ivoire and Morocco where there are ongoing social conflicts, when as Mannheim (1985, 40) has suggested, "the collective unconscious of certain groups obscures the real condition of the society both to itself and to others and thereby stabilizes it."[3] I begin by examining the reception of the monuments in the press and the ways that scholars have attempted to articulate the relationships between power, architectural styles, and political domination of the masses. I also explore how the practices of using architecture to dominate the masses were consolidated in colonial times and carried over to the postcolonial era under the guise of state ceremonies and rituals.

In Chapter 1, I describe the monuments, how one experiences them, and the social settings in which they were conceived and appropriated. Chapter 2 focuses on the ideologies, architecture styles, and urban design ambitions of the two monuments, as well as the architects themselves. Chapter 3 covers the relationships between the leaders, the monuments, and the peoples of the countries where the monuments are located. The concluding section in Chapter 3 reviews utopian art and architecture in Africa from 1960 to 2000, focusing on specific national monuments that were intended to endow many African countries with new national identities.

This book is concerned with the semiotic intentions of the architecture of the two monuments within the contexts in which they were produced. Differentiating the contexts in which each monument is produced asserts historical boundaries between the basilica and the mosque, regardless of the fact that they share several similarities as far as political leadership is concerned. Moreover, the method eliminates the risk of presenting both objects as the culmination of the activities of French colonialism in the Côte d'Ivoire and Morocco. My approach does not imply that art is a total cultural, economic, and political "index of society," but it does emphasize the uniqueness of every edifice and the multiple uses of monuments like Our Lady of Peace Basilica and the Hassan II Mosque.[4] As E. H. Gombrich (1960/1989, 6) has observed, "works of art are not mirrors, but they share with mirrors that elusive magic of transformation which is so hard to put into words."

ARCHITECTURE AND POWER IN AFRICA

The print media was the first to hammer at the replicatory ambitions of the two edifices. It particularly focused on the phenomenal costs and the grandiose scales of the projects, the styles of architecture they inaugurated, and the opulence of the ornamentation in both buildings. It vociferously delineated an artistic culture that guaranteed a triangulated, dubious relationship between the monuments, the rulers of the respective countries in which they were sited, and the citizens of the countries. As self-appointed judges of the two buildings, the media indicted the two leaders who had commissioned them, maintaining that they had injected their private fantasies into the public spheres of their countries in order to maintain social inequality, stifle democracy, and extinguish social movements that threatened the existence of the regimes.

It is therefore not surprising that the urgency to comprehend the cultural meanings, political power implications such as maintaining the status quo, and other socioeconomic effects that the basilica and the mosque might have on the Ivorian and the Moroccan societies, respectively, inspired press from around the world to boisterously celebrate and denounce the two edifices from the times their foundation stones were laid to the dates that they were inaugurated.

When reviewing the inauguration of the Hassan II Mosque, the Algerian paper *Le Soir* (29 August 1993) was interested in presenting the technological and physical wonders of the mosque, emphasizing that it was the tallest in the world. In Tunisia, both *La Presse* and *Le Renouveau* (29 August 1993) covered the story of the mosque's inauguration focusing on the scale of the edifice and its technological marvels. In Mali, *L'Essor* (2 September 1993) also praised the marvels of the edifice, suggesting that it was the result of the devotion of human genius to the glorification of God. Writing for the Côte d'Ivoire government-controlled newspaper *Fraternité Martin* (10 September 1993), Ibrahim Sy Savane called the Mosque "la perle de Casa" (the pearl of Casa). The *Libreville* (4–5 September 1993) of Gabon praised the edifice and noted the most conspicuous guests at the inaugural ceremony, the presidents of Gabon, Mali, and Guinea. The Kenyan press followed similar tones: *The Nation* (1 September 1993) focused on the great site of the mosque, while *The Standard* (1 September 1993) and *Kenya Times* (30 August 1993) praised it as the most modern mosque on earth. In the Gulf states, the theme of the "modern" was prevalent in the press, particularly the *Arab Times* (1 September 1993), the *Kuwait Times* (29 August 1993), and the *Times of Oman* (30 August 1993). In Pakistan, India, Japan, and as far west as Mexico, the most common reports in the press were about the scale, the religious theme that inspired the location of the edifice at the edge of the water, and its "modern" significance.

The British press also had its views on the mosque. *The Guardian* (31 August 1993) gave it the caption "mighty Mosque lends spiritual dimension touching the most high," and the *Observer* (1 September 1993), pricing the mosque at £528 million, commented on the more than eighty thousand worshipers who had attended the inauguration of "one of the biggest Islamic monuments." *The Daily Telegraph* (30 August 1993) called the mosque "Morocco's beacon of faith" and predicted that it would boost the king's stature as "the leader of Morocco's Moslems, based on claimed descent from the prophet." But many newspapers were quick to point out the controversial aspects of King Hassan II's project.

Writing for *The Times* (30 August 1993), Michael Binyon noted that the edifice was a sign of political stability in the kingdom but commented that the vast expense of "Hassan's treasure on earth" (which he estimated at about £357 million) "has proved controversial in a country where the average annual income is about $500 US." *The Independent* (31 August 1993) dubbed it "King Hassan's message to God and man," cynically pointing out that since the people of Morocco are renowned neither for their affluence nor for their piety, "the expenditure by King Hassan of almost £400 million on a Mosque that is one of the most impressive monuments in the Islamic world must be explained in reasons other than an extravagance born of opulence or the glorification of God."

Our Lady of Peace Basilica did not receive less attention from the press. When Gerald Bourke (1990) prepared his report on the consecration of the basilica for *West Africa* magazine, his headline read: "Pope Paul Consecrates a Controversial $200 million Basilica." His subtitle was just three words: "Beauty or Beast?" Bourke's article drew attention to the key issues about the complex such as the fact that a sixty-room marble mansion was built for Pope John Paul II, just for a one-night stay, during the consecration of the basilica on 9 and 10 September 1990. He reminded the reader that less than 10 percent of the country's twelve million inhabitants are Roman Catholics. The most subversive article about the basilica, by Tournier and Kpantindé, sneered: "Houphouët offre au pape sa 'belle dame" (Houphouët offers the Pope his beautiful lady).[5] In this report, the basilica, "Houphouët's beautiful lady," was represented as a sexual object, suggesting that poor, innocent, celibate Pope John Paul II had been cornered into accepting the "beautiful lady" and compromising his celibacy. The perpetrator of this abominable crime against the innocence of the pope was the politically savvy president, Houphouët-Boigny, who played the role of a pimp in the "belle dame" transaction between himself and the pope. It was a transaction that the Vatican was not proud to accept. But, for its own reasons, it could not reject it either. According to Tournier and Kpantindé, the "belle dame" transaction was so scandalous that it divided world opinion either for or against the edifice, especially among Catholics. The divisions ran along multiple lines: the clergy, class, political affiliation, nationality, and religious conviction. "At the center of the debate is the $300 million US which the belle dame cost."[6] The huge price was a source of embarrassment to the Vatican—considering that the "belle dame" was financed by a country that was plagued by huge foreign debt and a dismal standard of living.

The most socially indicting of all the essays about the basilica are by Murielle Szac-Jacquelin (1992, 34–36) in the left-wing Paris-based weekly *L'Evenement*. Szac-Jacquelin's essay condemned both the edifice and the newly built town of Yamoussoukro as products of the phantom dreams of Houphouët. Szac-Jacquelin was against the fact that the president went to his birthplace, the village of Yamoussoukro, where no urban infrastructure existed before, and built a new town. Calling the edifice a replica of St. Peter's Basilica in Rome, Szac-Jacquelin outlined the extravagance of the project by reviewing the scale, the materials, and its huge cost. Accusing the president of corruption and cruelty, he emphasized the structure was built when the economy was in a downturn, and the majority of the people of Côte d'Ivoire were living from hand to mouth. Joseph Vandrisse called the basilica "the challenge of Yamoussoukro" in *Le Figaro* (10 September 1990), reasoning that Africa had too many economic problems, and the last thing the continent needed was a basilica like Our Lady of Peace. Vandrisse's essay put the burden of proving that the edifice was needed on its planners. In *Le Monde,* Patrice Claude's essay (9–10 September 1990) was along the same line as that of Vandrisse, pointing out that the basilica was the most expensive, the largest, and the most contested church building in the world. *U.S. News & World Report* (24 September 1990) was incensed that President Houphouët-Boigny spent $300 million of his impoverished country's money to build "the world's largest Catholic church." *Time* magazine called it a "monumental dispute,"[7] while in the *New York Times,* Kenneth Noble called it a "mammoth Basilica" suggesting that the "opulent Ivory Coast Church is reviled by many as an insult to Africa's poor."[8]

There are several studies by scholars on the subject of power, political domination of the masses, and architectural styles to justify the strong alarm raised by certain segments of the media against the two monuments. Such studies also explore how architecture is employed as a tool for fudging postcolonial national identity in many newly independent African states. Professor Udo Kultermann's books *New Architecture in Africa* (1963) and *New Directions in African Architecture* (1969) drew attention to the fact that many newly independent African states were trying to develop their countries by constructing universities, secondary schools, and civic buildings in a modernist-inspired architectural vocabulary. Kultermann's work has been followed by many others (Brian 1980; Vansina 1984; Moughtin 1985; Blier 1998; Coquet 1998) who have fleshed out the idea that the concepts of power and the deployment of art as a tool for political manipulation and domination of the masses have been part of Africa's social practices since antiquity. This point is eloquently articulated by Eric Hobsbawm (1995/1996, 11), who observes that "art has been used to reinforce the power of political rulers and states since the ancient Egyptians, though the relationship between power and art has not always been smooth." Such social practices, the scholars argue, continue in the politics of contemporary Africa.[9]

Jane Guyer (1995) observes that wealth is often displayed to consolidate social status in many African societies, such as the Igbos and the Yorubas of southern Nigeria.[10] Among the Igbos, membership in exclusive societies in which the individual is bestowed with a title such as *Ozor* provided occasions for the display of wealth as well as the consolidation of social hierarchies among the beneficiaries of the titled society. Citizens who are not initiated and bestowed with *Ozor* are not allowed to enjoy the privileges that the titled members reserved for themselves. Such is the case in the Ogboni societies in Yoroba land. Sometimes, performances that celebrate specific traditions such as the masquerade dance are exploited as the occasion for the display of wealth and political power in the community. During certain masquerade performances, the participants who choose to exploit the occasion for the display of their power and status in the community camouflage the lines between ceremonial performance and political maneuvering in the ritual dance.

For example, in "The Sublime Dance of Mende Politics: An African Aesthetics of Charismatic Power,"[11] William Murphy (1998, 565) observes that the primary relationships between the Mende concept of "wonder" and the Western concept of the "sublime" are on the "formal dimension of visible effects and invisible forces," suggesting a dialectic of power essential to the study of "African art and aesthetics." Commenting on the notions of "public effects" and "hidden meanings" among the Gola people of Liberia, Murphy notes that there are behaviors and objects that arouse a sense of hidden meanings, have public effects, and sometimes present exaggerated versions of reality. These objects can range from amulets, walking sticks, bracelets, necklaces, clothing, harts, masquerades, to large objects such as buildings.[12] According to Murphy (1998, 566):

> The dialectic of extraordinary effects and mysterious forces links the aesthetic theory of the sublime with the political theory of charisma. Both the sublime and charisma refer to powers transcending normal routines and expectations. Both are signified by the responses of wonder and astonishment at the effects of this transcendence. And both unite politics and aesthetics through a dialectic of extraordinary power.

Murphy (1998, 568) adds that "in aesthetic theory, the concept of the sublime provides a tool for developing the idea of power as wondrous and filled with awe, and offers a heuristic for understanding the logic of power by examining power's aesthetics." The gist here is that the architects exploited architectonic vocabularies in order to consolidate desired visual effects for the personalities of the leaders. Personality is used here to suggest that "art is a form of expression, a projection of the psychological patterning of the individual."[13]

It is therefore not surprising that both leaders aspired to cast themselves as unique individuals who were endowed with creative powers from the supernatural world. Numerous scholars of African art have also explored this notion of the artist as a mystic.[14] At Casablanca and Yamoussoukro, the two leaders intended that their works of art, the basilica and the mosque, should be accepted not just as religious buildings but as reflections of themselves and their ranks in their respective society. This latter point ties in to the leaders' beliefs that their edifices would act as systems of signs and hierarchies of social representations and also would function as settings where state-sanctioned rituals capable of influencing the behaviors of the public could be enacted and performed.

Turner (1986, 75) reminds us that ritual is the "performance of a complex sequence of symbolic acts . . . a 'transformative performance revealing major classifications, categories, and contradictions of cultural processes.'" It is not just the rituals that are important, but the various categories that influence human interactions when they are performed in settings like the mosque and the basilica. Turner also reminds us that human beings are "self-performing animals," and their "performances are, in a way, reflexive." In performance, people reveal themselves to themselves and to other people. The basilica and the mosque are "performances" in the sense that they are attempts to reveal the personalities of the men who commissioned them.[15]

Several layers of issues need to be elucidated here. First, the president's edict to erect a basilica vested all design powers in the hands of architect Pierre Fakhoury, in order to meet the president's economic, political, spiritual, and social exigencies. Likewise, the king's undebated edict to build a mosque in Casablanca vested all design powers in the hands of architect Michel Pinseau, for the same purposes. Fakhoury synthesized certain Greco-Roman architectural elements from the much earlier St. Peter's Basilica and applied them to the basilica at Yamoussoukro.[16] Moreover, since the later basilica is called Our Lady of Peace, people can also conflate the name with "Le Père de L'Etat, Le Père de La Paix, and La Mère de La Paix," the multiple names with which the president identified and projected himself to the world. The metonymy invented by architect Pinseau in Casablanca is less subtle: The mosque bears the king's own name as the Hassan II Mosque, and the architectural ideology promoted there does not allow any room for distancing the king from the edifice. Instead, it strengthened him to declare himself the *Al Amir al Mumineen*—Commander of the Faithful—who guards the Western frontiers of the Islamic world. The title came into use after the reign of Caliph Abu Bakr (A.D. 632–634). It specifically applied to the three immediate successors of Abu Bakr: Caliph Umar (A.D. 634–644), Caliph Uthman (A.D. 644–656), and Caliph Ali (A.D. 656–661) during the formative years of the kingdom. In another metonymized construction the title came to mean both "Commander of the Faithful to God" and "Commander of the Faithful to King Hassan II." Thinking about this deliberate conflation of names and meanings compels us to take note of the observations of Charles Jencks (1995, 21), who argues that "power is aphoristic," and that there are always difficulties in defining or separating the architect's power from the power of the buildings that the architect produces.

Thomas Markus (1995, 8–20) expands on Jencks's points by drawing a parallel between architecture and language, arguing that a building is like a narrative: "From the moment it is conceived, through its design, production, use, continuous reconstruction, in response to changing use, until its final demolition, the building is a developing story, traces of which are always present." On a similar topic Kim Dovey (1995, 36) discusses the issues of place, ideology, and the mechanism by which architecture wields its power. According to Dovey, architecture exploits metaphor and history to construct "mythology through the politics of representation." Scale can be manipulated to deliver colossal or insignificant objects for the purposes of intimidation and domination. Stability and change, disorientation and reorientation, surveillance and privacy, segregation and access, and simulation and distortion can all be manipulated in designs to display the relationships between power and architecture. Dovey (1995, 40) reaches the conclusion that architecture is a "highly political and social art." As a result, "the value of architectural practice is revealed in the everyday experience of the place it creates, constrained as they may be by the imperatives of ideology and power" (Dovey 1995, 40).

Dovey's contribution emphasizes the point that the manipulation of architectural design vocabularies, such as scale, mythology, and elements that suggest a building's stability, can empower or disempower a building, depending on what the architect and the patron want to achieve. Dovey underscores the point that to be effective, the design elements have to adopt specific architectural "styles" that can promote the mythology and ideologies that are intended to be advertised by the building. Such design practices depend a great deal on semiotic representations of "styles" as tools for delineating relationships and differences in design concepts and precedents. I use the term "style" along similar lines as Meyer Schapiro (1994, 51) and Jan Vansina (1984), who suggest that it can serve as a "system of forms" capable of possessing characteristics and significant expression by which we can learn about the personalities of the artist and the outlooks of the society. As a conduit of social expression, style can also influence the moral, political, and religious values of a group through the "emotional suggestiveness of forms." However, architectural styles require that the landscape on which the buildings are situated should be considered. Unlike other kinds of visual arts, such as most sculptures and paintings, buildings cannot be seen completely at a glance. Goodman and Elgin (1988, 45) have observed that a building has to be put together and explored from a multiple range of visual and kinesthetic experiences: "from views at different distances and angles, from walks through the interior, from climbing stairs and straining necks, from photographs, miniature models, sketches, plans, and from actual uses." Accordingly, Eva Blau and Edward Kaufman (1989, 13) suggest that "architectural images, whether in the form of drawings, prints, photographs, illustrations in books and magazines, or the transient images of film, video, or computer screen, are usually produced and used in groups," in order to endow them with the intended visual effects.

The process of exploring a building's architectural style is therefore like reading an ensemble of an architectural text that is inscribed on the landscape, the site where its buildings are located. All users and visitors to buildings of any sort consciously and unconsciously engage in the process of "reading" the architectural ensemble of the building they are visiting in many different ways: from finding the entrance of the building, looking for restrooms, or looking for a place to sit, to actually spending time observing the style of architecture, the material, and the technical manner in which the building is put together (Rapoport 1977, 109–177; Hall 1969). Each of these activities involves making decisions that are inherently tied to the landscape on which the building is located. A landscape, as Duncan (1990) observed, has a rhetoric that we read consciously and unconsciously. Designers of monumental cities and structures are aware of the potential of the rhetoric of landscape as sources of semiotic signs. Moreover, designers also recognize that audiences are always consciously and unconsciously confronted with decisions that relate to way-finding and admiring the aesthetics of building designs in their day-to-day dealings with the built environment.[17]

According to Duncan (1990, 19), the rhetoric of the landscape is important because "it raises questions about the processes whereby the landscape as a text is read and thus acts as a communicative device reproducing the social order." An effective landscape can function as a visual mode of step-by-step enculturation, containing tropes "which encode and communicate information by which readers may, or may not be entirely persuaded of the rightness, naturalness, or legitimacy of the hegemonic discourses." Duncan suggests that our inability to "read our artifactual remains," our affliction with a sort of mass "cultural amnesia," makes the landscape a powerful ideological tool that can be exploited by leaders through the manipulation of architectural motifs.[18] Leaders can invoke artifice and make landscape part of quotidian existence, something people take for granted: "By becoming part of the everyday, the taken-for-granted, the objective, and the natural, the landscape masks the artifice and ideological nature of its form and content. Its history as a social construction is unexamined. It is, therefore, as unwittingly read as it is unwittingly written." The system of signs contained in a landscape, Duncan (1990, 20) goes on to say, functions in much the same way as an allegory—what Jameson (1981, 29) calls "the opening up of the text to multiple meanings, to successive rewritings and over writings which are generated as so many levels and as so many supplementary levels." Although Duncan's essay is about how the kings of the Kandyan Kingdom exploited the landscape to tell allegorical stories about themselves, after examining the scale at which the king and the president built their monuments, it is plausible to apply his thesis to the Hassan II Mosque and the Our Lady of Peace Basilica. As such, one can suggest that the king and the president exploited Casablanca's and Yamoussoukro's landscapes, respectively, in order to tell allegorical stories about themselves.

In the same vein as Duncan's (1990) and Jameson's (1981) contributions, Rapoport (1982, 80–81) suggests that the environment communicates through a whole set of cues depending on the choices to be made. The cues facilitate the situations and contexts, and they enhance appropriate emotions, interpretations, behaviors, and transactions. "The environment can thus be said to act as a mnemonic reminding people of the behavior expected of them, the linkages and separations in space and time—who does what, where, when, and with whom. It takes the remembering from the person and places the remembering in the environment" (Rapoport 1982, 81). Thus, the edifices have the potential to become effective mnemonic devices that can communicate desired messages about the king and the president to the Moroccan and the Ivorian peoples. According to Rapoport (1982, 82), the need for information processing will be highly reduced, and one does not have to think everything out from scratch. "In effect, one can routinize many behaviors and make them habitual." Rapoport's observations confirm Duncan's (1990, 19) suggestion that the landscape can be as "unwittingly read as it is unwittingly written," once it becomes part of the quotidian experience.

If the basilica and the mosque are analyzed as systems of signs and hierarchies of social representations, it is not hard to see how such systems can be deployed and manipulated to serve as tools for "cultural" solidarity among various groups, tools employed for distancing, belonging, and exclusion in the production and the reproduction of social interactions. "These things are needed preeminently to enable the production of material life—to fix an order in which men and women can make their living and have some confidence that they will continue to do so."[19] Rapoport (1969, 2) concurs that monumental architecture and urban design projects are built to "impress either the populace with the power of the patron, or the peer group of designers and cognoscenti with the cleverness of the designer and good taste of the patron." Rapoport's observations apply to Our Lady of Peace Basilica and the Hassan II Mosque. After all, most of the built forms that have the greatest impacts on people's lives on a daily basis are houses and other objects that belong to the majority of the people in the society. According to Rapoport (1969, 2), the "folk tradition" of building "is the direct and unselfconscious translation into physical form of a culture, its needs and values—as well as the desires, dreams, and passions of a people." The construction of edifices radically different from folk tradition, such as the basilica and the mosque, suggests social settings where, in the production and reproduction of social interaction, "agents" depend on structural elements of social systems such as signification "(meaning), domination (power), and legitimation (sanctions)" (Giddens 1985, 19). Monumental architecture, such as the basilica and the mosque, can be considered as settings for human interactions that are privileged with certain representational powers capable of influencing the behavior of the public.[20]

THE PREMISE

To fully understand the ideological trajectories that inspired the construction of the basilica and the mosque, we must reach back to the colonial times and examine the architectural legacies that the two leaders inherited from their former colonizers before we can examine the period after independence through the times the edifices were planned and constructed. With this context in mind, this book investigates the relationships between social hierarchy, national memory, architectural style, and the elite who made the decision to build the two monuments.

During the colonial era, the notion of "abnormal environment" enabled the advancement of certain narratives that equated traditional African architecture with the primitive man who was the "responsibility" of the European colonizer on a "civilizing mission."[21] Such ideas of the African and his building traditions were reinforced by colonialists who built houses, Christian missions, and administrative infrastructures to provide a contrast to "primitive" African "huts" and to present examples of "the new civility in all its propriety."[22] In countries like Morocco, where there was a long tradition of monumental buildings, the

French colonialists practiced *arabisance,* the process of camouflaging beaux arts–inspired French buildings with Islamic façades in order to give them legitimacy, and to make it easier to domesticate the Moroccans. The sites of "civility" and domestication presented to the Africans by the Europeans, including Christian missions, schools, and administrative infrastructures, became nodes of transformation and acculturation of the African into colonial memory. Mudimbe (1994) writes that the process of domestication involved the physical alienation from the African population, the physical reconstruction of the environment, and the erasure of the cultural memories. The objective was to situate the African between his people and the colonizers without completely reducing him to either side. Mudimbe also suggests that: "throughout this long period of acculturation, an average of fifteen years, the candidate learns, in a Foucauldian sense, how to become 'a docile body.'"[23] This statement suggests that the nodes of "civility" that the Europeans introduced to Africa were designed to function as points of tension between the elements that define a person's identity and his or her spatial, temporal, and cultural memory.

Social historians have identified certain colonial architecture ideologies in Africa that vindicate Mudimbe's position: (1) Architecture ideology as an instrument of social oppression and urban segregation.[24] (2) Architecture ideology as a vehicle for fulfilling colonial bourgeois ambitions and exotic desires that could not be fulfilled in Europe, but could be fulfilled in Africa.[25] (3) The application of imported colonial architecture forms for the specific purpose of subverting the colonized subject's cultures, and as tools for creating centers to domesticate colonial subjects.[26] (4) Architecture ideology as a tool for formulating collective, colonial memories among distinct ethnic groups of Africans, binding them into pseudocolonial subjects through verbal, visual, symbolic, and conversion processes (processes that often took advantage of practices of "neutralization, re-creation, and rearrangement of a site, of its geography, and of the values by which a tradition distinguished it.[27] And above all, (5) architecture ideology as a metaphorical "citadel" of hope, a symbolic motif for fudging postcolonial national identity and unity, and as a template for structuring national development policies.[28]

The historical discourse between colonialists and anticolonialists created a "cultural nationalism"[29] among African leaders. Inspired by the ideology that architecture could provide models for national development, and "citadels of hope" for a continent that was struggling to free itself from colonialist oppression, African leaders used the nationalist movements to promote indigenous cultural and social practices, and marketed wares in various aspects of life—food, cloth, fashions, marriage systems, and religious beliefs—while calling for the boycott of colonial ways of life and beliefs. One of the intellectual movements of that era of African cultural retrieval was *Négritude,* a movement led by Francophone Africanists from the continent and the Caribbean. Négritude was founded by Léophold Sédar Senghor, Aimé Césaire, and Lyon Dama of French Guyana in 1934, with the objective of using poetry to counter French colonial assimilation policy, and to advocate the existence of a vibrant African culture.

The French policy of assimilation was based on the notion of the ultimate equality of all human beings but of the superiority of European culture and civilization (with the French culture and civilization considered the finest). Assimilation policy operated on the paradigm that education can remove all racial and cultural differences. Moreover, any African or colonial subject could be a French citizen with all the rights enjoyed by the citizens in metropolitan France as long as he or she were grounded in French culture and civilization. Colonial education policy in Francophone Africa and metropolitan France was designed to breed citizens who would perpetuate the French colonial bureaucracy and ensure political stability in the colonies.[30]

Although motivated by a variety of factors, cultural nationalism resulted in two competing views on the arts and architecture of Africa. One camp believed in the relevance of traditional building precedents in the development of African architecture. The other believed that traditional African buildings, which primarily figure as huts, had no place in the future Africa that they were about to set free from colonial bondage.[31]

Following independence, leaders like Houphouët-Boigny and Hassan II began to rebuild their countries with several ambitious, nationalist-inspired projects. First, they had to address the economic realities of underdevelopment that plagued their countries. They knew that they needed outside economic aid to develop, and to stay in power. As a result, they began to entrench their aristocratic and bourgeois concerns by taking sides in the most important conflict to dominate global events since the end of World War II: the cold war. The president's stance was in direct opposition to the socialist ideology of the Ghanaian prime minister, Kwame Nkrumah. Woronoff (1972, 11), drawing on the ideas espoused by Houphouët at Abidjan in April 1957, concludes that "Houphouët was the spokesman for mutual dependence between Africa and metropolitan countries. He proclaimed a Franco-African community based on equality and fraternity, rather than self-government." Woronoff explains further that Houphouët-Boigny was even skeptical of Ghana's independence because he did not believe that it was a viable option—he did not believe that Africa could develop without the help of Europe, particularly France. "Nkrumah disagreed. Freedom and independence came first. Ghana could have all this as a free member of the Commonwealth, but he doubted whether French Africa would obtain it with Houphouët's policy." According to Woronoff (1972, 154–157), Houphouët-Boigny was so committed to the West, and resentful of the Eastern Bloc, that by 1965 he had already become a McCarthyite.

In fact, President Houphouët-Boigny renounced his association with the Communist Party within the territories of France as early as 1950, following intensive discussions with then French overseas foreign minister Francois Mitterrand, whose election victories under the Socialist Party banner would be despised by Houphouët-Boigny several decades later.[32] Despite the fact that both heads of state had served together in a number of French governments prior to Ivorian independence, as *The Economist* Intelligence Unit (1988, no. 2, 6) observes, "President Félix Houphouët-Boigny is ideologically closer to Jacques Chirac, the defeated right wing contender." The ideological relationship between President Houphouët-Boigny and Mr. Jacques Chirac was so warm that the first overseas visit Mr. Chirac made, immediately after he was elected prime minister in 1986, was to Yamoussoukro.[33] Their friendship has its roots in General de Gaulle, whom Houphouët-Boigny praised during his address to the nation on 7 August 1960, when his country became independent from France. In his speech, the president emphasized to the French delegation in his country that he was committed to following the illustrious examples that he had learned from France, particularly from de Gaulle, who had given freedom to the Ivorian people.[34]

It was highly lucrative for Houphouët-Boigny to clearly align himself with an anti-Nkrumah ideology because it brought him favors from the countries that were totally anti-Soviet. In return, these countries did as much as they could to sustain his stay in power, ignoring his human rights violations against opposition members. He earned financial, military, and surveillance blessings from his allies during the cold war by labeling members of the opposition communists.

The king exploited similar tactics against the opposition in his country. The favors that Houphouët-Boigny and Hassan II gained from their "Western Allies" enabled them to maintain control over their respective countries, using governance models that are quite outdated in the "West." The West was willing to ignore the obvious inconsistencies as long as Houphouët-Boigny and Hassan II fought those it perceived as its communist enemies.

But unlike their allies, who were at the forefront of the cold war and also helped bring it to an end, in the late 1980s and the early 1990s, neither the president nor the king could boast of nuclear missiles, or of any technological contribution that led to the defeat of communism. This denigrated their status to mere pawns in the service of other wealthy interests in the industrialized centers of the world. Such conceptions in the eyes of their fellow citizens emboldened their opponents to challenge their monopoly on state powers in their respective countries. In addition, there were no more communists to be blamed for social disturbances in either country, and several liberal movements in the West were also becoming increasingly vocal on human rights issues.

Subsequently, restoring their status among the most prominent leaders of the twentieth century became preoccupations of the king and the president, who knew that this would also bolster their political status at home. These two powerful postcolonial African leaders resorted to myths that they derived from religion and ancient architectural orders, with the objectives of producing two of the most conspicuous religious monuments of the twentieth century. The unique history of Morocco allowed the king to adopt a cultural nationalist approach to the construction of his mosque, by requiring that indigenous motifs be included in his edifice. On the other hand, the president believed that African tradition did not have a place in the church he was creating. The cultural outcome of the two approaches differs greatly.

I am aware of the complexity surrounding the term "postcoloniality," but it is used here to define the condition of what we might "ungenerously call a comprador intelligentsia of relatively small, Western-style, Western-trained, group of writers and thinkers who mediate the trade in cultural commodities of world capitalism at the periphery" (Appiah 1992, 240). This small, elite group presents a specific view of Africa to the world through their writings and trade, and a specific view of the West to Africa as "modern civilization." As the emergent bourgeois who took up the leadership mantle following the departure of the colonialists, they have begun to occupy different positions across all the professions and leadership positions in their respective countries. As Susan Vogel (1994, 11) has observed,

International art is made by artists who are academically trained or who have worked under the guidance of a European teacher/patron. These artists live in cities, often represent their governments in international gatherings, are more widely traveled than other artists, and have a higher standard of living. Their works are shown in exhibitions, and may be sold to foreigners and international businesses as well as to the governments and to the elite of their own countries. Their works can be concerned with the issues of form, and the meanings can be obscure to the uninitiated.

The president and the king, as members of the newly emergent bourgeois, are like the artists described by Vogel. Our Lady of Peace Basilica and the Hassan II Mosque were intended to gain them international prestige—their monuments, although African objects, are a part of what Vogel describes as "international art."

Are the ideological intentions of these two versions of Africa's contemporary "international art" different from those of their colonial predecessors?

NOTES

1. Davis defines replication as "the sequential production of similar morphologies—made or imagined material forms that are always 'artifacts' and often images that are substitutable for one another in specific social contexts of use" (Davis 1996, 1).

2. I am using "icon" in this context to suggest that the popularity of Houphouët-Boigny and King Hassan in their countries qualifies them as "visual representations which have achieved compelling prominence through frequent repetition in sacred and secular" realms. See Cole (1989, 12) and Panofsky (1974, 26–54).

3. Ideology is a subject that has been addressed by a number of scholars. In relation to architecture, see Tafuri (1976). The work of Lawrence Vale (1992) has numerous examples of nationalist ideologies and architecture. Karl Mannheim (1985, 40) also has approached the subject in relation to larger social issues.

4. See Haskell (1993/1995, 213).

5. See Tournier and Kpantindé (1990, 14).

6. This figure was translated from the 40 millards F CFA that the authors of the article presented as the cost of the Basilica.

7. *Time,* "A Monumental Dispute," 17 September 1990, 136, no. 12, 61.

8. Noble in *New York Times,* 10 September 1990.

9. I also wish to add that African scholars are not the only ones who have observed the phenomena of exploiting art for political gains. In the exhibition *Art and Power, Europe under the Dictators 1930–45,* Eric Hobsbawm (1995/1996, 11) observed that "art has been used to reinforce the power of political rulers and states since the ancient Egyptians, though the relationship between power and art has not always been smooth." Hobs-

bawm (1995/1996) elucidated how political power can make enormous demands on art, and how art found it difficult to escape the "demands and controls of political authority." Hobsbawm also observed that 1930–45 was a period when several European states and their arts were in "public confrontation," one of the most characteristic forms in which "art and power collaborated during the era of bourgeois liberalism." Like Duncan, Hobsbawm believed that the arts under consideration can be read as systems of signs and hierarchies of social representations. He concluded that the objects in exhibition lent prestige to the countries concerned, despite the fact that, "what they had celebrated was not the state but civil society, not political power but economic, technical and cultural achievement, not conflict but the coexistence of nations." Moreover, in *The Aesthetic Arsenal, Socialist Realism under Stalin,* Alanna Heiss (1993/1994, 5) observed that the art produced under Stalin is "conveniently labeled as propaganda art, commercial art, or simply bad realism," because they were exploited for political gains. According to Heiss (1993/1994, 5) the social contexts in which the Stalinist art was produced "recalls a time of political turmoil and tragedy, of repression of ideas and vision, and of the lost lives of hundreds and thousands of people."

10. See Guyer (1995).

11. Murphy's (1998) study explored the dialectics of power from the Kantian tradition through the postmodern applications, especially in the works of Lyotard (1984, 78). Readers should explore the full text to see the contexts in which it can be personality performances in several African cultures.

12. Jane Guyer (1995) notes that these are wealth in the African society and they are saved for special occasions. Also, they can be exchanged for food or currency or used to solve problems just like cash.

13. See Hatcher (1985, 97); Greenstein (1992, 355–375); Schapiro (1994, 51); Vansina (1984, 78); and Rapoport (1969, 2).

14. See for instance, Sarah C. Brett-Smith (1994), in *The Making of Bamana Sculpture;* Paula Ben-Amos (1995), in *The Art of Benin;* and Suzanne Preston Blier (1998), in *The Royal Arts of Africa, The Majesty of Form.*

15. Also, Mannheim's (1985, 40) concepts of "ideology" can be expanded here to include the construction of the basilica and the mosque as ritual performances that stabilize the society in times of crises, especially when established rules, customs, and symbolic frameworks exist, but they operate in the presence of areas of indeterminacy, of ambiguity, of uncertainty, and manipulability. Order never fully takes over, nor could it. The cultural, contractual, and technical imperatives always leave gaps, require adjustments and interpretations to be applicable to particular situations, and are themselves full of ambiguities, inconsistencies, and often contradictions (Turner 1986, 78). Although writing on different subjects, Richard Leppert's (1996, 5) statement that all meanings "results from social practices that are in a constant state of flux and are under challenge by people holding diverse, often conflicting interests," and T. J. Clark's (1986, 6) view that "society is a battle of representations, on which the limits and coherence of any given set are constantly being fought for and regularly spoilt," also confirm Turner's (1986) observations.

16. *Synecdoche* is defined here as "the employment of a part to stand for the whole, or the whole to stand for the part," while *metonymy* is a "figurative relationship in which a word or an icon stands for something else, to which it is related by contiguity" (Duncan 1990, 20–21).

17. There is a lot of work on semiotics and environmental behavioral studies (EBS). It is a vast field that depends on psychology and knowledge of urban design and anthropology. See Rapoport (1977).

18. Although I obtained this concept from Duncan (1990, 19–20), it should be studied in relation to Pierce Lewis (1979, 12), whom Duncan cited in his book.

19. Although T. J. Clark (1986, 6) was writing on a different subject, the questions he raised pertaining to the exploitation of art for the consolidation of different levels of social hierarchies can be applied to these two contexts as far as political leadership, national economics, and the production of wealth are concerned.

20. The author is aware that T. J. Clark (1986), Rapoport (1969), Giddens (1985), Mannheim (1985), Schapiro (1994), and Vansina (1984) are writing about different subjects. Nevertheless, the essays cited here implicate social practices that suggest that monumental architectures are not neutral.

21. See Mudimbe (1994, 105).

22. See Okoye (1993, 13).

23. See Mudimbe (1994, 121).

24. Janet Abu-Lughod (1980), Gwendolyn Wright (1991), Frantz Fanon (1963), Zeynep Çelik (1997), and Peter Abrahams (1954) are among those who spoke and wrote against colonial exploitation of architecture as a tool for oppressing people and are African literary scholars. Often, the authors expressed their feelings in larger narratives that capture the social status of the African people compared with that of their oppressors. The most damaging impact of those oppressive experiences were more psychological than physical, something that Fanon would echo more eloquently than anybody.

25. Professor Mazrui explains how European middle-class men and women fulfilled some of the architecture ambitions they could not fulfill in Europe. They built big mansions on the continent of Africa and staffed them with African servants. Also, they were introducing new modes of consumption to the Africans through their lifestyle. See Ali Al Amin Mazrui, *The Africans: A Triple Heritage,* a commentary written and presented by Ali A. Mazrui; produced by Peter Bate; a coproduction of WETA-TV and BBC-TV, 1986. Robinow (1989), Culot and Thiveaud (1992), and Cohen and Eleb (1998) also are good sources for this subject.

26. Colonial authorities applied architecture and spatial designs to abrogate certain cultural fabrics in the colonized communities. These includes erotic interpretations of dressing conditions that were once neutral, and the exploitation of the condition of colonized subjects as sex objects. See Malek Alloula (1986). Also see Barbara Harlow (1986, ix–xxii) and Mudimbe (1994). Please see Béguin et al. (1983). Béguin et al. delineate how the

French deliberately camouflaged buildings that have beaux arts–inspired plans with façades that make gesture to Islamic building decorations.

27. The literature on the subject of architecture as an instrument of colonial oppression and postcolonial national identity is vast, and it could be approached from a number of interdisciplinary studies. See V. Y. Mudimbe (1994, 134). In "Concerning Violence," Fanon (1961, 35–106) explores how urban layout and psychological oppression is a form of violence in the colonial city. Janet Abu-Lughod (1980) explores the consequences and the sources of the segregated cities of Morocco, especially Rabat. On the other hand, the works of Norma Evenson (1966), Ravi Kalia (1987), and Lawrence Vale (1992), and the essay of Wole Soyinka (1990) reflect how certain countries deployed architectural ideology for the purposes of consolidating their national unity and identities.

28. The theme of the citadel is a popular one in African literature. In reference to colonial urban injustice, it is often presented as the towers or citadels of oppression, connoting the strongholds of colonial capital cities or administrative headquarters. Also, African authors use the term to suggest stronghold of hope and peace and progress, strength. See Diop (1970).

29. See Ehiedu E. G. Iweriebor (1990, xi).

30. See Crowder (1967). This material explores the origins of the French assimilation policy in Africa and how it was applied for the purposes of creating an African culture that is subservient to the French culture.

31. See Okoye (1993, 13).

32. See Woronoff (1972, 11) and Toungara (1990, 30).

33. See *Fraternité Matin*, Abidjan, 7 April 1986, and *The Economist* Intelligence Unit, no. 2, 1988, p. 6.

34. His announcement as a loyalist to the West was in 1959, when he was already the prime minister of Côte d'Ivoire. In 1962, he paid a visit to the United States, Great Britain, and then Western Germany in order to cement his loyalties and economic ties, particularly to President John Kennedy who received him very well and gave him financial and technical assistance. These early relationships with the West were continued throughout the epic years of the cold war, resulting in favors from President Ronald Reagan and Prime Minister Margaret Thatcher in the 1980s. The visit of the American Secretary of State George Schultz to Yamoussoukro during the Reagan years and the red-carpet reception given to him in the Reagan White House are testaments to the ideological relationships between President Houphouët-Boigny and a highly established clique of international bourgeoisie. With the aid of the large French community the president led his country through a period of consistent economic growth from the time of independence until 1977–78 when cocoa and coffee (the two most important export products of the country) prices dropped sharply. Before the drop in commodity prices in 1977–78 and also during the years of structural adjustment programs of the 1980s, and early 1990s when the basilica was inaugurated, Côte d'Ivoire was regarded in the international com-

munity as one of the success stories in "black Africa" since independence. Most of the praises that were showered on the country's economic performance were attributed to political stability that enabled the Côte d'Ivoire to borrow heavily during the boom years. By the late 1980s and particularly in 1990, when the basilica was inaugurated, the country had the largest debt per capita in black Africa, and it had to suspend its debt servicing obligations to the International Monetary Fund and the World Bank (Doucet 1987, 1094; Crook 1990, 649). One of the reasons cited by scholars for the poor performance of the economy is the legacy of the stability that encouraged heavy borrowing. More important, the president was no longer able to manage the economy or deal with the financial lenders as his health began to fail rapidly, and he refused to discuss the succession issue.

REFERENCES

Abrahams, Peter. 1954. *Tell Freedom.* New York: Knopf.

Abu-Lughod, Janet. 1980. "Origins of Urban Apartheid." In *Rabat, Urban Apartheid in Morocco,* 131–149. Princeton, N.J.: Princeton University Press, 1980.

Alloula, Malek. 1986. "The Orient as Stereotype and Phantasm." In *The Colonial Harem,* ed. Malek Alloula, trans. Myrna Godzich and Wald Godzich, 3–36. Minneapolis: University of Minnesota Press.

Appiah, Kwame Anthony. 1992. "The Postcolonial and the Postmodern." In *In My Father's House: Africa in the Philosophy of Culture,* 221–254. London: Methuen.

Béguin, Francois, et al. 1983. *Arabisances, Décor Architectural et Urban en Afrique du Nord, 1830–1950.* Paris: Dunod.

Ben-Amos, Paula Girshick. 1995. *The Art of Benin.* London: British Museum Press.

Blau, Eve, and Edward Kaufman. 1989. "Introduction." In *Architecture and Its Image: Four Centuries of Representation, Works from the Collection of the Canadian Center for Architecture,* ed. Eve Blau and Edward Kaufman, 13–15. Montreal: Canadian Center for Architecture/Centre Canadien d'Architecture; Cambridge, Mass.: MIT Press.

Blier, Suzanne Preston. 1998. *The Royal Arts of Africa: Majesty of Form.* New York: Harry N. Abrams.

Bourke, Gerald. 17–23 September 1990. "Pope Consecrates a Controversial $200m Basilica, Beauty or Beast?" *West Africa,* no. 3812: 2480.

Brett-Smith, Sarah C. 1994. *The Making of Bamana Sculpture: Creativity and Gender.* Cambridge: Cambridge University Press.

Brian, Robert. 1980. *Art and Society in Africa.* London: Longman.

Çelik, Zeynep. 1997. *Urban Forms and Colonial Confrontations. Algiers under French Rule.* Berkeley: University of California Press.

Clark, Timothy J. 1986. *The Painting of Modern Life: Paris in the Art of Manet and His Followers.* Princeton, N.J.: Princeton University Press.

Cohen, Jean-Louis Cohen, and Monique Eleb. 1998. *Casablanca Myth et Figure d'Une Aventure Urbaine.* Casablanca: Éditions Hazan.

Cole, Herbert, M. 1989. *Icons: Ideals and Power in the Art of Africa.* Washington, D.C. Published for the National Museum of African Art by the Smithsonian Institution Press, 12.

Coquet, Michèle. 1998. *African Royal Court Art,* trans. by Jane Marie Todd. Chicago: University of Chicago Press.

Crook, Richard. 1990. "Politics, the Cocoa Crisis, and Administration in Côte d'Ivoire." *Journal of Modern African Studies* 28, no. 4: 649–669.

Crowder, Michael. 1967. *A Study in French Assimilation Policy.* London: Methuen.

Culot, Maurice, and Jean-Marie Thiveaud, et al. 1992. *Outre-Mer. Architecture Francais.* Institute Francais D'Architecuture. Paris: Mardaga.

Davis, Whitney. 1996. *Replications Archeology Art History Psychoanalysis.* With the editorial assistance of Richard W. Quinn. University Park: Pennsylvania State University Press.

Denyer, Susan. 1978. *African Traditional Architecture: An Historical and Geographical Perspective.* London: Heinemann.

Diop, David. 1970. "The Vultures." In *New African Literature and the Arts,*Vol. 2, ed. Joseph Okpaku. New York: Thomas Y. Crowell.

Doucet, Lyse. 8 June 1987. "Côte d'Ivoire Unable to Pay." *West Africa,* no. 3643: 1094–1095.

Dovey, Kim. 1995. "Place/Power." *Architectural Design* 65, no. 3/4 (March–April): 36–40.

Duncan, James, S. 1990. *The City as a Text: The Politics of Landscape Interpretation in the Kandyan Kingdom.* Cambridge: Cambridge University Press.

Evenson, Norma. 1973. *Two Brazilian Capitals: Architecture and Urbanism in Rio de Janeiro and Brasília.* New Haven, Conn.: Yale University Press.

Fanon, Frantz. 1963. "Concerning Violence." In *The Wretched of the Earth,* trans. Constance Farrington, preface by Jean-Paul Sartre, 35–106. New York: Grove Press.

Giddens, Anthony. 1985. *A Contemporary Critique of Historical Materialism: Nation State and Violence.* Volume 2. Berkeley: University of California Press.

Gombrich, Ernst Hans. 1969. *Art and Illusion: A Study in the Psychology of Pictorial Representation.* 2d ed. Princeton, N.J.: Princeton University Press.

Goodman, Nelson, and Catherine Elgin. 1988. *Receptions in Philosophy and Other Arts and Sciences.* Indianapolis and Cambridge: Hackett Publishing.

Greenstein, Fred. 1992. "Personality and Politics." In *Encyclopedia of Government and Politics,* ed. Mary Hawkesworth and Maurice Kogan, 355–375. London and New York: Routledge.

Guyer, Jane I., ed. 1995. *Money Matters: Instability, Values, and Social Payments in the Modern History of West African Communities.* Portsmouth, N.H.: Heinemann; London: J. Currey.

Hall, Edward Twitchell. 1959. *The Silent Language.* New York: Doubleday.

———. 1969. *The Hidden Dimension.* Garden City, N.Y.: Doubleday.

Harlow, Barbara. 1986. "Introduction." In *The Colonial Harem,* by Malek Alloula, trans. Myrna Godzich and Wald Godzich, ix–xxii. Minneapolis: University of Minnesota Press.

Haskell, Francis. 1993/1995. *History and Its Images: Art and the Interpretation of the Past.* New Haven, Conn.: Yale University Press.

Hatcher, Evelyn Payne. 1985. *Art as Culture: An Introduction to the Anthropology of Art.* New York: University Press of America.

Heiss, Alanna. 1993/1994. "Foreword." In *The Aesthetic Arsenal, Socialist Realism under Stalin.* New York and Moscow: Institute for Contemporary Art, P.S.1 Museum, and *Pravda.*

Hobsbawm, Eric. 1995/1996. "Foreword." In *Art and Power, Europe under the Dictators 1930–45,* comp. Dawn Andes et al. London: Hayward Gallery.

Iweriebor, Ehiedu. 1990. *Radical Nationalism in Nigeria: The Zikist Movement and the Struggle for Liberation, 1945–1950.* Ph.D. diss., School of Arts and Science, Columbia University, 1990, p. xi.

Jameson, Fredric. 1981. *The Political Unconscious: Narrative as a Socially Symbolic Act.* Ithaca, N.Y.: Cornell University Press.

Jencks, Charles. 1995. "Aphorisms on Power." *Architectural Design* 65, no. 3/4 (March–April): 21–35.

Jewsiewicki, Bogumil, ed. 1989. *Art et Politiques en Afrique Noire.* Canada: Association Canadienne des Études Africaines.

Kalia, Ravi. 1987. *Chandigarh in Search of an Identity.* Carbondale: Southern Illinois University Press.

Kultermann, Udo. 1963. *New Architecture in Africa,* trans. Ernst Flesch. London: Thames and Hudson.

———. 1969. *New Directions in African Architecture,* trans. John Maass. New York: George Braziller.

———. 1999. *Contemporary Architecture in the Arab World.* New York: McGraw-Hill.

Leppert, Richard D. 1996. *Art and the Committed Eye: The Cultural Functions of Imagery.* Boulder, Colo.: Westview Press.

Lyotard, Jean-François. 1984. *The Postmodern Condition: A Report on Knowledge,* translated by Geoff Bennington and Brian Massumi. Minneapolis: University of Minnesota Press.

Mannheim, Karl. 1985. *Ideology and Utopia: An Introduction to the Sociology of Knowledge.* New York: Harcourt Brace.

Markus, Thomas. 1995. "What Do Buildings Have to Do with Power?" *Architectural Design* 65, no. 3/4 (March–April): 8–20.

Moughtin, J. C. 1985. *Hausa Architecture.* London: Ethnographica in association with Institute of Planning Studies, University of Nottingham.

Mudimbe, V. Y. 1994. "Domestication and the Conflict of Memories." In *The Idea of Africa,* 105–153. Bloomington: Indiana University Press.

Murphy, William, P. 1998. "The Sublime Dance of Mende Politics: An African Aesthetic of Charismatic Power." *American Ethnologist* 25, no. 4: 563–582.

Okoye, Ikem. 1993. "Good News for Modern Man? Architecture as Evangelical Mission in Southern Nigeria." *Passage* 4, no. 1 (Fall): 13.

Ostling, N. Richard. 3 July 1989. "The Basilica in the Bush; The Biggest Church in Christendom Arises in the Ivory Coast." *Time* 134, no. 1: 38.

Panofsky, Erwin. 1974. "Iconography and Iconology: An Introduction to the Study of Renaissance Art." In *Meaning in the Visual Arts: Papers in and on Art History,* 26–54. Woodstock, N.Y.: Overlook Press.

Prussin, Labelle. 1969. *Architecture in Northern Ghana; A Study of Forms and Functions.* Berkeley: University of California Press.

———. 1986. *Hatumere: Islamic Design in West Africa.* Berkeley: University of California Press.

———. 1995. *African Nomadic Architecture: Space, Place, and Gender.* Washington, D.C.: Smithsonian Institution Press, National Museum of African Art.

Rapoport, Amos. 1969. *House Form and Culture.* Englewood Cliffs, N.J.: Prentice Hall.

———. 1977. *Human Aspects of Urban Form Towards a Man Environment Approach to Urban Form and Design.* New York: Pergamon Press.

———. 1982. *The Meaning of the Built Environment.* London: Sage.

Robinow, Paul, 1989. "Techno-Cosmopolitanism." In *French Modern,* 277–319. Cambridge, Mass.: MIT Press.

Schapiro, Meyer. 1994. *Theory and Philosophy of Art: Style, Artist, and Society. Selected Papers.* New York: George Braziller.

Soyinka, Wole. 1990. "Development *and* Culture." In *Challenges of Leadership in African Development,* ed. Olusegun Obasanjo and Han's d'Orville, 153–191. London: Crane Russak.

Szac-Jacquelin, Murielle. 12–18 November 1992. "Côte d'Ivoire: Folies Africaines aux Frais de Qui?" *L'Evenement,* no. 419: 34–36.

Tafuri, Manfredo. 1976. *Architecture and Utopia, Design and Capitalist Development,* trans. Barbara Lui La Penta. Cambridge, Mass.: MIT Press.

The Economist Intelligence Unit. 1988. *Country Profile Côte d'Ivoire,* no. 2, p. 6.

Time. 17 September 1990. "A Monumental Dispute," 136, no. 12: 61.

Toungara, Jeanne Maddox. 1990. "The Apotheosis of Côte Ivoire's Nana Houphouët-Boigny." *Journal of Modern African Studies* 28, no. 1: 23–54.

Tournier, Pascal, and Francis Kpantindé. 1990. "Houphouët offre au Pape sa "Belle Dame." *Jeune Afrique,* no. 1549: 14.

Turner, Victor. 1986. *The Anthropology of Performance.* New York: PAJ Publications.

U.S. News & World Report. 24 September 1990. "Felix Houphouët-Boigny." 109, no. 12: 23.

Vale, Lawrence. 1992. *Architecture, Power, and National Identity.* New Haven, Conn.: Yale University Press.

Vansina, Jan C. 1984. *Art History in Africa: An Introduction to Method.* New York: Longman.

Vogel, Susan. 1994. "Foreword." In *Africa Explores 20th Century African Art,* ed. Susan Vogel, assisted by Ima Ebon, 8-13. New York: Center for African Art, New York and Prestel.

Woronoff, Jon. 1972. *West African Wager: Houphouët versus Nkrumah.* Metuchen, N.J.: Scarecrow Press.

Wright, Gwendolyn. 1991. "Introduction." In *The Politics of Design in French Colonial Urbanism.* Chicago: University of Chicago Press.

Chapter 1

Experiencing the Monuments

THE PROCESS

Keeping in mind that the process of exploring a building's architecture is like reading an ensemble of an architectural text on the landscape, a process that requires a wide range of visual and kinesthetic experiences, does the location of the Hassan II Mosque and the basilica of Our Lady of Peace enhance or inhibit the pedestrian's ability to experience the edifices? Are the urban and architectural designs in harmony with their respective surroundings, or are they out of contexts? Since movement is an experience in time through a succession of spaces, and one of the most fundamental functions of architecture is "the articulation of space so as to produce in the participator a definite space experience in relation to previous and anticipated space experiences,"[1] do these edifices facilitate participators' comfort and enhance the performance of their intended activities in the buildings? Does the architectural design enhance or diminish the way that people experience light and shade, void and delimited spaces, hot and cold, color and texture, and noise and silence within the complexes? Do the designs provide the appropriate cues for religious activities and behavioral patterns in specific spaces, as the patrons and the designers claimed?

Hassan II Mosque

Realized at an estimated price of US$400 million to US$700 million,[2] is the Hassan II Mosque a citadel of hope for the people of Morocco? As it stands today, the mosque accidentally recaptures the hide-and-seek mysteries and the auras of the labyrinthine medieval city, even though it is located in Casablanca, a carefully laid out city in the baroque style.[3] Unless a visitor happens to be in one of the newly built high-rise structures in the town, the location of the mosque does not provide any warning that the individual is about to arrive at one of the tallest religious buildings of the twentieth century. As a pedestrian, the only way to view the minaret of the structure from a distance is to approach the complex on the roads that border the Atlantic Ocean: from the west, on the beautiful, meandering Boulevard Corniche, which becomes Boulevard Sidi Mohammed Ben Abdellah and terminates at the roundabout that abuts the southern terminus of the complex (Fig. 3). From the northeast, it is along Boulevard Des Almohads, which begins at the junction of the Port of Casablanca and Boulevard Félix Houphouët-Boigny. The two streets end at the roundabout at the eastern terminus of the complex. The coastal road between Boulevard Sidi Mohammed Ben Abdellah and Boulevard Des Almohads is underground in order to direct the traffic to and from the parking structures below the complex, and also to enable the continuous flow of traffic along the coast. From either direction, one can walk into the complex grounds without passing through the main gate. These side entrances lead into the esplanade, a void that covers an area of 30,000 square meters and can hold up to 80,000 people during prayers.

The main entrance is on Rue de Tiznit. Compared with the scale of the complex, it is obscure, and it is flanked on the west by the library and on the east by the museum (Figs. 2, 3, and 4). Both structures were planned and built when the mosque was under construction. Together, the three structures form the Hassan II Mosque complex. The library and the museum are two identical L-shaped structures facing each other (Figs. 3 and 4). The long wings of the two structures make up the eastern and western boundaries of the esplanade, while the short wings enclose the complex grounds along Rue de Tiznit. The most prominent structures on either side of the main entrance are the walls of the short wings of the library and the museum (Fig. 4). Each end wall is attached to a semicircular arcade that consists of multiple horseshoe-shaped arches that are linked to one another by clusters of columns (Fig. 2). It is the first object to intercept the

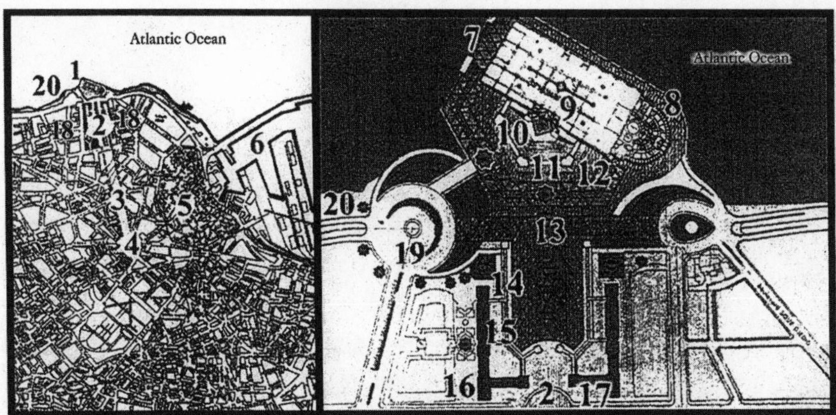

Fig. 3. A sketch of the part of the city of Casablanca showing: (1) the location of the Hassan II Mosque, (2) main entrance on Rue de Tiznit, (3) the proposed boulevard from Hassan II Mosque to the center of the city, (4) a major axis inside the city leading to the mosque through the proposed boulevard, (5) the Old City or Casbah/Medina, (6) the Port of Casablanca, (7) the first floor plan, (8) the *madrassa,* (9) the minaret, (10) the stepped courtyard, (11) the arcade separating the courtyard from the esplanade, (12) one of the three bastions of the arcade of the courtyard showing the fountain, (13) the esplanade, (14) the arcades that screen the library and the museum, (15) courtyards between the library, the museum, and the arcades, (16) the library, (17) the museum, (18) Rue de Tiznit, (19) roundabout, and (20) underground bypass.

person who walks from Rue de Tiznit into the complex grounds. Here, imagine the arcade as a large funnel, with its mouth facing Rue de Tiznit and its long tube (the pathway into the complex) pointing in the direction of the esplanade. It gets wider as one walks further into the esplanade, and it turns into an L shape like the library and the museum (Figs. 3 and 4).

Pinseau's design for the entrance to the complex has do with the manner in which he wanted visitors to the shrine to experience the spaces. First the arcades run parallel to the library and the museum. The one nearest to the library works in harmony with it to form multiple courtyards, and it screens in the spaces between them. The same applies to the museum, leaving the esplanade as the most centrally enclosed space. Second, as one proceeds into the esplanade from Rue de Tiznit, the arcades frame the view of the expansive esplanade and focus the attention on the main edifice that lies straight ahead (Fig. 4). Third, the configuration of the arcades with clusters of double columns amplifies the rhythm of

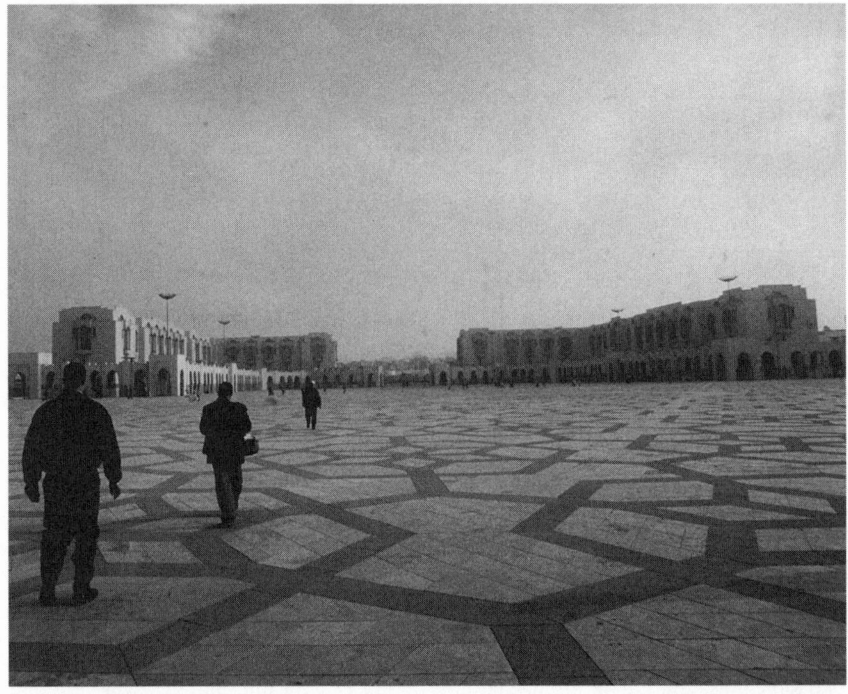

Fig. 4. Walking south across the vast esplanade toward Rue de Tiznit. The museum is on the left (east) and the library is on the right (west). Photo by Nnamdi Elleh, 1998.

interlaced multiple horseshoe-shaped arches and gives the pedestrian a sense of transition through multiple interconnected spaces.

The esplanade expands into a void once the individual arrives at its center. At this point, the library and the museum appear as small structures because of the overwhelming scale of the esplanade, and another arcade that separates the courtyard of the mosque from the esplanade clearly comes in view (Fig. 5). This arcade screens the lower part of the southern façade of the edifice in order to arouse the curiosity of the individual to explore what lies ahead. The edifice is now the wedge between the person and the expansive ocean, which is visible in all directions except if the person is looking backward (south) toward Rue de Tiznit (Fig. 4). Here, the pedestrian's sense of security in a designed setting is broken. The individual feels like a tiny creature in the middle of a void (Fig. 5). In some plazas one can feel like an object on display and want to move closer to the edge, but standing at the center of the esplanade of the edifice is even more overwhelm-

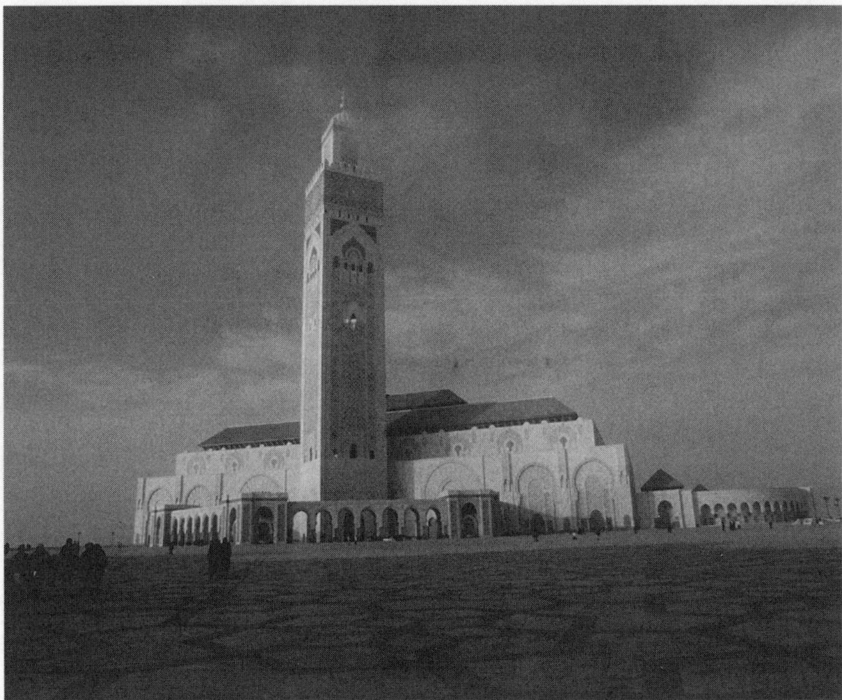

Fig. 5. The center of the expansive esplanade showing the main edifice on the edge of the ocean. South elevation. The arcade separating the esplanade from the courtyard of the mosque is in the foreground.

ing, especially when there are few people around. It dwarfs the individual, making him or her anxious to move closer to the mosque, the library, or the museum. When it is not too hot to be outside, the embankments around the complex provide better spaces for relaxation. They are decorated with tiles and have several planters and flowers around them. The rhythmic crashing of the ocean waves make these embankments ideal spots for meditation and daydreaming.

It is at a much closer proximity, just before one enters into the courtyard of the mosque, that one will begin to get a sense of the monumental scale of the edifice (Fig. 5). Here, people look very small when they stand next to the arcade, which encloses the courtyard of the edifice. It is as close as one can get to the edifice and still see the top of its minaret, which has two of its south façades tilted at forty-five-degree angles from Rue de Tiznit. The three major ornate bastions, which have two fountains each on the sides facing the esplanade, also become

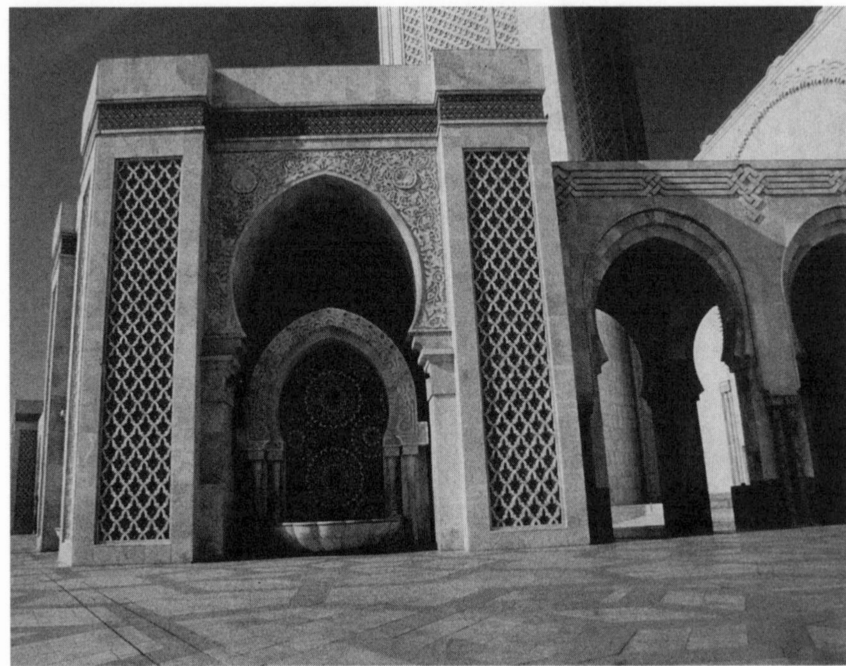

Fig. 6. Detail of the arcade that separates the esplanade from the courtyard of the mosque. It also shows one of the square bastions and its ornate fountain. Photo by Nnamdi Elleh, 1998.

legible (Figs. 5 and 6). On a sunny day, the granite pavements, the multiple colors of the *zellij*, the marbles on the walls, columns, and reinforcements; the green roof; and the curving blue ocean background are showered by sunlight, giving the ensemble the look of a large sculptured cube of gold, with multicolored spots and a green cap (Fig. 5).

The moment of transition from the vast esplanade into the courtyard of the mosque reveals the fact that the arcade of the courtyard of the mosque is maneuvering several angles in order to maintain the symmetrical design of the structure (Figs. 7 and 8). The overscaled minaret with its twenty-five-square-meter (fifty-six-square-foot) base forms the center of the symmetry. Inside the mosque's courtyard, the overscaled minaret is flanked on either side by extraordinarily large portals, and outside the courtyard by two slightly smaller ones (Fig. 5). Standing on the steps of the courtyard and looking west, one gets a glimpse of the main (southern) façade of the edifice—although one cannot see

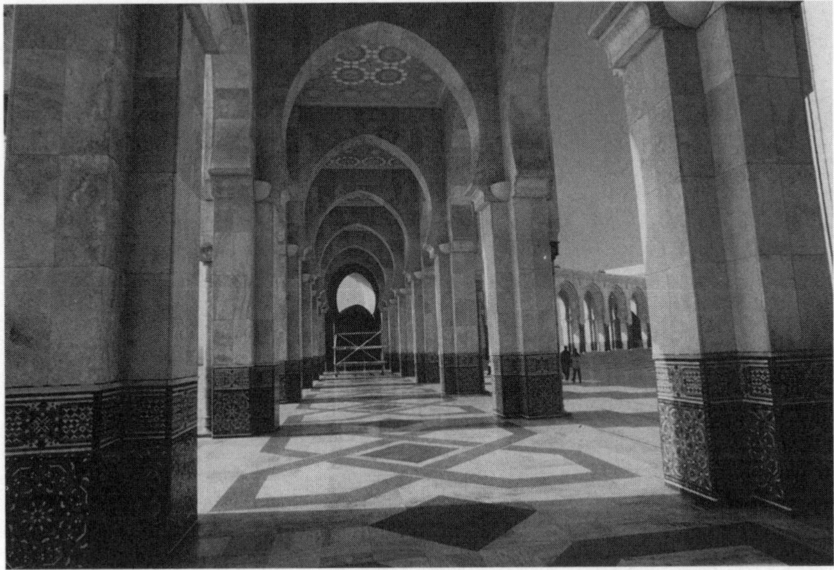

Fig. 7. Walking through the arcade that separates the esplanade from the courtyard of the mosque. Photo by Nnamdi Elleh, 1998.

all of it at once, because the colossal minaret obstructs the view (Fig. 8). Above all, the stepped courtyard and the large, ornate archways leading to the base of the minaret are finished so well that they hold one's attention for a long time.[4]

The minaret rises to a total height of 200 meters (650 feet) from its base, including the jamour, upon which the 15-meter (48.79-foot) copper finial is mounted (Figs. 2 and 9). The finial is equipped with a laser beam with a range of thirty kilometers (twenty miles). It points in the direction of the *qibla,* which always indicates the direction of Mecca. The laser beam also serves as a lighthouse for vessels coming into the Casablanca harbor. The copper finial on the top of the minaret shines brightly on a sunny day, to the extent that one can notice three major colors on the minaret: the white marble, the green *zellij,* and the shining golden finial. Intricately carved white marbles with diamond-shaped traceries make up the primary covering of the heavily reinforced concrete minaret. The two friezes on its tower are also visible from the ground. The frieze at the top of the tower consists of one large sixteen-point star *zellij,* which is filled in with numerous colorful stones. The sixteen-point star is flanked on both sides by two semicircular sixteen-point stars.

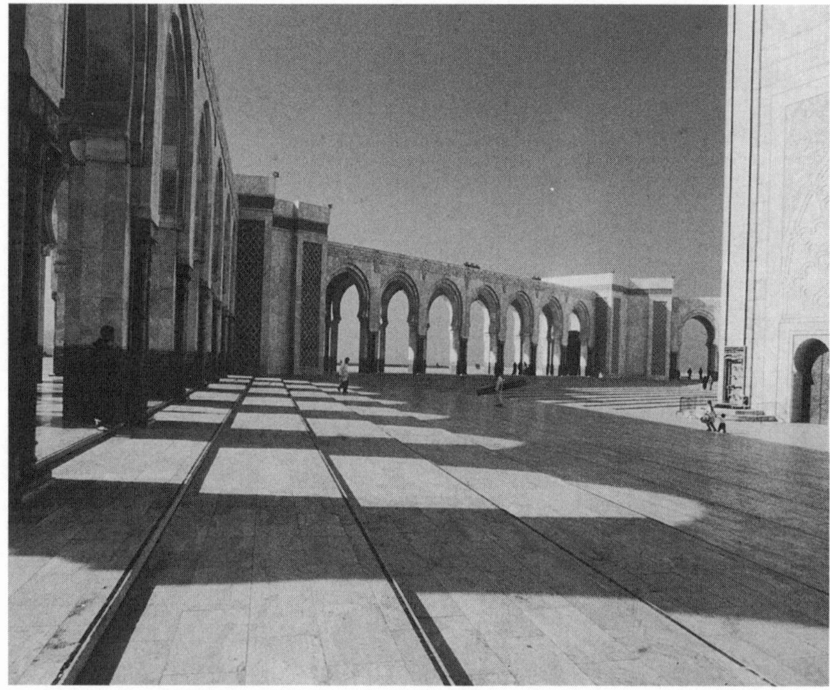

Fig. 8. The stepped courtyard of the mosque. The arcade and two of its bastions are visible on the left, while the protruding base of the minaret is on the right. Photo by Nnamdi Elleh, 1998.

The friezes above the tympanums of the minaret's archways are clad with delicate traceries of carved marble (Fig. 9). The archways of the minaret are closed with large intricately decorated titanium doors that glow with a dark brown sheen when the sun strikes them, and one cannot help but linger for a while to absorb the beauty of the sculptured doors and surrounding structures. The minaret is serviced by two elevators and a staircase up to the turret level. The walls of its vestibule are delicately garnished with green *zellij*, copper, polished granite, and gold-colored marble. The dome of the vestibule of the minaret is also lavishly decorated. It has intensive combinations of stucco, marble, copper, a rim that is woven into a hive of glowing stalactites, and a gigantic ornate chandelier from Italy. Over all, the tower is far too tall and heavy, and it is reported that the structure supporting the minaret's foundations "has four times the strength of the tunnel under the English Channel" (Holod and Khan 1997, 60).

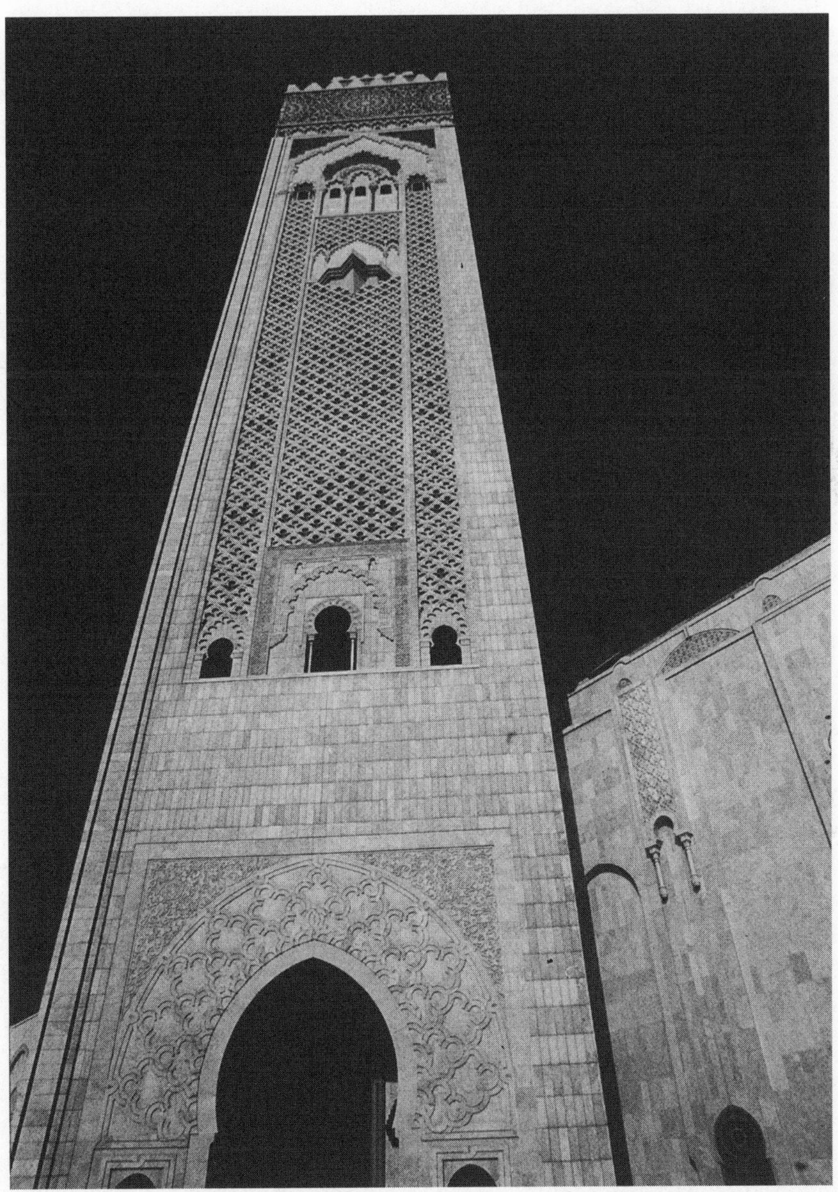

Fig. 9. The minaret. Photo by Nnamdi Elleh, 1998.

The next feature on the edifice that would hold the individual's attention in the courtyard is the huge portals on the south façade. The tympanum consists of a half cylindrical denture of carved marble, which rises to the frieze of the edifice. It is anchored on two pairs of green marble columns that have sculptured capitals. The portal is flanked by two smaller doors, one on each side, within recessed grooves, to emphasize the symmetry of the façade. The tympanums are made of a series of interwoven stars that are formed by chiseled marbles, which are filled with colorful *zellij* consisting of cubes of blue, green, and yellow stones. By leaving some of the chiseled points unfilled, shadows that give the illusion of dark stones are formed on the tympanums. The portals outside the courtyard have single columns underneath the tympanums, while those inside the courtyard have double columns. Also, the tympanums have different shapes, and the details on the doors are different. The overall effect of the lozenges during sunlight is that of a golden color over the dark brown titanium doors. Together, the minaret, the green roof, the arcade and its bastions, and the six large portals give the mosque its primary external character (Figs. 5–9).

As one moves east, outside the courtyard of the mosque, a large green *zellij* fountain in the shape of a twelve-point star forms a strong visual element on the ground. The large twelve-point star helps give a sense of transition as one moves toward the ambulatory veranda that wraps around the *madrassa* (Islamic school). Here, the articulation of the horseshoe-shaped entrance arches, which negotiate the semicircular turn from the eastern to the northern façade, also emphasizes the symmetrical intentions of the design (Figs. 5 and 10). This is achieved by giving primacy to three main arches that form part of the ambulatory arcade around the *madrassa.* The first arched portal of the madassa is located at the point where the southern façade joins the *madrassa.* The second is at the center of the eastern façade; and the third on the north elevation—at the point where the wall of the mosque also joins the wall of the *madrassa.* Of these three primary arches, the one directly on the eastern elevation is flanked on either side by smaller horseshoe archways to emphasize the symmetry of the design.

The northern elevation has nine bays that define nine portals. These are decorated like the two major portals outside the courtyard of the southern elevation. The northern elevation is missing a number of the elements from the southern elevation; for instance, there is no obstruction in the northern courtyard, so one can see the whole elevation at once. There is no arcade on the northern elevation like the one separating the vast esplanade from the courtyard of the mosque; in-

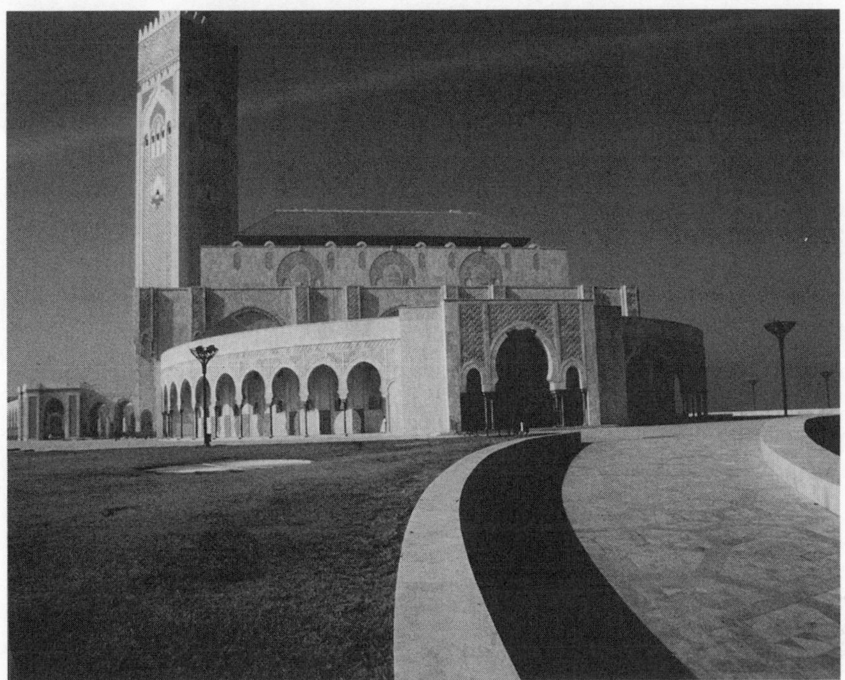

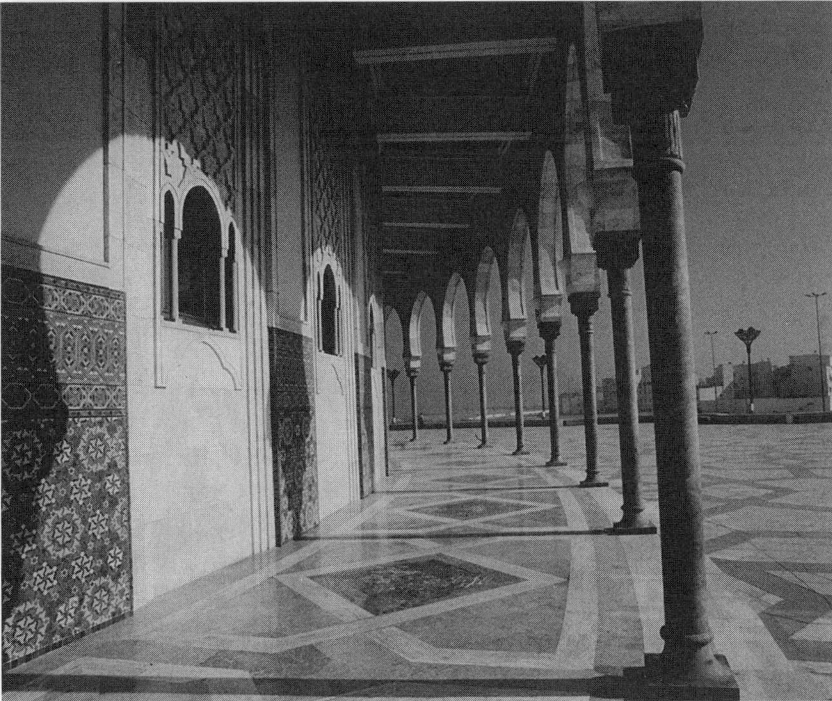

Fig. 10. Photographs of the eastern elevation. *Above*: the main portal, and the ambulatory arcade. *Below*: detail of the ambulatory arcade with *zellij* on the wall, the colored marble floor, and the city on the right side. Photos by Nnamdi Elleh, 1998.

stead there is a platform looking out on to the Atlantic Ocean that is used for prayers and other social gatherings. The western façade is primarily defined by three bays and three entrances whose finishes are variations of the finishes on the entrances on the southern façade. Individuals are already so overwhelmed by the time they have walked around the perimeters of the mosque that they have no resistance left for the things yet to be seen inside the building.

The ultimate part of the mosque is the prayer hall with a capacity of 25,000 worshipers in a 200-by-100-square-meter (650 by 325 feet) space. The plan is essentially a rectangle with three arched naves that are delineated by ten giant pairs of piers (Figs. 3 and 11). The two side naves are further subdivided by ten smaller piers that are nearer to the southern and northern walls. The piers that flank the central nave and the ones that are near the walls of the southern and northern façades are connected by a number of hanging, serrated, arched walls. Each pier is lavishly decorated with polished granite, marbles, plasters, and stuccos (Fig. 11). The decorations form hanging stalactites (*mouqarnas*), which consist of numerous lobes and arches. The *mouqarnas* are well defined by the addition of tiny columns along their edges, and by the intensity of the colors in the multiple lobes. The serrated arches that flank the central nave and connect the piers are also lavishly decorated with mouqarnas. The two side naves contain the galleries and the mezzanine for women, who can access the galleries directly from the ablution rooms in the basement. The fine woodworks that decorate the mezzanines on either side of the naves are further embellished with stuccos that radiate green, yellow, and white colors. The floor glows with the sheen of polished granite and marble. The giant retractable roof over the prayer hall is 65 meters (210 feet) above the floor, but the height of the ceiling drops to 38 meters (125 feet), and finally to 27 meters (90 feet). The roof is lavishly decorated with cedars that are embossed with gold, but its primary function is to bring natural light into the huge space when it is open. Even then, with a width of 100 meters and a length of 200 meters, natural light does not reach into all parts of the prayer hall. Rather it alters the interior atmosphere in a dramatic way quite different from when the stained glasses are the sources of light.

By the time one leaves the prayer hall, descends to the ablution rooms, and goes into the *hammam* (large heated pool, Moroccan bath) in the basement, any inclination for rejecting or celebrating an artwork has dissipated. But the information overload and the intensity of the interaction with the environment continues with the ablution fountains. Made of marble and beautifully carved

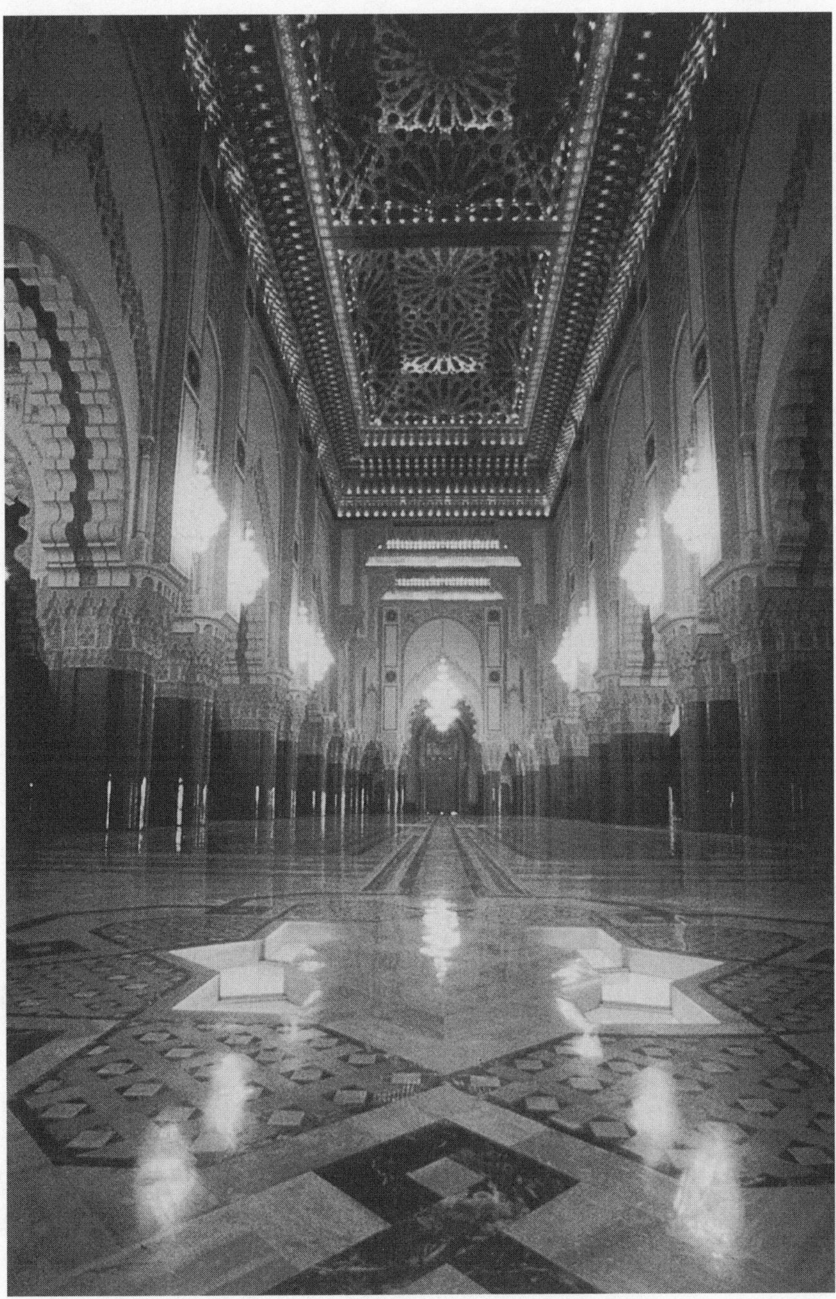

Fig. 11. Photo of the prayer hall when the mobile ceiling is closed.

like gigantic lotus leaves, the ablution fountains are arranged in a vast space, as if they were planted in a fantasy garden. The *hammam* does not make it any easier: the intensity of the *zellij,* the lighting of the space, both on the dropped decorated ceilings and underwater, gives the water a sparkling light green color, as if it is gentle rolling waves of liquid diamond. The sumptuous decorations, the steaming water, and its reflections combine to daze one into a subdued silence.

As one emerges from the basement of the edifice to the prayer hall, then to the courtyard, a reduction in the inebriating colors that bombard the senses brings relief. Heading back toward the esplanade from the courtyard of the edifice. The visitor has to first cross the arcade that surrounds the courtyard and the base of the minaret (Figs. 8 and 7) and make the long odious southward journey across the vast intimidating esplanade (Fig. 4), before arriving again at the main entrance/exit at Rue de Tiznit, which is a dead end. The dead end leaves one with the choice of going east (left) or west (right) on Rue de Tiznit. In Chapter 2, we will discover that this dead end was the most important factor in determining the urban design ambitions of the mosque. For my part, it was also a moment to contemplate what I had seen and to ask myself: How does one read the architectural design and art decor of the Hassan II Mosque?

Our Lady of Peace Basilica

> "Rome n'est plus dans Rome. Rome est à Yamoussoukro,"
> (Rome is no longer in Rome. Rome is in Yamoussoukro),
> —François Mathey, Conservateur en chef honoraire du Musée des Arts Décoratifs, 1990.

With an estimated price of US$150 million to US$300 million (15 percent of Côte d'Ivoire's national budget in 1987), this personal gift to Pope John Paul II and the Catholic Church holds a unique position in the history of architecture in Africa.[5] Like its Casablanca counterpart, its colossal excesses make it an edifice that will continue to attract controversy for years to come. The basilica is designed to seat 7,000 persons, with 11,000 standing on the central nave, and 30,000 standing on the parvis. The esplanade can hold 150,000 persons, who would be dwarfed by the 260 giant Doric, 12 Ionic, and 96 Corinthian columns. Together, there are a total of 368 columns. It has a 37-hectare (91.43-acre) garden that is planted with 400,000 species of flowers, shrubs, and trees, including

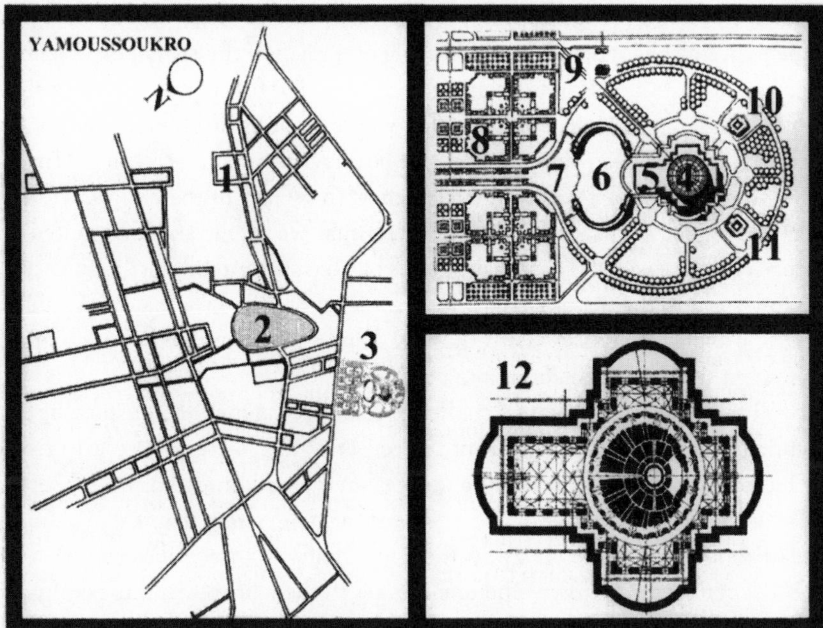

Fig. 12. Map of Yamoussoukro showing (1) the central business district where the bus station is located, (2) the lake, (3) the location of Our Lady of Peace from the center of the town, (4) the shrine, (5) the parvis, (6) the esplanade, (7) the peristyle, (8) gardens, (9) security station/entrance, (10) papal apartments, (11) the rectory, and (12) the floor plan of Our Lady of Peace

cocoa and other tropical cash crops. There is also a 25-hectare (61.78-acre) lawn around the monument. The total acreage of the land that the president provided for the basilica is 130 hectares (321.23 acres). Is this edifice a "beauty" or a "beast"?

Walking from the center of the town where the bus stop is located toward the edifice was a confusing experience for me (Figs. 12 and 13). For someone who grew up in both a West African village and a number of West African cities, a town like Yamoussoukro posed navigational problems. It was not the direction that was confusing, but the unusual feeling of not knowing whether I was in an African village or in a town. I wondered how the people of Yamoussoukro felt and related to their town, considering that they experienced, in a very short period (1982–90), massive expansions of infrastructure very different from what they were used to. Trying not to be nostalgic about the village life that I knew in the past, I also wondered, with tentative optimism, if the spatial experiences I was having at Yamoussoukro represented a model of future urban form, a sign of "progress," a new citadel of hope, that would be built throughout the continent to eliminate urban slums and village poverty. It is not a secret that African urban slums and villages are often characterized by lack of the basic amenities (electricity, good roads, and running water) that we often take for granted in some parts of the world. The image I got as I walked toward the basilica was that of a town where the people have attained a level of affluence that has enabled them to provide themselves with those basic necessities, and they built a great monument in order to celebrate their affluence.

This image poses the greatest challenge to understanding the purpose of the monument at Yamoussoukro. From the center of the town, particularly from the bus station, one can see two- and three-story buildings that house banks and state-owned enterprises on either side of the main street (Fig. 13). Although located about 2.5 kilometers away, the silver dome of the basilica can be seen from the center of the town, and one can get to the edifice without asking for directions. Because of its great height, the silver dome acts as a beacon for those who wish to visit the monument, mystically revealing itself as one gets closer to it.

Heading toward the silver dome, along the main street, in a northwest direction from the bus station, I made a left turn, and headed west on the first street that intersects the main street. The tempo of the town changed drastically as soon as I made this turn. Here, the road was not paved, but the street had been marked out and graded. Certain familiar village sites began to appear: cassava farms, lush cocoyam leaves, and several food crops. Unlike a typical village setting, the houses beside this street are arranged in multiple compounds in a linear order, suggesting urban settlement. Both sides of the street have compounds where people sit and cook as if they were in their villages. But the presence of automobile mechanic shops next to some of the compounds disrupts the idea of being in a village setting. In several African villages, there are bicycle repair shops, blacksmiths, carvers, weavers, and small provision stores that sell everything from medicines and soaps to apparel, but they are all located in the village square. Often, professional carvers work in the compounds where they learned their skills from older family members. At Yamoussoukro, everything is mixed up, and the visual transitions are incoherent. They consist of cultural and functional activities inextricably juxtaposed with one another.

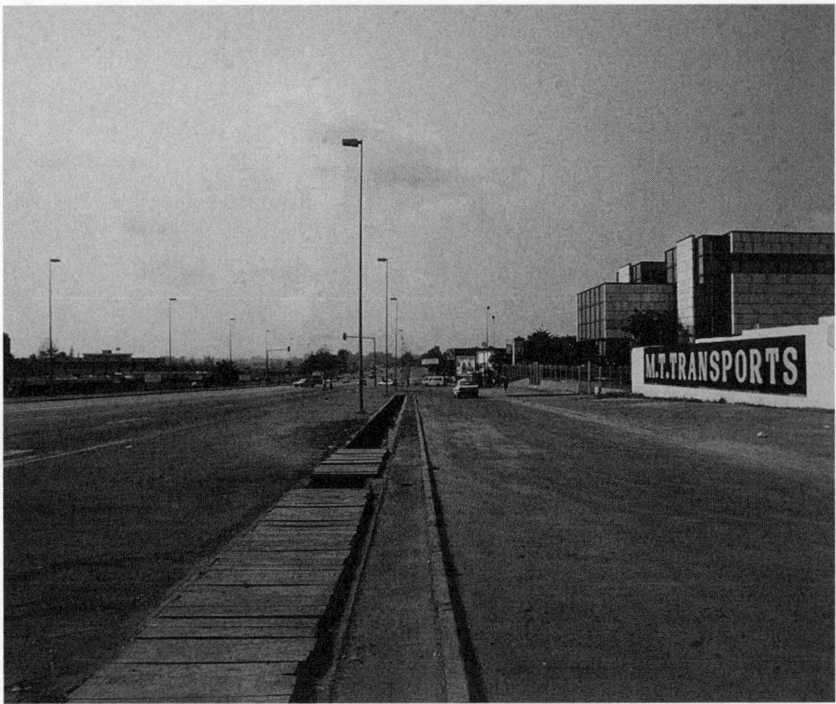

Fig. 13. Downtown of Yamoussoukro, showing the main street. The silver dome of Our Lady of Peace Basilica is directly behind the first light pole, left corner, in the distant left background. Photo by Nnamdi Elleh, 1998.

As I continued along the unpaved street toward the edifice, the indeterminate rhetoric of Yamoussoukro's landscape continued as well. The unpaved street now becomes wider; it has a median with an unplanted flower bed, and it terminates at the edge of a lake that overlooks the basilica in the distance (Fig. 14). From this juncture, the unpaved boulevard curves into another paved street where goats, sheep, and cattle are sold on both sides of the street, but the level of activity at the market is still that of a village—usually, animal markets in African cities are very boisterous. From this distance, the colossus increasingly commanded the surrounding landscape. It appeared to me as if all the natural and man-made elements in the area had been created to endow the peripheries of the colossal object with vegetation.[6]

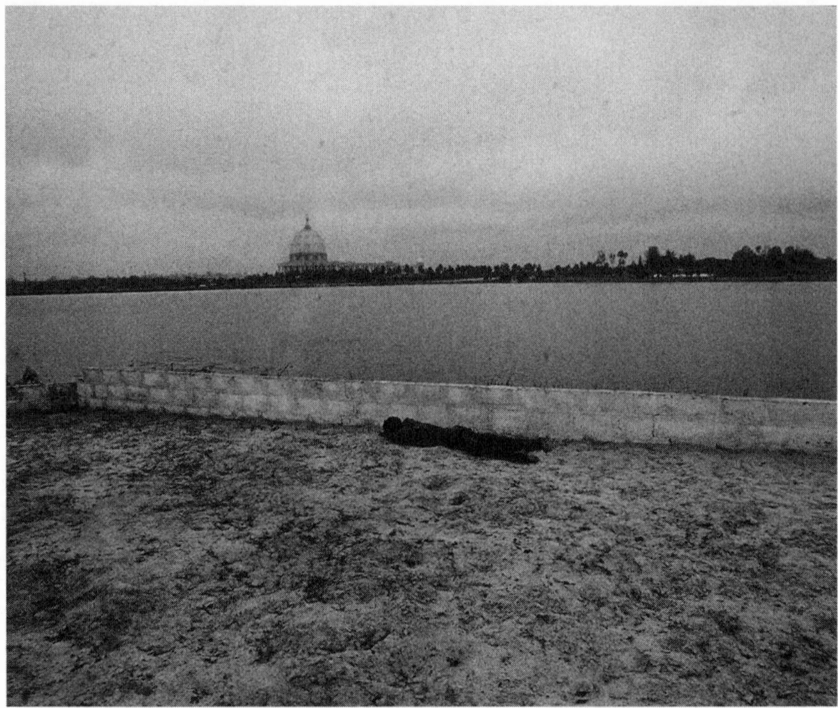

Fig. 14. The terminal of the unpaved boulevard, abutting a lake that overlooks Our Lady of Peace Basilica in the distance. Photo by Nnamdi Elleh, 1998.

Even then, the visitor does not yet realize the extent of the disorienting effects of the basilica until arriving at the gate, crossing it, and entering into the premises of the basilica. The disorientation comes from a grand illusion manufactured with the belief that, "Rome n'est plus pas dans Rome. Rome est à Yamoussoukro" (Rome is no longer in Rome, Rome is at Yamoussoukro).[7] Not only has there been an attempt to make an imported cultural edifice appear as if it were natural, the program also has incorporated a number of contradictions that undermine its naturalization efforts by imposing an emphatic difference between natural and man-made environments (Fig. 15). The natural and the man-made environments are differentiated from each other by a fence made of iron and concrete, in order to emphasize the superiority of art over nature. A closer look into the basilica's premises through the fence reveals its regimented

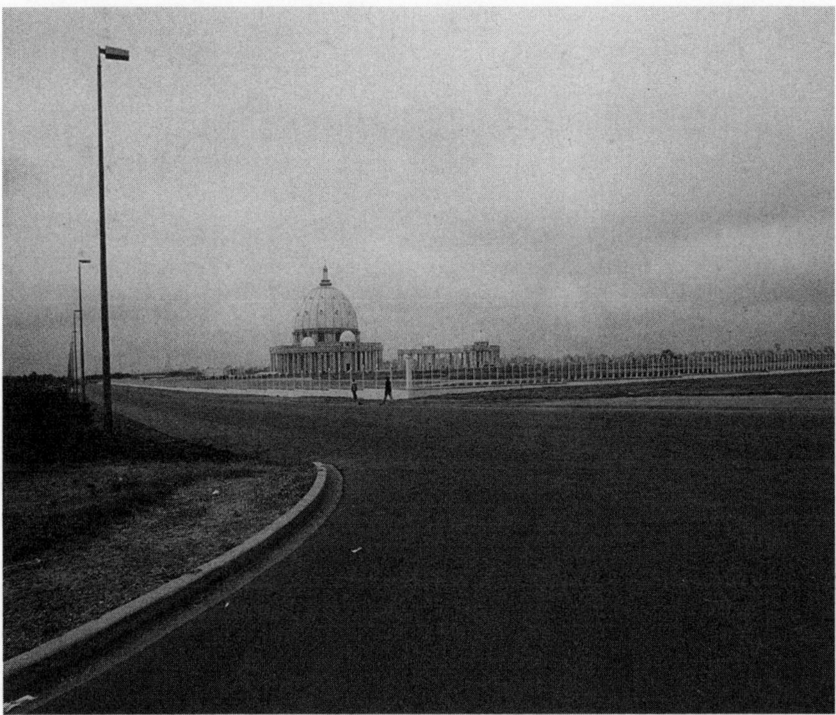

Fig. 15. The fence and a street demarcating the premises of the edifice from its surroundings. Photo by Nnamdi Elleh, 1998.

landscaping, giving one the impression that although nature is beautiful, it is accidental, haphazard, and inferior to art. As a result, the ordered garden, like the gardens at the Palace of Versailles, must be separated from the nature in the surrounding landscape. Moreover, as one glances at the edifice through the openings in the fence, the dramatic difference between the edifice and its surrounding, and the opulence of its architecture, speak less about church and religious piety than about cultural heritage (Fig. 15).

In the Casablanca project, cultural context is not an issue; there is no need to separate the mosque from the urban fabric, and the population is predominantly Moslem. At Yamoussoukro, by contrast, one might well ask: Why is the building there, and why is it on such a scale? More important, one might wonder what kind of personal gift this is to the Catholic Church. These questions undermine the whole experience of religious pilgrimage to the edifice; that is, they encourage the pilgrim to want to excavate the social context in which the basilica was constructed, rather than focus on experiencing the edifice in a similar manner to the Casablanca project. If the pilgrim's attention is so divided in the process of walking from the center of the town to the edifice, what will happen when he or she gets into the premises of the edifice?

The main gate is only opened when dignitaries visit with the head of state. But approaching the edifice from the main gate is not as dramatic as approaching it through the designated visitor's gate. From the main gate, one passes through the Versailles-like gardens into the esplanade before stepping onto the parvis. The main façade of the edifice and its esplanade are in view from the main gate (Fig. 1). On the other hand, standing at the visitor's gate, Houphouët's colossus is partially obscured from view until one has passed through a modest one-story symmetrical building, whose architecture forecasts the neoclassical intentions of the main edifice that lies beyond. From the gate, it is also obvious that, like Michel Pinseau at the Casablanca project, architect Pierre Fakhoury was highly concerned about controlling how the pilgrim experiences the edifice.

Upon going through the passage, one is thrust into a path that leads to an intersection near the end of the eastern arcade that encloses the esplanade of the edifice. One does not have the opportunity to experience the scale of the edifice until after arriving at the intersection, and one begins to follow the path that leads to the edifice (Fig. 16). This is also the point where the eastern arcade makes its outermost curve in order to complete the oblong shape of the esplanade.

From here, each step that one takes is dwarfed by the pacing of the double Doric columns of the arcade. Whether a person walked slowly, very fast, or even ran, he or she would know, just by being near those columns, that he or she had been outpaced and dwarfed. Individuals have no choice but to accept the reality that they are being subdued and dominated by an ensemble of stones, glasses, and other kinds of building materials. Moreover, the size of the columns and their articulations seem to have endowed the structures with a certain magnetic force, which pulls one toward them and makes one feel their presence to such an extent that one's body seems to rub around the edges of the bases of the columns while walking by.

Each column stands straight, like a colossal, glittering "ivory tower." Each is completely sculptural and majestic, and each gives the impression that it would be

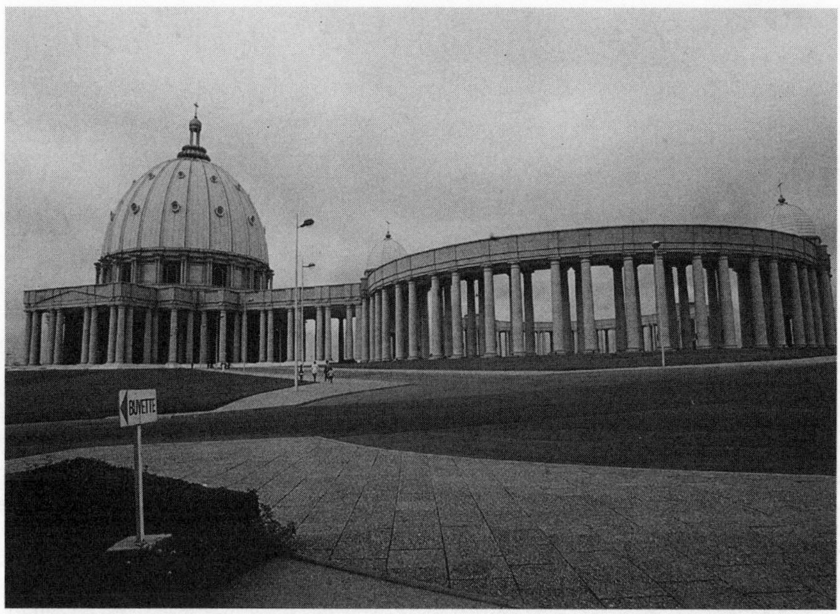

Fig. 16. The southeast elevation of Our Lady of Peace Basilica as one emerges from the entry house. Photo by Nnamdi Elleh, 1998.

confident to stand alone if the whole ensemble were to be taken apart and the columns replanted in different locations. The multiple columns in the ensemble are cynosures. They fixate one's attention on themselves in order to exhibit the multiple component parts of their capitals, trunks, and bases (Figs. 16 and 17).

Unlike the Casablanca project where one walks from Rue de Tiznit into the esplanade and experiences the feeling of void at its center, the esplanade at the basilica uses the arcades as screens to slightly conceal itself. The formal side entrance, which meets the edifice at an angle, also keeps the edifice out of view for a while (Fig. 16). Moreover, directing individuals to the parvis of the edifice at an angle also enables them to see the arcades without being inside, creating a visual suspense and a curiosity in the mind of the pilgrim (Fig. 16). There is also a sense of transition into another space at the point where one walks by the smaller dome of the eastern arcade and starts to climb the steps of the main structure (Fig. 16). The scale of the basilica becomes overwhelming as one ascends the steps leading to the parvis, and one realizes that the bases of the giant columns are almost at eye level (Fig. 17).

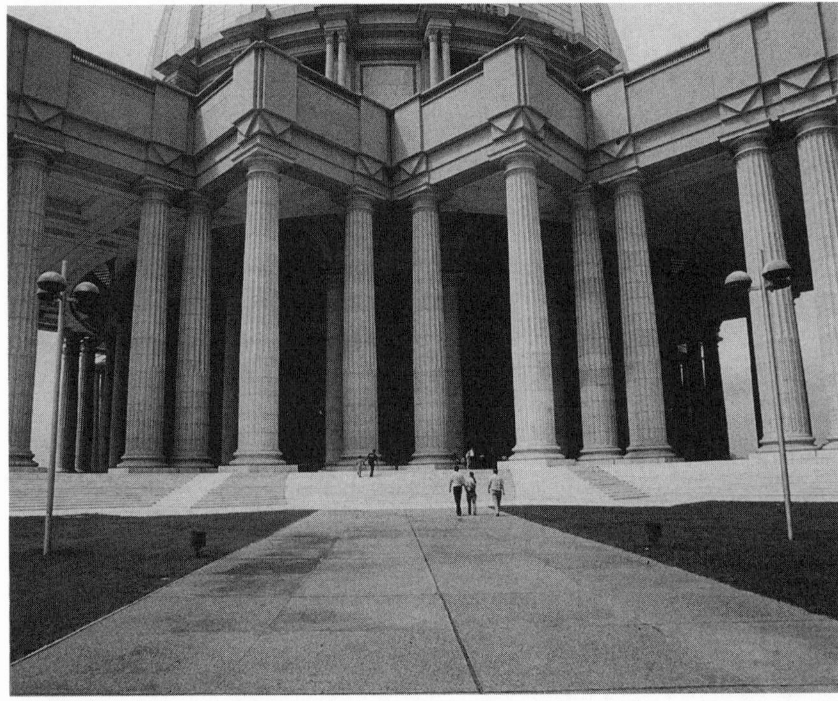

Fig. 17. Climbing the steps to the parvis of the edifice and the parvis showing the clustered Doric columns. Photo by Nnamdi Elleh, 1998.

Once on the parvis, the structure exhibits itself in component parts that together form a unified whole. In Casablanca, the columns of the arcade that separates the courtyard of the mosque from the esplanade are in a linear formation and at different angles. But on the parvis of the basilica the columns are in clusters, which helps highlight the cross shape of the edifice. The cross shape of the terrace and its cuffed ceilings are clearly visible. The gigantic columns can be viewed individually and collectively as they hold the floor of the terrace above, while the flutes of their shafts stress their muscles, their strength, and, above all, the stability of the edifice. An ambulatory skylight wraps around the main shrine to separate the balcony from the tambour, creating a well-defined transition space between the parvis and the interior of the shrine (Fig. 18). The transition space is further highlighted by a layer of marble that veils the stained-glass drum of the shrine at the lintel level, acting both

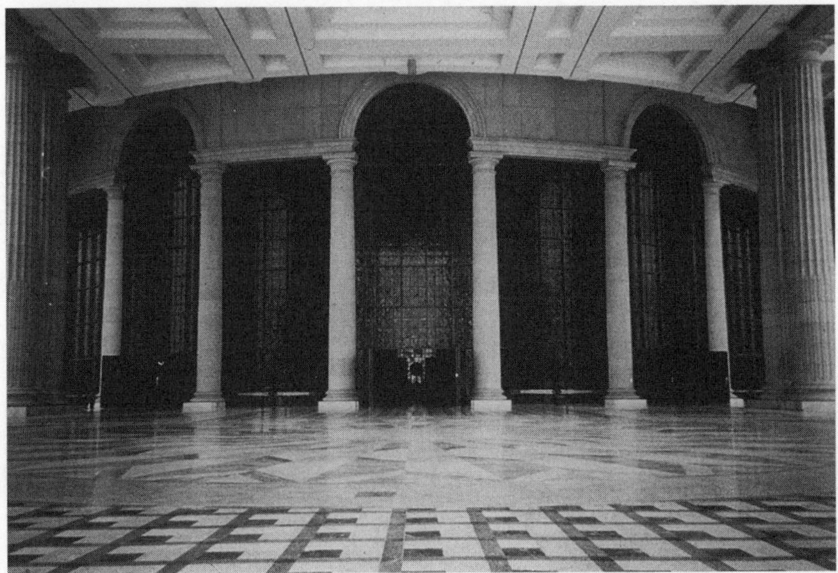

Fig. 18. The ambulatory shrine wrapped in stained glass (vitrail). Also, one of the main portals is open. Photo by Madame de Luengas, 1999.

as a protective shield for the stained glass and as a transitional demarcation from the parvis (Fig. 18). The marble screen around the stained glass is held in place by a set of columns in a circular formation to further reinforce the transition into the interior of the shrine. Twelve rectangular bays of stained glass of 21 meters (68.25 feet) high by 11 meters (35.75 feet) wide, along with twelve cylindrical bays of 28 meters (92 feet) high by 11 meters (35.75 feet) wide, form the circumference of the interior of the shrine. The largest of the windows is the Holy Spirit window on the dome, which measures 40 meters (130 feet) wide, resulting in a total stained-glass surface area of 7,400 square meters (24,050 square feet).[8] Each window is luxuriantly colored to mimic the African vegetation, especially the palms. The treatment of the parvis culminates on the interspaced rectangular and linear stained-glass bays that enclose the cylindrical shrine, especially the enormous doors (Fig. 18). Like any other part of the edifice, the floor of the parvis makes its own statement. It is a cross whose four arms are spread to the directions of the four cardinal points. But this cross is not ordinary. It is lavishly decorated with highly reflective ivory-white, ochre,

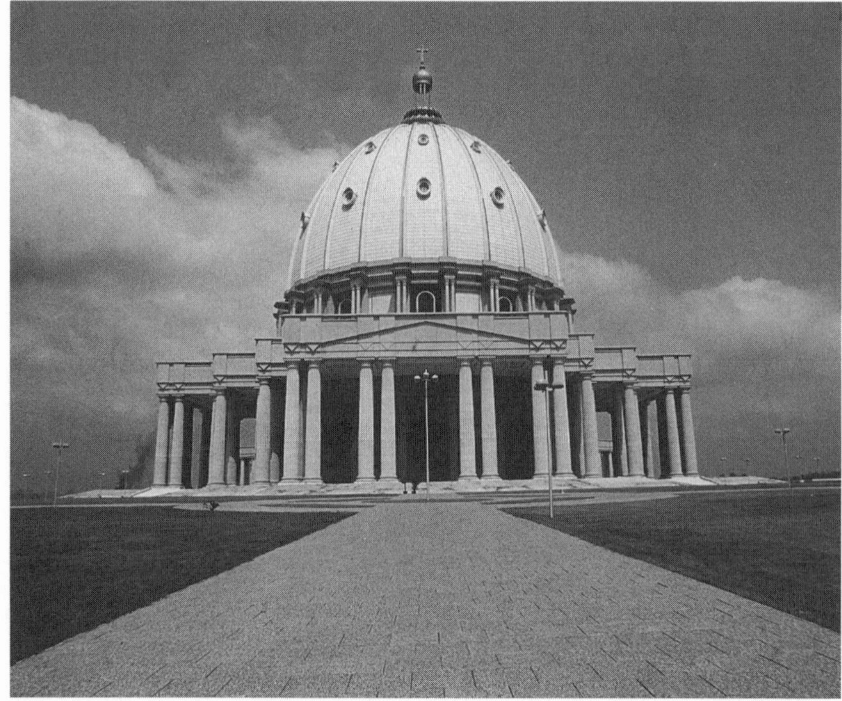

Fig. 19. The south façade of the edifice. Photo by Nnamdi Elleh, 1998.

and brown marbles, which reflect one's image as one walks on them. These colored marbles continue on to the esplanade, creating a sense of continuity and relatedness of the spaces.

A careful observation of the southern façade of the edifice shows six major segments that constitute the superstructure of the basilica from its base to the top (Fig. 19):

1. A crucifix-shaped platform, consisting of a white base, which is raised above the surrounding fields by layers of steps.
2. A cloister of majestic rose-colored Doric columns that give volume and shade to the platform.
3. A rose-colored terrace that forms the frieze and the porticoes of the edifice following the crucifix plan.
4. A rose-colored tambour braced with pairs of Corinthian columns.

5. A silver dome with double-spaced oculi on its panels.
6. A golden copular surmounted with a golden cross.

Three elevations of the edifice have the basic superstructure delineated in the preceding, except the northern façade, which has an elaborate esplanade, and is differentiated from the other façades by the oval-shaped arcades (Fig. 1). Each of these arcades seems to spread out its arms in welcome as the visitor approaches the esplanade from the main gate. One cannot resist the experience of the movement from the esplanade into the parvis. From here, one steps into more replicated artifacts, a domain of ecclesiastical magic that is facilitated by twentieth-century gizmos.

The canopy in the center of the basilica is the first structure to strike anyone who walks into the interior of the shrine. It has four spiraling, treelike columns, of polished bronze and brass, which are topped with a large dark blue chandelier, whose center and edges are trimmed by strings of brilliantly lit elongated crystals. This is the indisputable cynosure in the whole ensemble (Fig. 20). The church authorities believed that the chandelier lit the "throne of God." The glistening, burgundy-colored pews of African iroko wood follow the circular form of the plan of the shrine's interior. Unlike the hall of the mosque, whose interiors are free of furniture, the pews here are wooden gems, delightfully, delicately, and at the same time solidly made to reflect the extravagance of the entire enterprise.

Next is the dome. Rising more than 60 meters (195 feet), and with a diameter of 90 meters (292.5 feet), it is made primarily out of laminated aluminum panels that are installed on a frame of galvanized steel (Fig. 19). It is also crowned by a waterproof stained glass at its pinnacle, upon which a stainless steel golden lantern of 38 meters (123 feet) tall is installed. All together, the dome weighs 320 tons.

To demonstrate the scale of the president's achievement, the architects prepared three drawings comparing the basilica with three major monuments from around the world (Fig. 21). In the first sketch Our Lady of Peace Basilica is juxtaposed to the largest church in the Christian world, St. Peter's Basilica in Rome. Whereas the dome of St. Peter's Basilica is 42 meters (138 feet) wide, Our Lady of Peace Basilica has a dome that spans 90 meters (292.5 feet) wide, more than twice the width of the dome of St. Peter's. The juxtaposition of the cross sections of the two images demonstrates that the dome of St. Peter's could easily fit into the interior of Our Lady of Peace

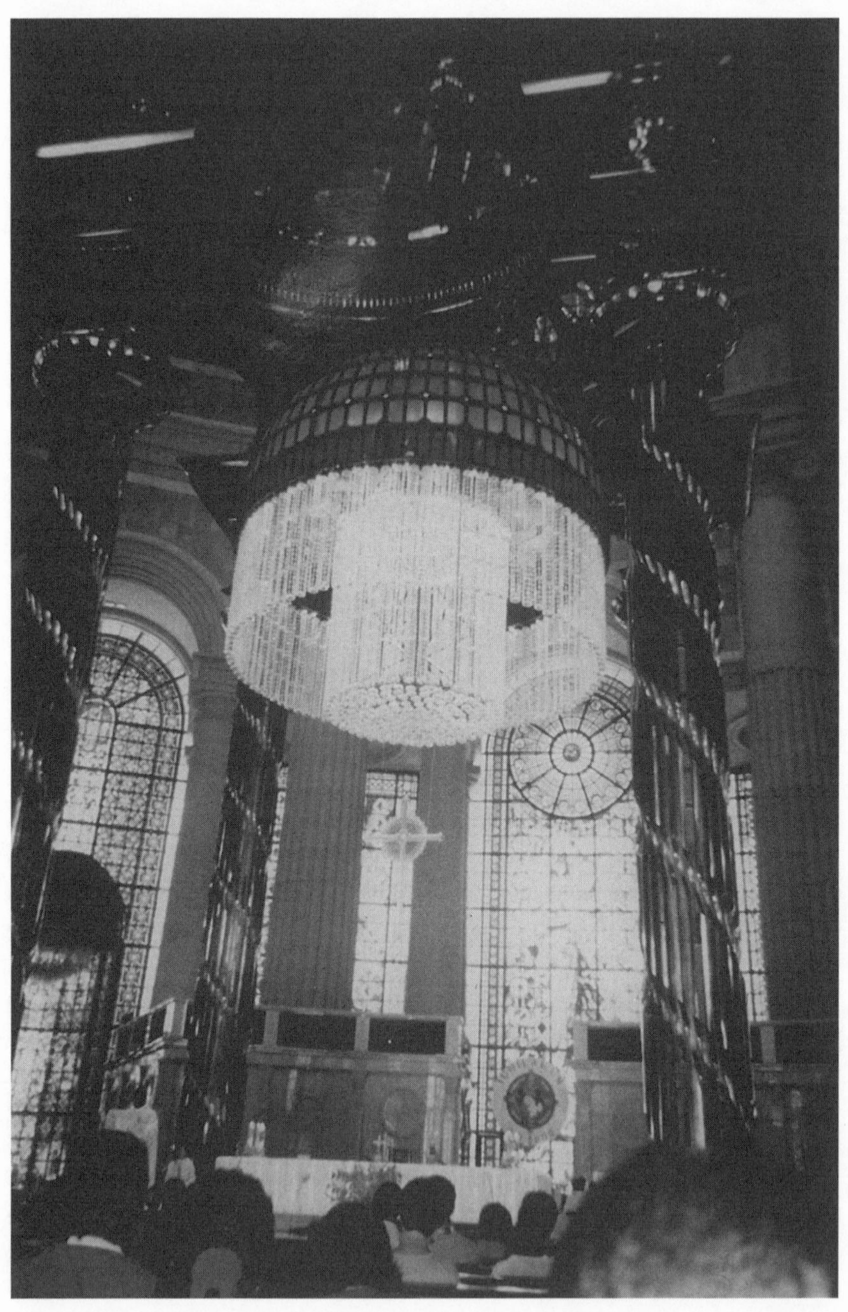

Fig. 20. The canopy (baldachin). Photo by Madame de Luengas, 1999.

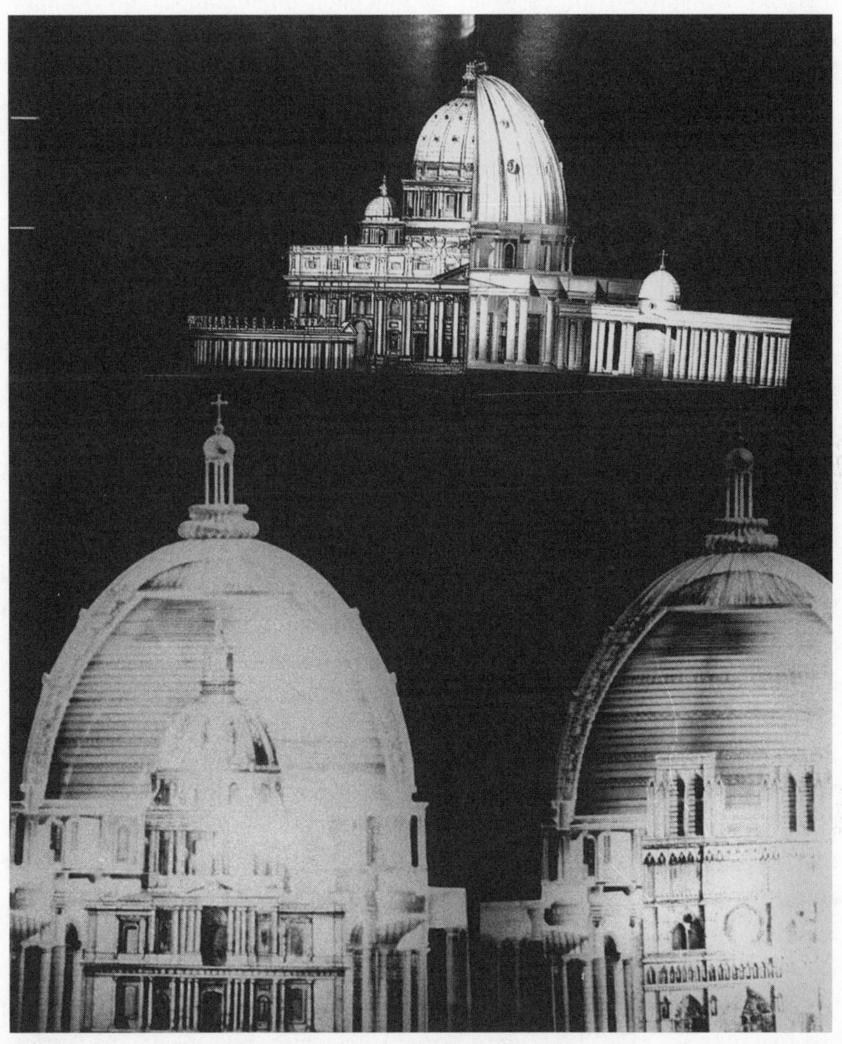

Fig. 21. Photos of three architects' sketches: The *top image* shows how Our Lady of Peace compares with St. Peter's Basilica in Rome. Left: St. Peter's Basilica. Right: Our Lady of Peace. *Bottom left* shows how Our Lady of Peace compares with St. Paul's Cathedral in London. *Bottom right* shows how Our Lady of Peace compares with Notre Dame of Paris. Photos by Nnamdi Elleh, 1998.

Basilica. When I observed the disparity between the width of the dome of Our Lady of Peace Basilica and the width of the dome of St. Peter's, I dismissed the disproportion between the new monument and the most important shrine of the Christian world as an insignificant technical solution. However, when I considered the heights of Our Lady of Peace and St. Peter's, I began to suspect that perhaps when the president was planning his colossus, he also intended to stage an architectural coup d'état against the Vatican. Whereas St. Peter's rises to a height of 123 meters (404 feet) to the top of the lantern, Our Lady of Peace Basilica rises to a total height of 158 meters (513.5 feet) to the top of the lantern (Fig. 21). The second drawing shows an elevation of St. Paul's Cathedral in London inside Our Lady of Peace Basilica in Yamoussoukro, leaving plenty of room on the sides of the latter. In the third sketch, Notre Dame Cathedral in Paris appears like a small church inside Yamoussoukro's basilica.

At the terrace, the first thing that draws one's attention is the tambour and its forty-eight Corinthian columns (Fig. 19). Next are the stained glasses, which are finished in each window with selected biblical narratives. In the ambulatory balcony around the tambour, in the interior of the shrine, there are twelve bays of apostle windows, which are 13 meters (42.25 feet) high and 8 meters (26 feet) wide. As one wanders around the interior balcony, the giant Corinthian pilasters that delineate the apostles window bays, read very well. Most important, the tinted air from the surrounding colorful stained glasses that enclose the shrine gives the entire ensemble the look of a giant jewelry box. Moreover, one obtains a perspectival view of the rotunda and its cylindrical pews, especially the drum of the base of the balcony that is carried by twelve hybridized Ionic columns. There is a series of twelve ornately cuffed barrel vaults held by four Doric columns each. Three giant Ionic columns have elevators inside them to whisk people to the ambulatory balcony along the tambour. It is indeed a "merveilleux" spectacle, as Francois Mathey (1990, 1) has remarked.

One can see why Tournier and Kpantindé (1990, 17) called Our Lady of Peace the "belle dame." It is also easier to sympathize with the pope and his Vatican flock for not being able to resist the gift. The "dame" is beautiful. She is a sculptured wedding cake whose seductions betray the piety of the Vatican and its flock, especially the tastes of her donor.

In contrast with the mosque, where the surrounding buildings and the streets in the vicinity give the impression that the complex is located on a constricted site, the Côte d'Ivoire edifice presents a different scenario due to the dominance of the basilica over the landscape. It appears as if the entire land is an extension of its grounds. This view becomes obvious as one looks at its surroundings from the terrace. The symmetrical location of the papal and bishop palaces, identical to each other and each with sixty rooms, within an inscribed circle mapping out one of the outlines of the premises of the edifice, reinforces the suggestion that the basilica was designed to dominate its surroundings and, at the same time, to differentiate itself from the surroundings (Figs. 12 and 22).

How does one evaluate the urban and architectural intentions of the Yamoussoukro edifice?

DEPLOYING THE PERSONALITIES IN THE MONUMENTS

Keeping in mind that art is a form of "self-expression and a projection of the psychological patterning of the individual that is called personality" (Hatcher 1985, 97), I will draw on the numerous publications of recent years on late President Houphouët-Boigny[9] and King Hassan II[10] to locate the specific scenarios in which the personalities and the monuments coalesced into inseparable entities in the public spheres of the respective countries. I would like to emphasize in this section that the biographical sketches I am providing here do not encompass all the achievements of the leaders—they delineate the relationships between the leaders and their monuments within the specific social contexts in which the objects were produced.

King Hassan II and the Cult of Antiquity

The mosque demonstrates how the king ritualistically replicated architectural elements from antiquity to assert his legitimacy to the throne, reinvent his monarchy, consolidate his power, and secure its survival into the future. The king ensured that whatever visual elements he incorporated into the structures of the mosque were understandable to the Moroccan people. These visual elements strengthened his claim to the throne by linking him to the traditions and achievements of his ancestors in the glorious years that were long gone.

To understand the mosque as a ritual, one needs to review the king's justification for its construction. We should remember Thomas Markus's (1995) ob-

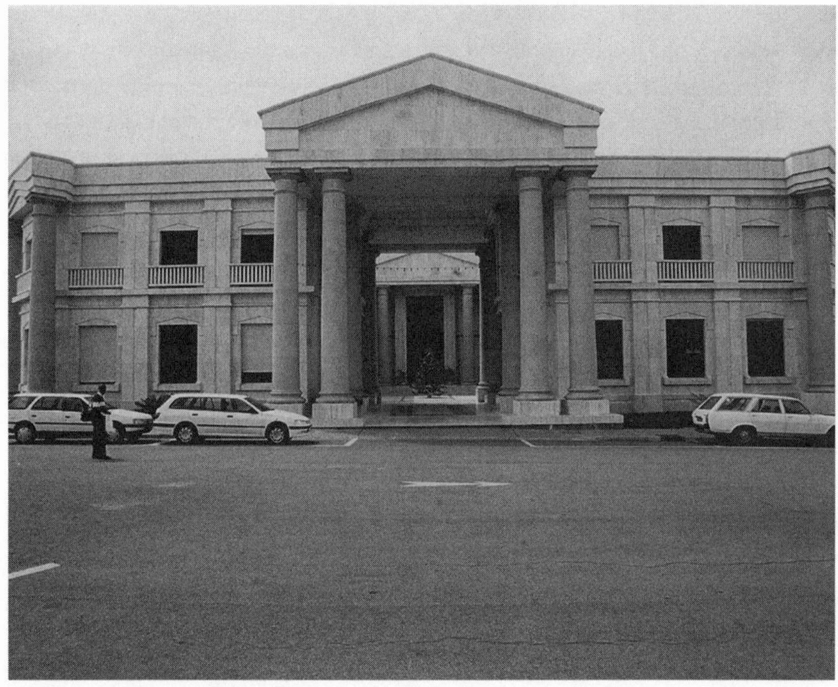

Fig. 22. One of the two identical marble sixty-room palaces for the pope and the bishops. Photo by Nnamdi Elleh, 1998.

servation that architecture is like a language and that every building is like a narrative from the moment it is conceived. The king constructed his mosque with a mythological and a historical narrative grounded in religious authority. During the declaration speech for the construction of the edifice on 9 July 1988, the king said that he wanted to build the mosque to fulfill one of the prophecies in the Holy Koran (Sourate XI, Verse VII-Hud): "And his throne was over the waters."[11] According to the king, the edifice would benefit those "subjects who will pray in it, meditate in it as well as praise the Creator while being on firm land, and may contemplate God's sky and Ocean."[12]

The king's proclamation is not too different from Combs-Schilling's (1989, xii) observation that power, ritual, and sexuality have played key roles in reconstituting the Moroccan society following major crises since the 1500s. The rituals celebrated are "the Prophet's Birthday, the popular celebrations of first marriage, and the Great Sacrifice." Correspondingly, some of the reasons given for the construction of the edifice include: (1) the founding of the Moroccan monarchy since A.D. 789; (2) the founding of the Alwalid Dynasty in the 1600s, of which the king is the sole representative; and (3) the king's sixty-third birthday; and, most important, (4) celebrating the Prophet Mohammed's birthday.

There is a lot of validity to Combs-Schilling's observations, especially since the mosque was consecrated on 30 August 1993, the eve of the anniversary of the birth of the Prophet. Moreover, it has been acknowledged within the official circles of the Moroccan government that consecrating the mosque on the eve of the anniversary of the birth of the Prophet would provide certain advantages to the king. First, it grounds his origins in the lineage of Prophet Mohammed, and dates his ancestors to about A.D. 571 in the Arabian Peninsula. It also connects him to Idris (788–829), a member of the first Moslem dynasty in Morocco who claimed descent from Prophet Mohammed. One of the most important functions of the consecration ritual was enlisting the king's followers to participate in the activities. Full participation symbolizes loyalty to the throne. As Combs-Schilling (1989, 31) observes, "those who participate in ritual are real performers in real-life dramas."

The consecration ceremony dramatizes all the king's victories and all the tribulations that threatened the survival of his kingdom since he assumed power in 1961. Such a ritual also reenacts the triumphs of the king's predecessors over their enemies, from the time the kingdom was founded by Idris (A.D. 788) until the king inherited the throne. As a result, one of the primary objectives of the ritual is to visually demonstrate to the citizens of Morocco and to the people of the world that the Moroccan monarchy is an institution that has endured many difficulties for centuries and will continue to prosper in the future. Thus, the mosque aspires to convey images of the king's supremacy and longevity by consolidating an impression of the monarchy as invincible in the collective experience of the Moroccan people, through the senses of sight, smell, sound, taste, touch and the visual abstractions that are familiar to them.[13] These goals were achieved through the conflation of the symbolic meanings of the mosque and the personality of the king into an indistinguishable single entity.

The most obvious example of this conflation is on the newly issued twenty dirhams currency, which first caught my attention when I was entering the country at the Mohammad V International Airport, Casablanca. On one side of the twenty dirhams currency lie two symmetrically juxtaposed images, one of the king and the other of the newly built mosque (Fig. 23). Both im-

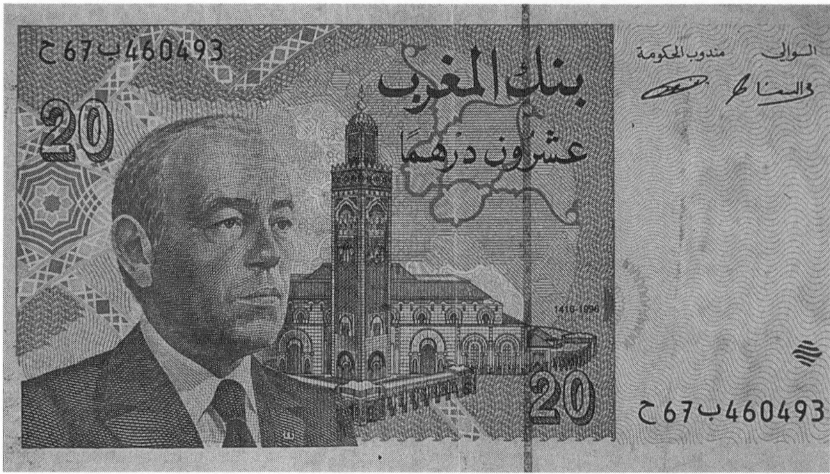

Fig. 23. Front side of the twenty dirhams currency note showing the portrait of King Hassan II juxtaposed with his mosque. Studio photo by Roman Stansberry, Department of Art History, Northwestern University, Evanston, Illinois, 1999.

ages are flanked by an image of the unmistakable bluish waters of the Atlantic Ocean—accounting for the name the mosque has been given by some of its advocates, "the Floating Mosque of Casablanca." Although the images of the king and the mosque are symmetrically juxtaposed, keeping the king's image in the foreground of the note makes it the most prominent object on the currency. The king's image is delineated in a reddish-brown cross-hatching technique that allows one to recognize his outfit as that of a modern head of state. It displays a low-cut hairstyle, a slightly flattened forehead that curves gracefully on its sides, and carefully contained bulging eyes that are centered, and that stare into the distance without maintaining eye contact with the viewer. There are dimples on both sides of his face that converge diagonally between the nose and the lower eyelids, spreading downward to melt into a smoothly shaven chin. Finally, there is the jacket and matching necktie that top the white shirt around his collar and provide visual equilibrium for both sides of his body.

Behind the king, the looming image of the ornate minaret of the mosque balances the king's image, while the mosque itself serves as a solidly articulated visual background for the entire composition. However, the date

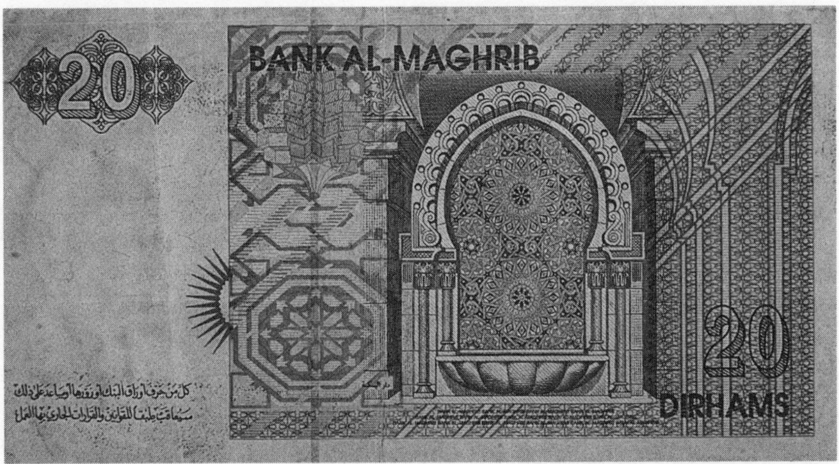

Fig. 24. Back side of the twenty dirhams currency note showing the fountain from the newly completed King Hassan II Mosque, 1986–1993. Studio photo by Roman Stansberry, Department of Art History, Northwestern University, Evanston, Illinois, 1999.

"1416–1996," on the lower right corner of the bill anachronistically destabilizes the entire composition. We know that the building was planned in 1985 and inaugurated in 1993. So what do these dates mean in this context of the mosque?

The answer to the question just raised is related to the inscriptions on the back of the currency. A boldly inscribed "Bank Al-Maghrib" tops a fountain framed by a columned horseshoe-shaped niche and given depth by a one-point perspective on the right corner that has been added to the column on the right-hand side (Figs. 6 and 24). The major feature of the fountain, warranting its placement on the back side of the twenty dirhams bill, appears to be the delicate ornate tiles that are inscribed in two major circles and about six semicircles that are subtriangulated in an interlacing manner. This juxtaposition is, once again, highly problematic, since one cannot tell whether the fountain and the spaces represented in the perspective are elements in the building(s) of the Bank-Al Maghreb or elements from the newly completed Mosque. Besides, the uninformed reader might not be able to tell whether the fountain is from the building of Bank-Al Maghrib in Rabat, the one in Casablanca, or from a branch of the bank in another major city of Morocco. We may be assured that the fountain comes from the newly completed mosque, not from the Bank Al-Maghrib as the images seem to indicate.

I am aware that several countries use images from their heritage or their contemporary achievements as their national symbols. Most of the time such representations are chronologically logical. The lack of logical chronology and deliberate visual conflation suggest that the image of the mosque is used for reasons other than as a site of worship as the king might like us to believe, and that this use has a deliberate effect on many essential aspects of Moroccan people's daily experiences. Since it is something that people handle on a daily basis, money is an ideal tool to impress the desired images of the king on the Moroccan people through the visual abstractions that are familiar to them. This is one of the reasons why it is imperative that we understand the social context in which this object was planned, produced, and deployed in the public sphere as part of the king's personality.

President Houphouët-Boigny: The Incarnate of Baoulé Ancestors

> Whether he is called Le Sage (the Wise Man), Le Vieux (the Old Man), or more recently Nana (a Boualé term for grandfather), the veneration implied by these words is unequalled by any other leader in West Africa today. (Toungara 1990, 23)

Unlike the Casablanca project, which was inspired by a long-standing tradition of monarchy and by the need to perpetuate that monarchy into the distant future, the Yamoussoukro basilica has no historical or political motive for its conception. Rather it speaks of spontaneity: an attempt to make what was essentially local and provincial become national; what was temporary, permanent; what was once secular, sacred; and what was common, exclusive. We can see how the president's personality interacted with his pet project in order to abrogate these poles from two stances: his position as an African chief, and his holding the office of the presidency of his country.

The president's worldviews, and the role he saw himself playing for his country as a guarantor of peace would derive partly from the meaning of his name, and from his role as a Baoulé chief. According to Toungara (1990, 27), the name "Dia Houphouét" combines the designation of diviner-healer, "dia," with the name given to a child born to its mother after a succession of deaths, "houphouët," meaning "one who must sweep away lingering evil spirits."

Houphouët added the family symbol, "boigny" (which means "ram") to the name after 1945. The most important events in his early years were the deaths of his maternal uncle Kouassi N'Goh and of his mother in 1935. His uncle was a French administrator (a *chef de canton*), a position that Houphouët inherited at the age of five, although he did not assume the role until later. He did not assume the name Félix until the age of eleven, after his conversion to Catholicism. By 1925, he had completed a medical program in Senegal at École William-Ponty, returned to Côte d'Ivoire as a doctor, and set up his first coffee plantation at Abengourou. At Abengourou, he organized cocoa farmers' boycotts to protest against the low prices they received for their crops. It was also in Abengourou that he married his first wife, Khady Sow, who was the daughter of a Senegalese merchant and the sister of the paramount chief of Agni of Abengourou, Boa Kwasi II. Boa Kwasi II became Houphouët's confidant and helped him learn the ways of Akan rule.

According to Toungara (1990, 28), "the President's initiation to power came as a result of his appointment in 1940 as Chef de Canton of the Akoué, a small arena of power, but adequate to serve as a training ground for the authority he would eventually exercise at the national level." Besides accumulating some of his own wealth, the president also inherited land, gold artifacts, and family heirlooms, which made him one of the richest persons in his country.[14] Toungara (1990) suggests that Houphouët-Boigny's views of how a government should work were shaped mostly by values of kingship based on Baoulé traditions, which are an extension of Akan governing tradition. The Baoulé people of Côte d'Ivoire believe that their ancestors migrated from the Akan Kingdom of Ghana toward the end of the eighteenth century. Scholars suggest that the migration myth might be plausible, but the immigrants were unable to create a state that was as prosperous or socially organized as the Akan society that they left in Ghana.[15] Nevertheless, they were able to bring with them certain Akan traditions that influenced their arts, religion, and social organizations. According to Toungara (1990, 28), Houphouët-Boigny's speech in reference to his position in the French Cabinet in 1956 implies that he saw his public office, and those who were associated with him, as an extension of his family and ancestral traditions. Such views were in accord with the concept of extended family in Akan/Baoulé tradition.

The president practiced Akan/Baoulé governing methods in the national government of Côte d'Ivoire, resulting in "neo-patrimonialism," a contemporary phenomenon that is rooted in ancient traditions, but which needs to adapt to present economic and political conditions.[16] In neo-patrimonialism, the line between the private and public domain is blurred, as rulers treat public institutions as their personal estates. In a one-party state like Côte d'Ivoire, neo-patrimonialism has been described by Fatton (1992, 46) as a government with a presidential monarch "whose capacity to survive depends on their ability to suppress alternative centers of authority." Fatton's view is given credence by Jackson and Rosberg (1982), who believe that there are contemporary princes and authoritarian rulers of Africa who combine traditional governance and modern governance to form political "oligarchy." However, "the legitimacy of the modern African Prince depends upon his respect for the private understanding and agreements he has made with those whom he rules. It is not only their power that he respects, but also his informal agreement with them." Potholm (1976, 184) has described Houphouët-Boigny's government as "authoritarian" but "less despotic" than the government of late President Kamazu Banda in Malawi.

In the Ivorian clientalism, those who are placed in the highest cadres of the government have monopolistic control of the state, and they have great resources for patronage, just as we observed in Morocco. "They can confer to their clients political office and public employment," (Fatton 1992, 53), enabling them to obstruct the organization of resistance among subordinate members of the society who are often isolated from one other, because of their personal loyalties to the big men who support them. Modeling his government after the traditional Akan methods of governance results in what Toungara (1990, 33) describes as the "Akanisation of the Nation-State":

> Just as an Akan chief is considered to be the ultimate authority over his people, so Houphouët has exercised almost total control over local affairs. With the nation as his Kingdom, he has proclaimed paramountcy over its diverse ethnic groups in what might be called an "Akanasation" of power in Côte-d'Ivoire. This type of domination in new states has been referred to as "neo-patrimonialism."

Scholars who have studied Akan political organization recognize that the chief is for life and cannot be deposed or challenged except by consensus within the council of chiefs. The Akan, by extension, and the Baoulé ethnic group to which the president belonged, have a concept of power known as *tumi* or *tum,* which Hagan (1981, 57) defines as the capacity to act and achieve a desired objective. Tumi embodies ritual, social, religious, and political powers that are vested in the hands of the paramount chief who mediates between the ancestors and the living. The chief is also vested with the powers of maintaining law and order so that the society will be at peace and enjoy a high level of productivity. Legal and religious issues, which often depend on oaths and libations administered by the chief through mediation with the ancestors, are binding to all parties who engage in them.[17] Therefore, the Akan or Baoulé chief has a great need to be near to his ancestors and often sees himself as somebody who holds an oath of peace with the ancestors. The president's concepts of peace and leadership were colored by the chief's role as mediator between the ancestors and the people. This is a point that Toungara (1990) makes, noting that the concept of peace was transferred from the ancestors' domain into the national and international scene during President Houphouët-Boigny's political tenure.

According to Toungara (1990, 52), Houphouët's desire to be recognized internationally as a peacemaker was promoted "by his own bureaucrats, party officials," and international agencies. Toungara (1990) views the UNESCO-sponsored international congress on "La Paix dans l'esprit des hommes," in Yamoussoukro, June 1989, as a step toward legitimizing Houphouët's self-glorification and deification as a man of peace in the international community. The conference was attended by the director-general of UNESCO, Frederico Mayor, who proposed a new peace prize in the honor of the president. The prize was confirmed at the November 1989 meeting of member states of UNESCO in Paris. According to the confirmation, "the Félix Houphouët-Boigny Peace Prize is to be awarded annually to an individual, institution, or organization having contributed to the promotion, search, safeguard, or maintenance of peace through educational, scientific, or cultural means."[18] The greatest praise singer of the president, the national newspaper *Fraternité Martin,* lauded the UNESCO move as the immortalization of the name of their president.[19] Toungara (1990, 52) also writes that Our Lady of Peace Basilica is the "most surreal of Houphouët's projects" that were designed to make him immortal.

If the president's concept of peace was mostly influenced by the traditional role that a king is supposed to play in Akan-Baoulé culture as the guarantor of peace, productivity, and the mediator between the ancestors and the living, why did he feel that it was necessary for him to mask his leadership model in Catholicism? In other words, why did he translate the concept of peace that he derived from Akan-Baoulé kingship into an architectural form that produced the basilica, knowing very well that the style of architecture he was adopting had absolutely no relationship with the visual symbols of Akan-Baoulé kingship?

It is also surprising that the papal visit to consecrate the basilica was highly opposed by the Catholic community, which one might expect to be the most enthusiastic to receive him in the country. Indeed, the most outspoken critic of the visit was Cardinal Bernard Yago, the archbishop of Abidjan and the primate of the Roman Catholic Church in Côte d'Ivoire. Cardinal Bernard Yago tried, right up to the last moment and contrary to the advice of the bishop of Man, Monsignor Bernard Agré, to dissuade the pope from consecrating the basilica.[20] It is important to note that, long before the construction of the basilica, Cardinal Yago was the only individual who could criticize the president without being sent to prison. The construction of the basilica at Yamoussoukro was one method by which the president could undermine the powers of the cardinal, who was the primate of the Roman Catholic Church in the country. Knowing very well that the pope would appoint a bishop at Yamoussoukro once he built such a grand church there, a church that he worked very hard to declare as the sister church to St. Peter's Basilica in Rome, it cannot be ruled out that one of the president's motives was to show the cardinal who the boss was, and he did it in a grand style. The possibility that the cardinal objected to the pope's consecrating the edifice because he knew that the edifice was intended to undermine his status in the country is unlikely; the cardinal had been a consistent critic of the president long before he conceived his basilica project.

Opposition to the papal visit to consecrate the basilica was so widespread that in July 1990 a French priest in Abobo, Abidjan, went on hunger strike to protest against the visit.[21] The timing of the papal visit (less than two months before the reelection of the president to a seventh consecutive five-year term on 28 October 1990) suggests that the president and the ruling Partie Democratique de la Côte d'Ivoire (PDIC) exploited the construction of the basilica for political gains.

It is appropriate to question the rush to complete the construction of such a grand monument in three years, and its inauguration in less than seven weeks before a national election that includes opposition parties, considering that multiparty elections had been banned in Côte d'Ivoire before 1990. Suggestion is borne out by the fact that the PDIC officials suggested to the electorate that the "incumbent had been blessed by God"[22] and therefore deserved to be reelected for the seventh term. Here, reference to God was obviously about the pope's visit.

A curious twist was added to the controversy surrounding the consecration of the basilica a few weeks before the elections. The president alleged that his men had uncovered a plot by the thirteen leaders of the opposition parties to kill the pope. The president's claim was seriously condemned by Cardinal Bernard Yago as a strategy to "drown" the opposition parties, particularly since no link could be established between the confessor to the plot (a Beninese national) and any members of the opposition parties. By accusing the opposition of involvement in a plot to kill the pope, the president put them on the defensive and effectively exploited the occasion to win the election for a seventh term.

What is important to this discussion is the manner in which the object functions as a consolidator of the president's image as "great leader." Yamoussoukro and its edifice seem to have been planned as the center from which images of the president would circulate and dominate the country's offices, shopping plazas, civic centers, public parks, television, radio, and, most important, public opinion. Unlike the Moroccan case, however, the gain was mostly short term. The president did not have any vision in mind, beyond being known as the builder of a Roman Catholic artifact and being affiliated with the pope for the immediate moment. The Moroccan king believed that he had ruled through his ancestors long before he was born, and that he would continue to rule through his children long after he was gone. The circulated images of the king are historical, organized, and consolidated. In the case of the president, the image and personality in circulation are haphazard, unorganized, and dispersed.

In Abidjan, along Boulevard de la Republique, across from the Ivorian National Assembly and the Nigerian embassy buildings, lie the exclusive entrances to the Stade Houphouët-Boigny. A portrait of the president dominates the wall of this exclusive entrance. It is easy to mistake the portrait for a photograph if one is looking at it from the street, but it reveals itself as a mosaic on a closer look (Fig. 25). The object is framed by planters that form the casing for the steps, the flowers on the planters, the tall date palms, the windows of the structure, and the portal directly below the object. The diagonally hatched palm leaves that form the background to the image and the leaves of the date palm on the planters harmoniously extend to each other in the frame, giving the image a consistent background. The extension of the plants into the image allows the object to stand out in a background that otherwise would have been difficult to manage.

Three themes dominate how the figure of the president is delineated: (1) the modern business man who conforms to international etiquette; (2) the sage, the wise man; (3) who is old, but ageless, because his aging has been frozen in time. The light cast on the president's forehead from the top left corner, while slightly

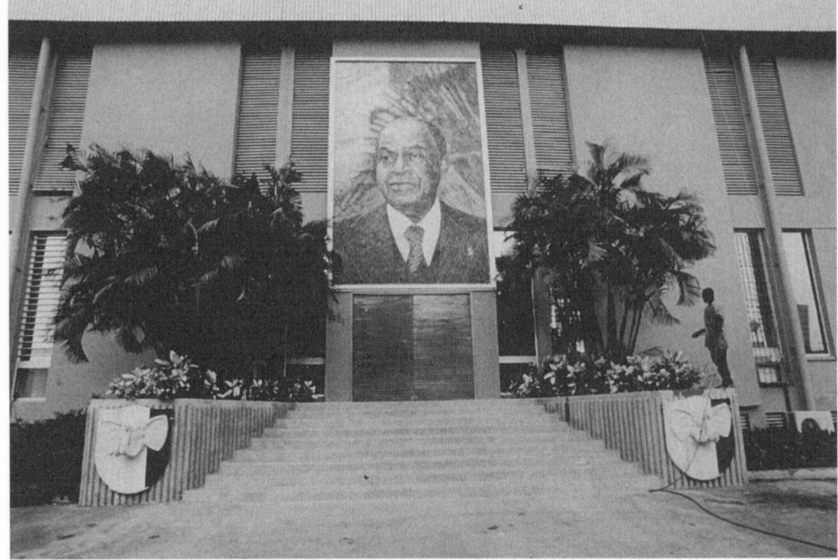

Fig. 25. Framed mosaic of the portrait of President Houphouët-Boigny at the VIP entrance to Stade Houphouët-Boigny in Abidjan. Photo by Nnamdi Elleh, 1998.

darkening the right side of the face, gives his restrained smile a seriousness that gives the image depth and mysterious aura. The image stares beyond the viewer into the distance. This lack of eye contact exaggerates its mystery. Apart from an air of mystery in the face, nothing in the image suggests that the president is also an African chief. Like his contemporary in Morocco, the president's face is hidden behind a modern European façade. How does this hidden face maintain balance with the president's African heritage?

THE SOCIAL SETTINGS

As Haskell (1993/1995, 217) has suggested, art is not a total cultural, economic, and political "index of society."[23] Nevertheless, we cannot ignore the role that certain art objects play to galvanize collective memories within the public space. Lefebvre's delineation of how social events and ideas can be transformed into "social spaces" in specific spans of time is also relevant here.[24] According to Lefebvre (1991), "(social) space is not a thing among other things, nor a product among other products: rather, it subsumes things produced, and encompasses their relationships in their coexistence and simultaneity—their (relative) order and/or (relative) disorder." Lefebvre argues that social space is the result of a "sequence and set of operations" that cannot be reduced to "a simple object." Similarly, we can argue that objects like the Hassan II Mosque and Our Lady of Peace Basilica constitute social spaces that are created out of sequences of events. When edifices like the mosque and the basilica are produced and deployed in the public sphere, these edifices constitute distinct kinds of social spaces, where dialogues and relations that are tied to formations of social hierarchy, production of material life, and consumption take place. To understand the nature of these spaces, one has to excavate the social sequences of events and enactment that paved the way for their construction. In this section, we look at how specific events, enactments, and ideas that circulated in the public spheres of the two countries were transformed into visual, architectonic ensembles within specific spans of time.

The Tribulations: Antiquity and Territorial Expansionism

Although the king announced the construction of his mosque in 1988, the social setting in which the edifice was produced dates to the period of Morocco's independence on 2 March 1956. Then, the seeds were sown for the two major events that would dominate the national scene in Morocco for the next four decades: (1) the struggle between political parties and the monarchy for the control of the Moroccan government, and (2) the territorial struggle for the control of the western Sahara, a region that was still under Spanish rule until the early 1970s.

After independence, the struggle for the control of the Moroccan government was mostly between Istiqlal, the party for independence, which was formed in 1943, and the monarchy, headed by Sultan Mohammed ibn Yousuf, King Hassan II's father.[25] The power struggle between the monarchy and Istiqlal was also due to the absence of a common enemy, the French. Before independence, Sultan Mohammed ibn Yousuf and Istiqlal united against French colonialism. After independence, the alliance broke because they no longer had a common enemy to fight. They began to fight among themselves along two broad divisions: The monarchists believed in the concentration of all state powers in the hands of the sultan, while the Republicans hoped that the newly freed Morocco would be a democracy. From that point on, the die was cast, and the confrontations snowballed into different forms that neither side could foresee.

Although Istiqlal had the majority in the government that was formed immediately after independence, Sultan Mohammed ibn Yousuf controlled it. The sultan reinforced the authority of his monarchy by announcing in July 1957 that his son, Prince Hassan, would be heir to the throne, and by declaring himself king in August of the same year. Meanwhile, the police and the army remained effectively under his control, enabling him to bully and divide the opposition forces. The measures which the sultan was taking put too much stress on the opposition forces, resulting in the dissolution of Istiqlal in September 1959 and the birth of a new independent party, the Union Nationale des Forces Populaires (National Union of Popular Forces—UNFP), led by Ben Barka (Bidwell 1994, 679). The advantages that the monarchy had over the opposition became clearer when the king made himself the prime minister in the new government that was formed in May 1960, while his son, Prince Hassan, was made his deputy prime minister.

The death of King Mohammed V in February 1961 paved the way for Prince Hassan to ascend the throne as King Hassan II, who also made himself prime minister. One of the earliest achievements of King Hassan II in the succession struggle was to legitimize his throne by ensuring that it was encoded in the constitution that Morocco was a kingdom governed by a monarchy. That constitution was approved by a referendum in December 1962. To further consolidate his powers, the king deprived members of the Istiqlal party of their cabinet positions in the government shortly afterward. Also, he formed the Front pour la Défense des Institutions Constitutionelles (FDIC) to represent his interests. Having consolidated his position, he resigned from the prime minister's post and installed a member of the FDIC in his place. Elections held in 1963 for the House of Representatives were unable to produce a clear winner. The Istiqlal and the UNFP were still in opposition. According to Bidwell (1994, 679):

> Several Istiqlal deputies were arrested for protesting against corruption and mismanagement of the election, leading the party to boycott further elections later in the year. Almost all the leaders of the UNFP were arrested in July 1963 in connection with an alleged coup attempt. Many of them were held in solitary confinement, tortured and eventually sentenced to death.

By 1964, political unrest, unemployment, and demonstrations by the urban workforce had escalated in Morocco. The king declared a state of emergency in June 1965, granting himself all the legislative and executive powers. The disappearance of the UNFP leader, Ben Barka, in France in October 1965, and the *in absentia* conviction of one of the king's strongmen, General Oufkir, by the French government, strained the relationship between France and Morocco. The king began to return the country to the electoral government in 1967, after relinquishing the post of prime minister to Dr. Mohammed Benhima. Two unsuccessful military coups followed, one in July 1971 and one in August 1972, by officers who wanted to establish a republic in Morocco. General Oufkir, the minister of defense and army chief of staff, was killed in a suspicious automobile accident immediately after the second coup. From then on the king took charge of the army and the defense portfolios. Suggestions to reform the government by the king were unacceptable to the Istiqlal and the UNFP, who demanded concessions that would have reduced his powers if he had agreed. The struggle for power between the monarchy and the parties rose to a crescendo in 1974 when there were several trials of opposition members in the country. The UNFP split in 1974, resulting in the formation of the Union Socialiste des Forces Populaires (USFP). The formation of the new party sowed the seeds for the emergence of more radical and religiously inspired opposition movements, which would haunt the king later in the 1980s and 1990s. But the king was still too engrossed with the immediate problems of the 1970s to consider what might be in store for him in the future.

Western Sahara seemed to be the only unifying element for the king and members of the opposition parties. The king took advantage of a combination of ancient myths and political history to raise the profile of the issue. The king and the opposition parties saw the whole of the western Sahara and Mauritania as extensions of their country since ancient times. The Moroccan authorities believed that the disputed territories belonged to them because the Sahrawi ethnic groups had always held political allegiance to their Cherifian monarchy, especially the Almoravid Dynasty, which dominated the region from A.D. 1184 to A.D. 1212.[26]

The facts were being stretched for a practical reason. The claim was probably a ploy that would enable the emergent Moroccan elite to gain access to the large phosphate deposits in the regions under dispute. A proven reserve of phosphate-rich rock was already yielding about six million tons a year for the Spaniards by 1975. "The only countries that exceeded that production level at the time were the United States and Morocco" (Lippert 1977, 48). It is also estimated that the production figure could exceed ten million tons a year because of the nearly thirteen billion tons of extremely rich phosphate rock (78 percent) reserves in the region. Moreover, the natural wealth of the region includes rich coastal fishing waters that the Spaniards had controlled for a long time.

The phosphate-rich regions of western Sahara have been contested by Morocco, Algeria, Mauritania, and the people of western Sahara. As early as 1967, the United Nations Assembly had urged the Spaniards who colonized the region in 1884 to adopt a policy of self-determination, based on a referendum that would enable the people of western Sahara to choose whether to be independent or to be part of either of the countries that were claiming the territory. It was a period when Algeria and Morocco were pursuing expansionist policies that encouraged both countries to lay claim to western Sahara. To spite Morocco, which had become the darling of France following their war of independence, Algeria supported the Popular Front for the Liberation of Saguia el-Hamra and Río de Oro (the Polisario Front), an independent movement that was formed on 10 May 1973. According to Lippert (1977, 46), the western Saharan conflict escalated after a UN investigation mission reported on 12 May 1975 that almost all the people it had consulted in the territory were "categorically for independence and against the territorial claims of Morocco and Mauritania." On 16 October 1975, the International Court of Justice in The Hague ruled in favor of self-determination for the Sahrawi people. But two days before this ruling, King Hassan ordered a march of 350,000 unarmed civilians (the Green March) to take possession of the Spanish Sahara. The crisis culminated in the invasion of the region by Moroccan troops on 1 November 1975.

There was clearly a Moroccan dominance of the military theaters of operation during the outset of the war in November and December 1975. The Moroccan army was better organized and equipped, and it anticipated victory within a short time. Besides, there was no military opposition from the western Saharans as it was occupying the towns and the military garrisons from which the Spaniards were withdrawing. One of the immediate outcomes of the invasion was the declaration of the Democratic Sahrawi Arab Republic (DSAR), by the Polisario Front, on 27 February 1976. Algerian and Libyan support for the Polisario Front turned the war to an indefinite guerrilla war that neither the Moroccans nor the Polisario movement could win. Taking advantage of their knowledge of desert terrain, the waterholes in the region, and edible vegetation and animals, the poorly armed Polisario army began to harass the better supplied Moroccan army.

By this point, as Lippert (1977, 57) reports, the king had gotten himself and his kingdom into an expensive military expedition that would last for several decades—a Moroccan Trojan war that was justified by appeals to distant history, but in reality was determined by hard business interests: phosphate and other mineral reserves in particular.

In May, 1976, Giscard d'Estaing visited Hassan II in Morocco, ostensibly to confirm their agreement of June, 1975. Also under the discussion was supplying of radar equipment, helicopters, "AMX" tanks and reconnaissance equipment. The Moroccans ordered twenty-five F-1 Mirages and took an option on fifty others, but since these could neither be delivered before twelve months nor Moroccan pilots trained to fly them, the French sent the Moroccans six transport planes (C130) and eighty helicopters.

Reports of large military expenditure by Morocco were already reaching the U.S. media by 1976. One of the reports suggests that "Morocco bought nearly $300 million dollars worth of arms in 1975 and projected buying $178 million dollars worth in 1976 and $150 million dollars worth in 1977" (Lippert 1977, 57)—a lot of money for a developing country to spend on armaments. The SPLA army of 5,000 was outnumbered by more than ten to one by the better equipped Forces Armée Royal (FAR). Despite the superiority of the Moroccan army, the Polisario Front was still able to infiltrate Moroccan lines, go deep into the country, and sabotage military convoys, equipment, and mining installations. Moreover, the financial benefit that was expected from phosphate mines in the western Sahara was not forthcoming, and the productive mines inside Morocco were also being sabotaged. It became clear to the Moroccan High Command that they were not just fighting a war in which they were on the offensive most of the time. In fact, quite the opposite was true. To make matters worse, the Moroccans had no idea when and where the Polisario Front *maquisards* (resistance) would strike next. The Moroccan High Command in the desert, led by General Ahmed Dlimi, took desperate steps to curb the guerrillas' success. They destroyed the support bases of the guerrillas among civilian populations and poisoned waterholes. It was a move that backfired badly in the international community, as the word got out.[27]

Five years afterward, the war dragged on with still no end in sight—the Green March adventure was becoming a great embarrassment to the king and his government. The war also began to produce dissent among the Moroccan people, including those who had enthusiastically taken part in the march when the king urged them to seize the territory before the Algerians got there. Dissent was common among the intellectuals, who voiced their opinions in the foreign press whenever they had the opportunity. Professor Abdallah Laroui, a historian, and a member of the USFP, had enthusiastically taken part in the Green March on

16 October 1975, but he condemned the Saharan war as ill-advised and remorsefully confirmed that he would no longer work for Moroccan nationalism. A former Moroccan military officer, Mohammed Ben Saïd, spoke against the war and the king's treatment of opposition party members who were either languishing in prison or were in exile.[28] Another opposition member writes that the Saharan war "was founded on *quid pro quo*," alluding to the dependence of the king on France and NATO for weapons.[29] The king used the weapons to combat France's number one enemy on the continent, Algeria, as well as fight his own wars against the Polisario Front and the opposition movements in his country.

The events that were unfolding in Morocco from the 1970s through the early 1980s began to isolate the king from the international community. In Africa, the Organization of African Unity, the OAU, took a stance in favor of self-determination for the people of the western Sahara by granting the SPLA a seat in the OAU in 1982. It was a move that made Morocco boycott the meetings of the OAU for several years.[30] In desperation, the king embarked upon what the press described as "une opération psychologique."[31] In an interview with a German magazine, *Der Spiegel*, in January 1981, the king said that he was sure that the war had ended. However, his suggestion was accurately described as "a premature hope." But while the king talked about the end of the war, both sides were consolidating their positions and gearing up for more battles for many years to come. The Polisario Front was still infiltrating phosphate mines and sabotaging equipment in Morocco.

By 1985, the high command of the FAR embarked on its most ambitious defensive project, the construction of a 2,500-kilometer wall of sand to reduce the infiltration of the Polisario Sahara People's Liberation Army (SPLA), which always came to Moroccan phosphate mines through Algeria.[32] The sand wall extended from the east of the garrison of Zaag in the Ouarkziz Mountains, all the way to the Atlantic coast, south of Boujadour, and was equipped with radar and observation posts. The Moroccan forces began to minimize the activities of the SPLA greatly after the construction of the wall. Although neither side of the warring enemies could claim victory in the war at that time, both sides became uncommitted to the United Nations and the OAU-sponsored peace plans. The king and his high command remained anxious to get the western Saharan crisis off the international agenda, with the hope that time would wear out the SPLA. But the SPLA was interested in keeping the issue on the international front pages, with the hope that, by winning the media battles, it could also wear out the resolve of the king to keep the territory. The 1960s through the early

1980s were the most difficult moments in the king's career as a monarch and a head of state.

There was less investment in the country following the king's economic policies of the early 1970s, which focused on the Morocconization of the economy—the nationalization of lands that were owned by foreign nationals, largely French citizens. The Moroccan economy was already experiencing severe problems before the Saharan crisis began. Morocconization worsened the economic situation to the extent that "by the late 1970s, Morocco was seriously in debt and had a current deficit on its balance of payments equivalent to nearly 17 per cent of its gross domestic product" (GDP) (Seddon and Lawless 1993, 710). The government's stabilizing measures in 1979 were ineffective due to an increase in oil price, increased interest rates, and low phosphate prices, as well as the western Saharan crisis, which was consuming about 20 percent of the country's GDP every year.[33] By the early 1980s, the government of Morocco was in serious negotiations with the International Monetary Fund (IMF) for its $13,800m debt. The imposition of structural adjustment programs required by the IMF in 1984 led to high levels of inflation, public discontent, and violent street protests throughout the country, especially in Casablanca. The structural adjustment program was temporarily abandoned until 1985. Unlike the 1978–80 and the 1981–85 development plans, which were entirely unsuccessful, the 1988–92 five-year development plan was anticipated to transform the current account from 1.5 percent of GDP in 1986 to a surplus equivalent of 2.9 percent of GDP in 1992.[34] The five-year development plan was followed by a privatization program of 112 government-owned companies. It was in the middle of the euphoria of this economic recovery that the king conceived his mosque. Hence, the Hassan II Mosque is not just a ritual object intended to rejuvenate a bewildered monarchy. It is also a celebration of the victories the king had won over his greatest tribulations.

A Ritualized Comeback to the World Stage

Was it an accident that the inspection of the construction site of the Hassan II Mosque was the premier cultural display to the visiting twenty-two heads of state of Francophone countries during the Casablanca Summit of December 1988?

King Hassan II took President François Mitterrand, President Omar Bongo of Gabon, and a number of the Moslem clergy on a tour of the construction site more than four years before the mosque was inaugurated. The visit to the construction site served as a prelude to the king's sixtieth birthday in July 1989.[35] The mosque was inaugurated on the eve of the birthday of Prophet Mohammed in August 1993, in the year 1414 of the Moslem calendar, 400 hundred years after al-Mansur inaugurated his Baadi Palace in Marrakech on the same anniversary occasion and in the same way.[36] Showing the mosque to international personalities, such as President Mitterrand and President Omar Bongo, was a reenactment of the ancient rituals that al-Mansur had performed several centuries before. The action indicates how ancient rituals can be adapted to contemporary circumstances for the purpose of renewing the monarchy after two decades of national instability. In this sense, some of the rituals that the king performed with his distinguished guests served as rituals of the rebirth of the Moroccan society, particularly of the monarchy itself, after so many years of tribulations. According to Combs-Schilling (1989, 10), the Moroccan monarchy began the practice of "ritually sacrificing a ram on the nation's behalf on the occasion of the Great Sacrifice ('Id al-Kabir). It was a dramatic reformulation, modeled on Mohammed's own performance, that placed Morocco's monarch in the position of the great collective sacrificer upon whom the good of the whole depends." Mohammed-Allal Sinaceur (Ploquin and Sinaceur 1993, 5) summed up the ritual role of the mosque as follows:

> The Hassan II Mosque springs from a rigorous faith, consecrates the renewal of Islamic arts, breaks with the visible world, and multiplies the images of the immeasurable.... It corresponds to the moment when the life of nations and history became more intense, united and back one another to generate a great action of work of art. The Hassan II Mosque means to prove and suggests, through anti-phrases, and in relationship to a world where all decisive conflicts are mainly part of the invisible order, the origin of the desire to last in the challenge of the unshakable faith faced to the strained shapes of the waves, recurring and renewing for ever.

Sinaceur's evaluation of the mosque concretizes the level of confidence in Rabat in 1988 after decades of tumult in the kingdom. Sinaceur's text also locates the mosque in a social setting that vacillated up and down, before it began to achieve some positive economic and political results in the mid-1980s. The high point of the positive results was the Casablanca Francophone countries' summit of December 1988, over which President Mitterrand of France presided. However, the positive results did not occur overnight; they were a culmination of a series of events that began in the mid-1980s. For example, Morocco's improved relations with Libya encouraged cooperation between the two countries until 1984, but in 1985, relationship between the two countries declined resulting in a unilateral breakup of the relations in 1986 by Morocco. In March 1985, the king dispatched emissaries to more than twenty countries in Africa and the Middle East to explain the Moroccan policies toward western Sahara. He also normalized diplomatic relations with several countries with which he had severed relations for recognizing SPLA. Morocco restored relations with Mexico in June 1985, followed by Angola in July of the same year.[37] In 1976, Morocco and Algeria broke diplomatic relations, but they resumed again "in May 1988, and reopened their frontier" (*The Economist* Intelligence Unit 1993/1994, 6). The normalization of relations between Algiers and Rabat in 1988 paved the way for the king to attend a summit of the Arab League and heads of states of Algeria, Libya, Mauritania, Morocco, and Tunisia, with the intention of developing a regional Maghreb Union.

Hence, 1984–88 were watershed years for the king, who felt more confident among his neighbors, despite the fact that the western Saharan war was not yet over. During this "breathing space," on 9 August 1988, the king announced the construction of his mosque in Casablanca, although the project had actually been in planning since 1985.

I completely agree with Hugo Sada (1989, 29) that the Casablanca Summit was "Morocco's grand return to the African Scene, following four years of diplomatic isolation from the OAU," and the rest of the international community. On that occasion, the king's grand mosque, which was still under construction, was the major celebration ritual.

A Victory in Western Façade

> A monumental symbol of his Europeaness now rises out of the bush in his home village, Yamoussoukro: a vast Roman Catholic Basilica, loosely based on St Peter's in Rome, finished in carved Italian marble and built a few years ago at a cost of $280m. Barely 15% of Ivorians are Catholic.[38] ("Le Vieux est mort," 1993, 45)

> "Since most of the Ivory Coast's 12 million people are non-Christians [63 percent animists and 25 percent Moslems] and only 10 percent are Catholics," [he explains], "we really don't need a Catholic Church that big. And right now, we just can't afford it." His sentiments are echoed by many Ivorians, but many support the Basilica. They dismiss some of the condescending references to "the Basilica in the bush" in the European and U.S. press as typical racist Africa-bashing. All of the big churches in United States and in Europe, including St. Peter's, were built with poverty all around them," says Ivorian student Miriam Djabla. "They are spoken of with great admiration. But the *moment* we Africans build a beautiful big church, we are called extravagant." (Massaquoi 1990)

We have seen that the Casablanca mosque can be located in a social setting that ritualistically celebrates the king's triumphs over his political enemies and social instability. The Côte d'Ivoire basilica, by contrast, cannot be located in a setting where there was continuous struggle with the opposition, despite the fact that the president's political career spanned more than fifty years, during thirty of which he served as the president of the country. More pressing is the reality of having a Roman Catholic Church on the scale of Our Lady of Peace Basilica at Yamoussoukro. Out of an estimated total national population of 12.91 million people, only about 10 percent are Catholics. This is in complete contrast with the Moroccan project, where Islam is the national religion and over 98 percent of the population are Moslems. Moreover, when the national population data of Côte d'Ivoire are broken down according to religious preferences, the scale of the project raises issues of social justice and power dynamics among Catholics, Christians of other denominations, Moslems, and practitioners of other religions. For example, 27.5 percent of the total population of the country are Christians, 40 percent are Moslems, 17 percent are ancestor worshipers, and the remaining 16 percent either practice other religions or are atheists.[39] The scale of the project suggests a strong political dominance of the country by Catholics who are only 10 percent of the population.

Unlike the continuous struggle that the king faced throughout his career, the president annihilated the opposition in his country in two steps. First, he installed a one-party state under the leadership of the PDIC when the country became independent from France in August 1960.[40] The monopoly of PDIC with respect to the political apparatus of the country was justified by the president as a measure to prevent competition that might tear the country apart, due to rivalries among the sixty-plus different ethnic groups. Second, the president further weakened the opposition in 1963–64 by arresting and detaining more than 100 senior opposition members, including some PDIC ministers whom he accused of plotting a coup against his government.[41] Richard Crook (1990) has explained that the alleged 1963 communist plot was designed to eliminate opposition to Baoulé (the president's ethnic group) dominance of the PDIC, particularly by Ivorians from the Bété region of the country, whose ethnically based movement Opposition Africain was seen as a threat by the president. Two localized rebellions led by Kragbe Gnagbe's Parti Nationalist Ivorien in the Gagnoa were interpreted as another military coup.

In 1970 government troops were dispatched to Gagnoa to put down a Bété revolt, and the ultimate death toll was believed to have been several hundred. That episode minimizes the President's chances of winning a much coveted Nobel Peace Prize, despite his recent nomination by some 300 French parliamentarians led by the leader of the right wing Front National, Jean-Marie Le Pen. (*The Economist* Intelligence Unit 1988, 5)

To be nominated for the Nobel Peace Prize by a group of fascists, led by Jean-Marie Le Pen, says a great deal about the positions that the president took in dealing with his political enemies. Analogies have been drawn between the use of human sacrifice and decapitation as methods of eliminating oppositions and rebellious figures in the ancient Akan kingdom, and the methods that the president employed to eliminate his opponents. According to this school of thought (Diarra 1997, 29), the fact that the president was an African doctor, a *chef de canton* of Akoué, and a wealthy grower of cash crops such as cocoa and coffee, encouraged him to see himself as both an "aristocrat and autocrat," as early as 1933, when he first became the *chef de canton* of Akoué. As an aristocrat, he felt that he was destined to rule his country, and the punishment for those who attempted to disrupt this destiny were severe. As a modern autocrat, he had to devise sophisticated means of getting rid of his opponents—which usually involved accusing them of treason. Subsequently, when confronted with an alleged communist plot to overthrow his government in 1963, the president decapitated his opponents in a manner similar to the methods employed by the Ashantene when they wanted to get rid of their opponents. The opponents he allowed to survive were those who accepted "a state of dependency" (Diarra 1997, 24; Toungara 1990, 31) on him, rendering them effectively impotent to oppose the president's one-man rule. Critics of the president following his death have gone as far as describing him as a paranoid man who set the trend that was followed by Nigeria's late General Sani Abacha, the Democratic Republic of Congo's Laurent Kabila, and a legion of African dictators.[42]

Another school of thought maintains that the president "would have been sacrificed for the superior interest of the nation"[43] had he not capitulated to the demands of the opposition parties by legalizing multiparty elections in 1990, when the basilica was consecrated. The activities of the president during the period leading to the inauguration of the edifice and the presidential elections suggest otherwise. He planned the basilica when the country was in its worst economic recession since independence. The planning and construction of the project was highly condemned by members of the opposition, but the president's confidence and security in his position encouraged him to go ahead with the construction of the edifice, justifying it as a personal gift to God, for the sake of peace on earth.

In fact, the president was able to travel abroad during those years, sometimes staying as long as three months in his palaces in Paris and Belgium before returning confidently to his country. During those years, the officials of the government shuttled back and forth between Abidjan and Paris constantly to consult with the president about crucial national decisions. No African head of state enjoyed such security. Many African heads of state are wary about traveling abroad for the fear of being overthrown. The security of President Houphouët-Boigny's position until he died can be attributed to the patrimonial/oligarchal structure that he had installed within the governing PDIC.

In addition, the question of a "dauphin," an heir to the presidency, preoccupied both journalists and politicians alike, in and outside Côte d'Ivoire (*Africa Confidential* 1984, 5; Bourke 1990b, 801; Dahmani 1982, 22; Diallo 1982, 20; Doucet 1987, 1094; Howard 1988), but it did not threaten the president's position. Instead, he contributed to the national anxiety about a possible successor by keeping silent over the matter, and by taking actions that made the succession question urgent. According to *The Economist* Intelligence Unit (1992/1993, 5), Phillipe Yacé was considered to be the heir apparent until he fell out of favor with the president and was deposed from that position. In 1985, the president eliminated the office of the vice president completely. A constitutional amendment was hurriedly made in November 1990, stipulating the transfer of power to the president of the National Assembly "in the event of a Presidential vacancy." In addition, the president took the position that "a Baoulé chief should not know the identity of his successor, meaning that the choice should be made only after his death" (*Africa Confidential* 1987, 2; Howard 1988, 55).

The construction of the edifice and the succession debate were taking place when the president was sinking deeper into senility and was unable to cope with the day-to-day management of his entrenched one-man rule. According to *Africa Confidential* (1990, 5), "President Félix Houphouët-Boigny, opening a recent session of Council of Ministers, asked why his old comrade Camille Alliale was late. Ministers had to explain gently that the President had retired Alliale during last October's reshuffle." Ministers were so concerned about the country being plunged into anarchy that some of them wished for a "medical coup d'état." It was the kind of strategy that facilitated the removal of the then senile Tunisian president, Habib Bourguiba, by his doctors. The same article reports that the president was also preparing for the end by giving away most of his real estate in Abidjan.

Considering that the basilica was planned in 1985, construction began in 1987, and it was completed in 1990, a record time (three years) for a project of that magnitude on the African continent, it is clear that the social setting in which the project was conceived and executed was dominated by the preparation for the aging president's death. In fact, the rush to complete the project in three years, when the country was broke, explains that the president wanted to see his pet project completed while he was still alive. So the planning and the construction of the edifice was an integral part of an elaborate preparation for his departure from political office and also from this world altogether. This observation gives credence to critiques of the president and his basilica such as that of Massaquoi (1990, 116):

> Some praise it as the most inspirational, most enduring symbol of love and peace in Africa. Others call it an obscene waste of money in a country beset by poverty. Some hail it as the embodiment of African technological achievement and pride. Others condemn it as a self-serving attempt by an old man to buy his immortality in heaven on earth.

Lack of decisive political motives like the ones we saw in the Casablanca project calls for us to further explore why the president wanted such an elaborate send-off party. Our point of departure is to investigate how the Baoulé people deal with the death of their chiefs.

The First Burial of a Baoulé Chief

In one of the official publications describing the canopy in the center of the basilica, the authors suggested that the canopy had to obey the "Roman and Byzantine empires' traditions,"[44] which says that the throne of the sovereign would be "decorated by a canopy supported by four columns,"[45] and that this decision was inspired by the need to emphasize the royalty of divine power. The authors of the text implied that the replication of a canopy that closely resembles the one at St. Peter's Basilica in Rome was done in order to obey the canon of "Roman and Byzantine empires' traditions." It is therefore not surprising to see how the four columns of the canopy of Our Lady of Peace Basilica were designed to resemble spiral tree trunks laced with liana stems like those of a tree in a "virgin forest" (Fig. 20). According to the publication, the canopy of Our Lady of Peace Basilica is the "royal Baoulé throne which becomes the throne of the King of Kings, Jesus Christ. Its sober form merges with traditional ornamentation, expression of African Art."[46] What is obvious about this text is the author's freedom to see the Baoulé throne as the throne of "Jesus Christ" and the throne of "Jesus Christ" as the Baoulé throne. It also suggests that the virgin forest from which the liana trees that decorate the columns of the throne were obtained might be a Baoulé virgin forest. More important, if the throne of Jesus Christ is the same as the Baoulé throne, then it is the same throne that the president occupied as a Baoulé chief. The authors of the text obviously do not make any distinction between the Catholic faith and the traditional Baoulé faith, which is rooted in ancestor worship. As in the Casablanca project, mythology and history are being deployed to justify the replicated items. Here, the throne of God is being conflated with the throne at the Vatican and the throne of the Baoulé people's chief.

The conflation of the throne of the "King of Kings" with the Baoulé throne indicates how the postcolonial African elite gives themselves cultural latitudes that enable them to simultaneously experience colonialist styles of life and rituals, and African styles of life and rituals, without really admitting that they are dealing with identity crises. Instead, they explain the identity crises as an essential lifestyle of "civilized people" who are smart enough to respect their cultural ways of life. These identity crises are carried through in all aspects of life: education, religion, bureaucracy, the public, and the domestic spheres of life. In fact, life becomes a series of juxtapositions, and effort is made to explain them as culture. In reality, they have little to do with culture, but more to do with what Jameson (1991), Clark (1986), Lefebvre (1991), and Ghirardo (1996) have clearly elucidated as the production of material life and social hierarchies through inclusive and exclusionary acts deliberately built into the productive process to delineate distinctions. The desire of the president to place himself on a higher level of social distinction in his country and around the world gives credence to critiques like those of Massaquoi (1990) and Toungara (1990), who suggest that the president used the basilica to buy his immortality on earth. Massaquoi's and Toungara's portrayals of the president's buying immortality also point to how funerary rights are held in the Baoulé culture for chiefs.

The writings of Thomas McCaskie (1989) and Vincent Guerry (1972) are particularly pertinent here, because they specifically elucidate Akan-Baoulé chieftancy funerary rites. Funerary rites of chiefs or prominent citizens in Akan-Baoulé culture are on multiple levels. As the custodian of law and order, the guarantor of agricultural and material prosperity, and the mediator between the people of Akan and the ancestors, the Ashantene is metaphorically equated and represented as *gyadua*, the large tree, which provides coolness (social stability), shade (*dwo*), and protection from enemies and evil spirits. Consequently, the death of the Ashantene is likewise metaphorically referred to as the falling of the large tree *(gyadua)*. As the Ashantene is the custodian of the earth, his death is also euphemistically referred to as the corruption of the earth. This latter point is emphasized by both McCaskie (1989, 422) and Guerry (1975, 126), who suggest that it is a capital crime to say that the Ashantene is dead; instead the people of Akan announce the death of their king indirectly.

It was commonly believed that the spirit of the Ashantene had to be prepared before it could be sent home. Until the preparation was completed, and the spirit was properly sent home to the ancestors, the Ashantene's spirit lingered around the whole community, and its presence could spell catastrophe for the people. In practice, the first burial takes place immediately after the death of the Ashantene. The death cannot be announced at this time. Instead, the body is secretly put away to decompose, sometimes for as long as two years. This period, when the spirit of the Ashantene lingers around, waiting to be sent home, is the liminal period. The second burial takes place when the preparation is complete. Then, the skeletons are exhumed from the secret grave, usually somewhere in the compound of the Ashantene, washed, and adorned with treasures, including golden objects, before the final burial takes place. The rituals involved could last for several months. In the olden days, slaves would be found to accompany the Ashantene to the grave—in order to serve him in the afterlife.[47]

The third burial has to do with changing the guard, usually the coronation of another Ashantene, metaphorically equal to the purification of the earth, and the rise of another giant tree, a new tree that would offer protection and lead the whole community to prosperity. The third burial might also be the period when the mourning for the passed Ashantene is over: The members of the immediate family, especially the wives, daughters, closest relatives, and the sons, are supposed to stop wearing their mourning robes. Usually, the most immediate family members of the deceased Ashantene dress in black and will not shave their hair for a long period. It is during the third burial that they can cease to wear their mourning robes and shave. Women may begin to plait their hair if they choose to do so. Also, they can begin to put makeup on their bodies. Such practices are prohibited during the mourning period.

Drawing from his understanding of Baoulé chiefs' burial ceremonies, and his belief that a Baoulé chief should not know who will succeed him, the president was actually taking charge of his own first burial when he constructed the basilica. More important is the aspiration to bury his name in history as a man who loved peace. In addition, this kind of practice also conforms to the kind of performances that many chiefs in sub-Saharan Africa have to undergo when they are at the peaks of their careers: They take titles. For this president, the title he wanted to assume was that of the recipient of the Nobel Peace Prize. As the name suggests, Our Lady of Peace Basilica is a self-styled first burial whose roots are deep in the ancestor worship of Akan-Baoulé chieftancy tradition. Combs-Schilling's (1989) and Turner's (1975) analogies with rituals can help us understand how the burial process of a Baoulé chief was metaphorically enacted by the president when he was constructing his basilica. The president understood that buildings are generally constructed in a step-by-step process, which requires physical planning and interaction with the earth, just as when we plant a tree or when we bury a deceased body.

FUNDING THE MONUMENTS

We will not be able to know the cost of the projects until the respective governments or agencies that were responsible for the construction of the edifices open their financial books. In both cases, the projects were funded by controversial mechanisms that enraged the oppositions—although the president suggested that he paid for the basilica from his own family fortunes that he earned from cocoa and coffee exports. Nobody really knows the worth of his assets accurately enough to be able to validate whether or not he was capable of funding the project by himself, as he claimed. *Africa Confidential* (1988, 5–6) observed that the 130-hectare site allocated to the basilica was carved out of the president's 450-hectare coconut farm. However, that does not account for the US$250–300 million estimated to be the cost of the constructing the project. *Africa Confidential* insists that "the most likely source of the money is two private accounts held by the President in the Public Treasury. Several billion Francs more than is officially allocated to the Presidency passed through these accounts every year. They were in effect bank accounts, on which payments may be made by checks drawn on the Treasury." *Africa Confidential* also suggests that the IMF is aware of the existence of the accounts, because as early as 1981–83 overspending drawn on those accounts upset fiscal stabilization policy that drew the IMF's attention. If anything, it is obvious that the secrecy surrounding the funding of the project actually reinforced feelings of opposition toward the edifice.

On the other hand, the mosque was funded through a public subscription that was as controversial as the funding of the basilica. According to the *Times* (30 August 1993), "government employees complained they were pressured to donate one month of their salaries to fund the project." *The Independent* (31 August 1993) agreed, suggesting that government employees were forced to "donate" parts of their salaries for the project, and businessmen who did not donate enough were embarrassed publicly by government officials. *The Guardian* (31 August 1993) continued along similar lines by suggesting that the king decreed the subscription in 1988, while telling the people that "he who constructs a Mosque where the name of God is invoked, for him the most high will build a house in paradise." *L'Express* (31 August 1993) also discusses the great financial drive following the king's speech in 1988.

Available evidence suggests that the financing of the edifices will remain a controversial subject for years to come. At least this will be the case until we know exactly how much the officials spent on each of the projects and the people of either country are free to express their opinions about the monuments.

NOTES

1. The questions I asked here have been explored in depth by scholars of urban design, environmental behavior studies, and architectural graphics and representation. See Rapoport (1977, 3), Bacon (1974, 21), and Ching (1996, 228).

2. *The Economist* Intelligence Unit, *Country Report, Morocco,* no. 4, 1988, estimated the price at over US$365 million, while Renata Holod and Hasan-Uddin Khan estimated the price between US$400 and US$700 million. Also see *Annuaire de L'Afrique Du Nord,* vol. 27, 1988, pp. 690–694 for how the funds were raised by national campaign and subscription.

3. It should be borne in mind that several city plans have been proposed for Casablanca by the French, although the most comprehensive one appears to be the 1917 project by Henri Prost. Henri Prost proposed several master plans for the city under the colonial French resident governor, General Lyautey. The 1912 Master Plan by Albert de Tardif, and the Plan of 1900 by Dr. Félix Weisgerber also should be kept in mind. The Weisgerber document only reviewed the existing Casbah; the Tardif plan actually extended the boundaries of the city beyond the Casbah. See Cohen and Elab (1998). Also see Wright (1991) and Robinow (1989).

4. The minaret negotiates many angles at its base, giving it multiple sides. One can estimate from seven to ten sides around the courtyard and the surrounding walls.

5. There is no formal financial accounting for this project due to the justification that it is a personal gift to the Church of Rome. However, several sources have been speculating on its overall cost, which is plausible considering the scale at which the project is completed. See *Time,* 3 July 1989, vol. 134, no. 1; and 17 September 1990, vol. 136, no. 1,

p. 61; *Côte-d'Ivoire Country Report,* no. 1, 1990, *The Economist* Intelligence Unit; Bourne (1990a); and *Africa Confidential* 29, no. 20 (7 October 1988): 5.

6. This can be likened to a process that Pratt (1986, 140) evaluates as "reductive normalizing." For Pratt, "reductive normalizing" involves the attempt to make both subjects and objects appear as fixed, codified, reified, to make what is patently cultural appear as if it were natural.

7. Mathey and Fackhoury (1990, 1).

8. See *Basilica of Our Lady of Peace* (1990, 125).

9. See Amondji (1984); Jen-Pieere Aye, "Notre-Dame de la Paix n'est pas Saint-Pierre," *Fraternite Martin,* 11 September 1990; Baulin (1962); Byrnes (1991, 43–89); Joure (1989, 33); and Siriex (1975).

10. One of the major sources of the activities of King Hassan II is the compilation called the speeches of King Hassan II, by the Moroccan ministry of information, Rabat. The series covers several years from the early 1980s.

11. See Ploquin and Sinaceur (1993, 11). Also see Holod and Khan (1997, 56).

12. See Basri (1993, 3).

13. So far, the most elaborate study of how the Moroccan monarchy is constantly renewed through ritual and the details of the ritual is by Combs-Schilling in *Sacred Performances* (1989).

14. See Toungara (1990, 23–54).

15. See Garrard (1993, 290–301). Also see Guerry (1975, 12–13).

16. Ibid. Also see Médard (1982, 162–192).

17. See Ayisi (1980, 190–209).

18. See Toungara (1990, 52).

19. Ibid. Also see *Fraternité Martin* 8 and 17 November 1989.

20. See Hoyle (1984, 41) and Rake (1984/1985, 459–463).

21. See *The Economist* Intelligence Unit, *Côte-d'Ivoire,* no. 3, 1990, p. 11.

22. Ibid.

23. Haskell (1993/1995). In this chapter, Haskell reviewed several examples of how artists and historians have learned from the past through the works of art. The belief that development in the arts, music, literature were inherently linked to the events that were taking place in the society was very common in the last year of the eighteenth century, and it lead to a proliferation of studies that looked to the arts as sources of information for events that happened in the past.

24. See Lefebvre (1991, 73).

25. Although Sultan Mohammed ibn Yousuf was once forced out of the throne by the French government on August 1953, he was allowed to return to it on 5 November 1955.

26. Anne Lippert (1977, 41–60) has a history of the events leading to the invasion of the territory and the consequences of the invasion.

27. Ibid, 53. Also see *Jeune Afrique,* no. 1004 (2 April 1980): 100.

28. See *Jeune Afrique,* no. 1004 (2 April 1980).

29. Ibid.

30. "Morocco: Digging In." *Africa Confidential* 26, no. 16 (31 July 1985).

31. "Sahara la guerre, est-elle finie?" *Jeune Afrique,* no. 1050 (18 February 1981): 20–24.

32. The construction of the defensive wall was covered in newspapers and magazines around the world. See Hermida (1993, 40–43). Also see *Africa Confidential* vol. 26, no. 8 (10 April 1985); *The Economist* Intelligence Unit, *Country Profile Morocco,* 1993/1994, London; and *Le Soleil,* Dakar, Senegal, 19 January 1985.

33. Two separate articles were prepared on the price of the Saharan conflict on the Moroccan economy by Raphaël Mergui (1980) and Phillippe Simonnot (1980) in *Jeune Afrique.* Also see Sanctucci (1992, 851–857).

34. See *The Economist* Intelligent Unit, *Country Profile, Morocco,* 1993/1994, p. 11.

35. See *Jeune Afrique,* no. 1461 (4 January 1989): 31.

36. See Holod and Khan (1997, 61), and Ploquin and Sinaceur (1993, 7).

37. See *Africa Confidential* 26, no. 16 (31 July 1985).

38. Different authors have different estimates for the number of Ivorians who are Catholic. The estimates range from 10 to 15 percent. Sometimes it is put at 12 percent. Also see *The Economist* (11 December 1993, 45).

39. Please see *The Economist* Intelligence Unit, *Country Profile, Côte d'Ivoire/Mali,* 1994/1995, London, pp. 2 and 10–11. Also see Synge (1990, 417). Gerald Bourke also wrote about this in *West Africa,* no. 3812, 17–23 September 1990, p. 2480.

40. See Synge (1984/1985, 457), and *The Economist* Intelligence Unitt (1994/1995, 8).

41. See Woronoff (1972).

42. Howard W. French's review of Samba Diarra's book: *Le Faux Complots d' Houphouët-Boigny* (Paris: Karthala, 1997) appeared in *Foreign Policy,* no. 114 (Spring 1999): 115–119.

43. See *The Economist* Intelligence Unit, *Country Profile Côte d'Ivoire,* no. 4, 17 December 1990, p. 11.

44. See *The Basilica of Our Lady of Peace.* B.P. 1888, Yamoussoukro, Côte d' Ivoire, p. 21.

45. Ibid.

46. Ibid.

47. See Guerry (1975, 127).

REFERENCES

Abu-Lughod, Janet. 1980. "Origins of Urban Apartheid." In *Rabat, Urban Apartheid in Morocco,* 131–149. Princeton, N.J.: Princeton University Press.

Africa Confidential. July 1984. "Ivory Coast: After Houphouët-Boigny." Vol. 25, no. 15. London: Computer Posting Limited, 5.

———. 10 April 1985. Vol. 26, no. 8. London: Computer Posting Limited.

———. May 1987. "Côte d'Ivoire: Rendering unto Cesareo." Vol. 28, no. 10. London: Computer Posting Limited, 2.

———. 1988. Vol. 29, no. 20. London: Computer Posting Limited, 5.

———. 9 March 1990. "Côte d' Ivoire: Houphouët-Boigny Prepares for the End." Vol. 31, no. 5. London: Computer Posting Limited.

———. 28 September 1990. "Côte d'Ivoire: The Labor of Hercules." Vol. 31, no. 19. London: Computer Posting Limited, 5.

Amondji, Marcel. 1984. *Felix Houphouet-Boigny et La Côte d'Ivoire L' Envers d'Une Legende*. Paris: Editions Karthala.

Ayisi, Eric O. 1980. *An Introduction to the Study of African Culture.* Ibadan and Nairobi: Heinemann.

Bacon, Edmond. 1974. *Design of Cities.* New York: Studio Book, Viking Press.

Basri, Driss, Minister of Interior and Information. 1993. *Hassan II Mosque Casablanca.*18 bd Rachidi, Casablanca—B.P. 16249. Morocco: Agence Uban De Casablanca, 3.

Baulin, Jacques. 1962. *La Politique Africaine D'Houphouet-Boigny.* Paris: Editions Eurafor Press.

Bidwell, Robin. 1994. "History." In *The Middle East and North Africa,* 678–697. London: Europa Publications.

Bourke, Gerald. 1990a. "Pope Consecrates a Controversial $200m Basilica, Beauty or Beast?" *West Africa,* no. 3812 (17–23 September): 2480.

———. 1990b. "Houphouët-Boigny Considers Constitutional Reforms." *West Africa,* no. 3794 (14–20 May): 801.

———. 1990c. "Houphouët's Heavy Hand." *Africa Report* 35, no. 2 (May–June): 13–16.

Byrnes, Riba M. 1991. *Historical Setting. Côte d'Ivoire. A Country Study.* Washington, D.C.: Library of Congress.

Ching, Francis D. K. 1996. *Architecture, Form, Space, and Order.* New York: Van Nostrand Reinhold.

Clark, Timothy. J. 1986. *The Painting of Modern Life: Paris in the Art of Manet and His Followers.* Princeton, N.J.: Princeton University Press.

Cohen, Jean-Louis, and Monique Eleb. 1998. *Casablanca. Mythes et Figures d'une Aventure Urban.* Paris and Casablanca: Édition Belvisi and Édition Hazan.

Combs-Schilling, M. E. 1989. *Sacred Performances. Islam, Sexuality, and Sacrifice.* New York: Columbia University Press.

Crook, Richard. 1990. "Politics, the Cocoa Crisis, and Administration in Côte d'Ivoire." *Journal of Modern African Studies* 28, no. 4: 649–669.

Dahmani, Abdelaziz. 27 January 1982. "L'attente Houphouët se porte mieux que le pays, mais l'avenir demeure incertain." *Jeune Afrique,* no. 1099: 22–25.

Debord, Guy. 1995. *The Society of the Spectacle,* trans. Donald Nicholson-Smith. New York: Zone Books.

Diallo, Siradiou. 27 January 1982. "Côte d'Ivoire: Le Fauteuil Vide." *Jeune Afrique,* no. 1099: 20–22.

Diarra, Samba. 1997. *Les Faux Complots d'Houphouët-Boigny fracture dans le destin d'une nation.* Paris: Edition Karthala.

Diop, David. 1970. "The Vultures." In *New African Literature and the Arts,* ed. Joseph Okpaku, vol. 2. New York: Thomas Y. Crowell.

Doucet, Lyse. 8 June 1987. "Côte d'Ivorie Unable to Pay." *West Africa,* no. 3643: 1095.

Fakhoury, Pierre. 1990. *La Basilique Notre-Dame de la Paix Yamoussoukro.* Liege: Magada.

Fatton, Robert. 1992. *Predatory Rule. State and Civil Society in Africa.* Boulder and London: Lynne Rienner.

Garrard, Timothy. 1993. "The Baoulé: An Introduction." In *Art of Côte d'Ivoire from the Collection of the Barbier-Mueller Museum,* ed. Jean Paul Barbier, vol. 1, 290–301. New York: Barbier-Mueller Museum.

Ghirardo, Diane. 1996. *Architecture after Modernism.* New York: Thames and Hudson, 1996.

Guerry, Vincent. 1975. *Life with the Baoulé,* trans. Nora Hodges. New York: Three Continents Press.

Hagan, Geroge. 1981. "Le concept de pouvoir dans la culture Akan." In *Le Concept de pouvoiren Afrique,* 56–83. Paris: UNESCO.

Haskell, Francis. 1993/1995. "The Artist as an Index of Society." In *History and Its Images: Art and the Interpretation of the Past,* 217–235. New Haven, Conn.: Yale University Press.

Hatcher, Evelyn Payne. 1985. *Art as Culture: An Introduction to the Anthropology of Art.* New York: University Press of America.

Hermida, Alfred. 1993. "The Forgotten Front." *Africa Report* 38, no. 3: 40–43.

Holod, Renata, and Hasan-Uddin Khan. 1997. *The Mosque and the Modern World. Architects, Patrons and Designers since the 1950s.* London: Thames and Hudson.

Howard, William. 1988. "The Succession Crisis." *Africa Report* 33, no. 3 (May–June): 53–55.

Hoyle, Russ. 16 January 1984. "Sweating It Out in Abidjan; Despite Setbacks, the Ivory Coast Remains a Rare Success Story." *Time* 123: 41.

Jackson, Robert H., and Carl G. Rosberg. 1982. *Personal Rule in Black Africa. Prince, Autocrat, Prophet, Tyrant.* Berkeley: University of California Press.

Jameson, Fredric. 1991. *Postmodernism, or, The Cultural Logic of Late Capitalism.* Durham, N.C.: Duke University Press.

Jeune Afrique. 2 April 1980. No. 1004: 97–112.

Joure, Kolo. 1989. "Felix Houphouet-Boigny et la Paix." Les Nouvelles Editions Africaines. *New African* (September): 33.

Lefebvre, Henri. 1991. *The Production of Space,* trans. Donald Nicholson-Smith. Cambridge, Mass.: Blackwell.

Le Soliel. 19 January 1985. Dakar, Senegal.

"Le Vieux est mort: Cotê d'Ivoire." 11 December 1993. *The Economist* 329, no. 7841: 45.

Lippert, Anne. 1977. "Emergence or Submergence of a Potential State: The Struggle in Western Sahara." *Africa Today* 24, no. 1: 41–60.

Markus, Thomas. 1995. "What Do Buildings Have to Do with Power?" *Architectural Design* 65, no. 3/4 (March–April): 8–20.

Massaquoi, Hans, J. December 1990. "An African Gift to the Vatican: The World's Largest Church (Félix Houphouët-Boigny, Basilica of Our Lady of Peace)." *Ebony* 46, no. 2: 116.

Mathey, Francois. 1990. "Preface." In *La Basilique Notre-Dame de la Paix Yamoussoukro,* by Pierre Fackhoury. Liege: Magada.

McCaskie, Thomas, C. 1989. "Death and the Asanthene: A Historical Meditation." *Journal of African History* 30: 417–444.

Médard, Jean-Francois. 1982. "The Underdeveloped State in Tropical Africa: Political Clientelism or Neo-patrimonialism?" In *Private Patronage and Public Power: Political Clientelism in the Modern State,* ed. Christopher Clapham, 162–192. New York: St. Martin's Press.

Mergui, Raphaël. 5 March 1980. "Rabat améliore ses position." *Jeune Afrique,* no. 1000: 22–25.

"Morocco: Digging In." 31 July 1985. *Africa Confidential* 26, no. 16.

Our Lady of Peace Foundation. 1990. *Basilica of Our Lady of Peace (La Basilic Notre-Dame de la Paix).* Yamoussoukro: Basilique Notre-Dame De La Paix, B.P. Yamoussoukro, Côte d'Ivoire.

Ploquin, Philippe, and Mohammed-Allal Sinaceur. 1993. *La Mosquée Hassan II* (*The Hassan II Mosque*). Photographiée par Philippe Ploquin et Francis Peuriot; textes de Mohammed-Allal Sinaceur; assisté par Mustapha Kasri, Ali Amahane, Houceïne Kasri. Drémil-Lafage: Editions D. Briand.

Potholm, Christian P. 1976. *The Theory and Practice of African Politics.* Englewood Cliffs, N.J.: Prentice Hall.

Pratt, Mary Louis. 1986. "Scratches on the Face of the Country; or What Mr. Barrow Saw in the Land of the Bushmen." In *"Race," Writing, and Difference,* ed. H. L. Gates, 138–163. Chicago: University of Chicago Press.

Rake, Alan. 1984–85. "Economy" In *Africa South of the Sahara,* 14th ed. London: Europa Publication.

Rapoport, Amos. 1977. *Human Aspects of Urban Form. Towards a Man–Environment Approach to Urban Form and Design.* New York: Pergamon Press.

Robinow, Paul. 1989. "Techno-Cosmopolitanism." In *French Modern,* 277–319. Cambridge, Mass.: MIT Press.

Sada, Hugo. 4 January 1989. "Afrique-France un succès pour Hassan II." *Jeune Afrique,* no. 1461: 31.

"Sahara la guerre, est-elle finie?" 18 February 1981. *Jeune Afrique,* no. 1050: 20–24.

Sanctucci, Jean-Claude. 1992. "Les limites de l 'ordré monétaire et financier: Le reflux de l'économique et la pression du social." In *Annuare de L'Afrique du Nord,* vol. 31, 851–857. Paris: CNRS Édition.

Schapiro, Meyer. 1994. *Theory and Philosophy of Art: Style, Artist, and Society. Selected Papers.* New York: George Braziller.

Seddon, David, and Richard Lawless. 1993. "Economy." In *The Middle East and North Africa,* 710. London: Europa Publications.

Simonnot, Phillippe. 5 March 1980. "Le bilan économique de la guerre." *Jeune Afrique,* no. 1000: 26–28.

Siriex, Paul-Henri. 1975. *Houphouet-Boigny: An African Statesman,* trans. Kevin Conlon. Les Nouvelles Editions Africaines.

Synge, Richard. 1984/1985. "Recent History." In *Africa South of the Sahara 1984–85,* 14th ed., 457. London: Europa Publications.

———. 1990. "Recent History." In *Africa South of the Sahara 1990,* 19th ed., 417. London: Europa Publications.

The Economist. 11 December 1993. Vol. 329, no. 7841: 45.

The Economist Intelligence Unit. 1994–95. *Country Profile, Côte d'Ivoire/Mali,* 1994–95, London: *The Economist* Intelligence Unit, 2 and 10–11.

———. *Country Report, Morocco,* 1988, no. 4. London: *The Economist* Intelligence Unit.

———. *Country Profile Morocco,* 1993/1994. London: *The Economist* Intelligence Unit.

———. *Country Profile Morocco,* 1991/1992. London: *The Economist* Intelligence Unit.

———. *Country Profile Côte d'Ivoire,* 1992/1993. London: *The Economist* Intelligence Unit, 5.

———. *Country Profile Côte d'Ivoire,* no. 3, 1990. London: *The Economist* Intelligence Unit, 11.

———. *Country Profile Côte d'Ivoire,* no. 4, 17 December 1990. London: *The Economist* Intelligence Unit, 11.

———. *Country Profile Côte d'Ivoire,* no. 2, 1988. London: *The Economist* Intelligence Unit, 6.

———. *Country Profile Côte d'Ivoire,* no. 1, 1989. London: *The Economist* Intelligence Unit, 7–8.

———. *Country Profile Côte d'Ivoire,* no. 3, 1986. London: *The Economist* Intelligence Unit, 10.

Toungara, Jeanne Maddox. 1990. "The Apotheosis of Côte d'Ivoire's Nana Houphouët-Boigny." *Journal of Modern African Studies* 28, no. 1: 23–54.

Tournier, Pascal, and Francis Kpantindé. 1990. "Houphouët offre au pape sa 'belle dame.' *Jeune Afrique,* no. 1549: 14–17.

Turner, Victor. 1975. "Death and the Dead in the Pilgrimage Process." In *Religion and Social Change in Southern Africa,* ed. M. West and M. Whisson, 107–127. Cape Town: David Philip.

Woronoff, Jon. 1972. *West African Wager: Houphouët versus Nkrumah.* Metuchen, N.J.: Scarecrow Press.

Wright, Gwendolyn. 1991. "Introduction." In *The Politics of Design in French Colonial Urbanism,* 1–13. Chicago: University of Chicago Press.

Chapter 2

Designing the Monuments and the Cities

THE ARCHITECTS

The primary roles of the architects, Michel Pinseau and Pierre Fakhoury, were those of urban ideologists, who took simple ideas such as "the throne of God is on the waters," and brought them to physical reality. In addition, they visually expanded and glorified the ideologies as divine decrees, in order to situate the king and the president as links between God and the citizens of the countries in which the objects are located. The function attendant on the architects' roles as urban ideologists was an important one for ensuring the immortality of the king and the president.

It has been established that "one of the hallmarks of man-environment research is the realization that designers and users are very different in their reactions to environments, their preferences, and so on, partly because their schemata vary" (Rapoport 1982, 15; Hall 1969). It appears to me that if the schemata of patrons, architects, and the public vary, ultimately, their design objectives will also vary. When monumental projects are involved, the architect might try either to please the client or to subvert the client's objectives by designing what might bring himself or herself architectural fame. Or in rare instances, he or she might truly try to design for the masses.

In light of the competition between patrons, designers, and the public, one may assume that the designs the architects produced for their projects were intended to be the finales of their individual careers. Pierre Fakhoury acknowledges that any reference to the basilica will also invoke the name of the architect who designed it long after his death.[1] The implication is that the designs of the monuments had several competing ideological agendas from the very moments that the projects were conceived. We are reminded once again that, as urban ideologists, architects who are involved in the production of monumental buildings such as Our Lady of Peace Basilica and the Hassan II Mosque create designs that will "impress either the populace with the power of the patron, or the peer group of designers and cognoscenti with the cleverness of the designer and good taste of the patron" (Rapoport 1969, 2).

Architect Pierre Fakhoury

Pierre Fakhoury was forty-seven years old when he was handpicked by President Houphouët-Boigny to design Our Lady of Peace Basilica at Yamoussoukro. He is Lebanese-Franco-Ivorian, a Parisian-based architect whose career was made in Africa. His major projects before the basilica include a cardiology center in Trenchville, a low-income neighborhood of Abidjan, a hospital at Yopougon, and the Hotel Ivoire in Abidjan, Côte d'Ivoire.

In the elaborate monograph *La Basilic Notre-Dame de la Paix,* which describes the Yamoussoukro project, Fakhoury's (1990) brief text suggests a lack of involvement in the project. He saw himself as man who was only carrying out orders from the president, and he believed that he had thoroughly executed his duties and deserved credit for a job well done. Fakhoury's text gives us some preliminary insights into reading his design. However, we need to go deeper into the architectonic layers of social hierarchy in Côte d'Ivoire to clearly understand where Fakhoury fits in the social schema of the project, and to analyze his design of the basilica beyond the façade that he has presented to us.

Dubbed "Builder of Eternity" by *Jeune Afrique,* Fakhoury's architectural portfolio does demonstrate certain qualifications that might explain why he was chosen by the president to design the basilica.[2] Nevertheless, his participation in the project also indicates the existence of a third layer of social hierarchy of people who manage the economy of Côte d'Ivoire, the Lebanese. While the president and the top officials of the PDIC constituted the first layer of social hierarchy in Côte d'Ivoire, the 100,000-strong French community, to whom the president entrusted the management of his economy since independence in the 1960s, constituted the second tier of hierarchy. The endless Lebanese Civil War has been encouraging the departure of large numbers of Christians from the country since 1974. Some of the Lebanese found their way to West Africa, and the largest number settled in the Côte d'Ivoire. Estimates of the number who settled in Côte d'Ivoire vary from "30,000 (an official figure, and far too low) to 300,000. The true total seems to be 100,000 to 200,000" (Bistoury 1989, 1329).[3] These groups, first predominantly Christians, but later joined by Moslems (especially members of the Shi'a), formed a distinct third layer of middle class above the Africans. The Lebanese left their countries with sufficient funds to enable them to get involved in all sectors of the economy: from import/export, to medical equipment, banking, transport, property development, supermarket proprietorship, textile, and street-side vending. The Lebanese community began to experience severe resentment from the Africans when the world's cocoa and coffee prices dropped in the 1980s, and recession hit Côte d'Ivoire severely, leading to the loss of national income. The highly pro-government newspaper *Fraternité Martin* (25 June 1986) began to take swings at Lebanese businessmen in its editorials, suggesting that they were corrupting the police, customs officials, and public officials in order to avoid paying taxes. An increase in social violence and agitation by students and political opposition movements in 1990, the year of the commissioning of the Yamoussoukro edifice, encouraged labor movements to circulate tracts asking for a boycott of jobs by Lebanese proprietors, especially taxi drivers, who drove for their Lebanese bosses.[4]

Although Ivorians began to resent the successes of the Lebanese business community during the economic crisis of the 1990s, the community actually consolidated its position in Côte d'Ivoire in the 1980s and obtained a high profile that boosted its ability to participate in certain political events in the country. Details of the community's involvement in world affairs are yet to be published; however, plausible connections have been sketched between the community and certain influential elements in Beirut. One of the Lebanese community leaders, Imam Adnana Zalghout, who was residing in Abidjan, was linked to Amal in Beirut. Also, a strong connection was established between Imam Jaafar El Saegh who resided in Abidjan and the Beirut Hizbollah.[5] It was suggested that these groups of influential Lebanese had access to the powerful Ayatollah Khomeini regime in Iran.[6]

Establishing the connections between certain influential Lebanese who were residing in Abidjan and certain influential Lebanese in Beirut was not really a surprise. However, connecting the president of Côte d'Ivoire to the clandestine activities of the influential Lebanese in Abidjan and Beirut was something else, particularly when the president was represented as a mediator between the Beirut hostage takers and the Western countries whose citizens were held in Beirut. Instead of coming out to publicly deny or substantiate the allegation that was circulating in the media that he was personally, secretly, involved in the negotiations for freeing of the American, British, French, German, and other Western hostages who were held in Beirut, the president chose to exploit the fact that Côte d'Ivoire was a point of convergence for the various groups who were heavily invested in the Lebanese crisis, including Palestinians and Syrians, following the Israeli invasion of southern Lebanon in 1982. When the president refused to state whether or not he was involved in the freeing of the hostages, he left it open to the media to speculate that the connections of the Lebanese community to certain influential people in their homeland, particularly Beirut, also translated into international political assets for the president. In this circumstance the press circulated information that the president used the links between the Lebanese-Ivorian Shi'a imams and their Beirut counterparts to free the hostages.

The president knew that it was lucrative to be perceived as a man who played the role of a peacemaker for the West, especially during the Ronald Reagan, Margaret Thatcher, and the Mitterrand governments. He wanted the world to believe that he had the ability to tap into the links between Imam Adnana Zalghout, who was residing in Abidjan and the Amal in Beirut, and to call on his connections to Imam Jaafar El Saegh who resided in Abidjan but also had strong links with the Beirut Hizbollah.[7]

It is not a secret that one of the ways in which the Beirut war was funded was by profit from hostages. Some of the hostage takers quit the business after they had made huge sums of money, went to the Côte d'Ivoire to enjoy their bounty, and invested in other businesses in the country. According to Bistoury (1989, 1329), "it seems clear that earnings in Côte d'Ivoire fund the activities of all sides in Lebanon's endless wars; fighters from both sides come to Abidjan for rest and recuperation." Possible involvement of Abidjan in freeing Western hostages from Beirut has also been noted by *The Economist* Intelligence Unit.[8] Commenting after a DC-10 belonging to the French carrier *Union des Transport Aeriens* went down over Niger on 19 September 1989 while on its way from Brazzaville to Paris via Ndjamena, *The Economist* Intelligence Unit suggested that:

There were allegations that extremist Lebanese Shia Moslems based in Africa were responsible for planting the bomb which caused the explosion, killing 171 people on board. In an article on the disaster, the right wing Paris based weekly *Minute* maintained that members of Côte d'Ivoire's 300,000 strong Lebanese community—the biggest on the continent—had strong links with Hizbollah. It claimed that the release of three hostages in Beirut just before the final round of voting in the French Presidential elections in May 1988 had been secured as a result of the intervention of its leaders. This paper also claimed that the killing of a French army colonel, Pierre Chirol, in Abidjan in June this year [1989] was not, as has been claimed, the work of armed robbers, but a politically motivated murder. Colonel Chirol, ostensibly on secondment to the Ivorian government as an adviser on Arab affairs, was, it maintained, employed by French intelligence to identify Shia terrorists. A month before his death, the paper went on, Chirol discovered that an extremist Shia terrorist group was planning attacks on French interests.

It would have been nice to have more proof of the role of Houphouët-Boigny in securing the hostages for the Western states. Nevertheless, such an idea cannot be totally dismissed despite the tenuous evidence—that is, if we take into consideration the strength and the activities of the Lebanese community in Abidjan and the obvious connections that these Ivorian-Lebanese have in their homeland—we can see how the president might have been tempted to exploit the connections between his Lebanese refugees and Beirut for his political gains. More important is the fact that helping secure the release of the Western hostages was not just a humanitarian project for the president. Acting as a participant in the negotiations for securing the hostages also helped give him the image of a man of peace in the eyes of the Western leaders, whose favor he desperately needed, if he was ever going to secure his Nobel Peace Prize.

Without minimizing Fakhoury's talent, it is apparent that if the Lebanese community helped elevate the status of the president in the eyes of the Western world, he had to give something back to the community besides being a gracious host to them. Thus, he was obliged to compensate the community by awarding it with numerous contracts, including the design of his largest project, the basilica. The award of the design contract for the basilica to Fakhoury confirms that the Lebanese community had infiltrated the Ivorian economy so well that it ranked next to the French community within the Ivorian social structure. That left the indigenous Ivorian business community in a fourth social hierarchy. As Fakhoury put it in a recent statement, "Le Président ne m'a pas donné la basilique. Il m'a accordé sa confiance. Et j'ai construit avec cette confiance" (The president did not give me a basilica. He trusted me, and I built the monument with his trust).[9] This exchange of trust between the Lebanese community and the president reflected what happened in the society economically and politically when critical decisions needed to be made. The French were always the first to be consulted, then the Lebanese, leaving the Africans clearly out of the decision process, except on ceremonial issues that had no power or economic benefit. We are further reminded by Fakhoury that the architecture of the basilica was addressed to a select international elite whom the president wanted to impress, the French community, and then the Lebanese community, and the final design of the project was created with this audience in mind.

The minimalization of the role played by African businessmen and bureaucrats by the president is confirmed by the appointment of a French construction "czar," Antoine Cesareo, as the director of the Direction et Controle des Grands Travaux, who was dubbed the emperor of the Ivorian construction industry during Houphouët-Boigny's last years. Antoine Cesareo was in charge of all government construction projects in Côte d'Ivoire. He was given so much power that he was only accountable to the president. Critics saw the move as the president's way of keeping all the lucrative construction contracts among his family and immediate followers. However, it was highly likely that it was the president's way of ensuring that all the construction projects he had begun were completed before he died, especially his pet project, Our Lady of Peace Basilica.[10] The losers in the administrative structure that the president had created were the Ivorian citizens—more specifically, their culture—when it came to the design of the edifice.

Architect/Engineer Michel Pinseau

Like Pierre Fakhoury, Michel Pinseau was a personal architect to the client he served. For many years, Pinseau was King Hassan II's director of public works, wielding enormous power that enabled him to control all the major constructions in the kingdom of Morocco. His last major project, before he began work on the mosque, was an estimated $300 million royal palace that was completed at Agirdi, a place where the king hardly went and that one Moroccan professor referred to as a "phantom palace."

Pinseau's role in the feasibility studies, the design, the construction, and the inauguration of the mosque was published in the lavishly illustrated book *Mosquée Hassan II,* which he coauthored with Abow Kakr Kaddiri under the guidance of the powerful minister of interior and information, Driss Basri.[11]

Michel Pinseau's statements as the principal architect and engineer of the project lend weight to the argument that ideologists are "nothing other than a 'class of cultural persons' who act as *freischwebende Intellektuelle,* as thinkers who provide but justification. Their job is solely the consolidation of existing reality" (Tafuri 1976, 52). Like Pierre Fakhoury, Pinseau confirmed that he did not question what he was told to do. He refused to acknowledge any responsibility for the mosque. According to Pinseau, he had designed the mosque according to the wishes of the king, who told him in October 1985 to do a study for a mosque, a museum, and a national library/archive.[12]

Moreover, Pinseau's description of the site during his feasibility study is in sharp contrast with the historically documented character of the city. Pinseau wrote that the king chose the site because he was inspired by the Koranic verse "the throne of God was on the water." Next, he interpreted the Spanish origin of the name of the city, *Casa-blanca,* the white house, which is a well-known fact. Pinseau's aim for tracing the origin of the name of the city was to endow the city with the character and the milieu of a holy ground. Characterizing Casablanca as a religious town was a front designed to make the construction of the colossal mosque appear as the appropriate project for a city that has been dominated by religious activities since the time it was founded. Nothing close to Pinseau's representation of the city of Casablanca as a holy ground that has always been dominated by religious activities can be found in the works of scholars (Cohen and Eleb 1998), who have documented the growth of the city as purely commercially inspired.[13] Once again, we can see an instance where religion, mythology, and history are exploited to convey the impression that the mosque is located where it is naturally meant to be. Pinseau emphasized that the entire design of the project and the supervision of the construction was done by the king, who laid the foundation stone for the edifice on 11 July 1986. To further his argument that the construction of the mosque was natural, Pinseau connected one of the design innovations that was introduced on its ceiling to religious rituals. The king insisted on the mobile ceiling because he wanted his subjects who would worship in the mosque to be able to contemplate both the ocean and the blue sky of God. Here the mobile ceiling is essentialized as an inseparable aspect of the kind of prayers that were intended to take place in the mosque.

Keeping in mind that more than 60 percent of the commercial activities of the kingdom take place in Casablanca, it is obvious that Pinseau's characterization of the city is particularly motivated by a desire to justify the edifice he had built. Pinseau's statement reinforces the fact that it was the king who made the choice of siting the project near the ancient *medina* (town/village/casbah) of Casablanca in order to bring it near to his people. He goes on to point out, significantly, that it was the king's ambition that the mosque combining old and new technologies in equal proportions would be the most beautiful Moslem structure in the world. Pinseau also tells us that the king's desire to build the most beautiful, grand, and certainly the most ostentatious mosque in the world was so strong that he rejected the first minaret that he had designed on the grounds that it was too short. He had to redesign the minaret by raising the height from 175 meters (568 feet) to 200 meters (650 feet). This inflated height of the minaret would have serious impact on the final design of the edifice, as we will see in the section on the architectural style of the structure.

Nonetheless, Pinseau's statement suggests a real contrast with what happened in Côte d'Ivoire, where the president, whose values and architectural taste were, in Fakhoury's words, essentially "Greco-Roman," had absolutely no consideration for Ivorian building traditions. But in one important way, the two architects had very similar attitudes about their projects: They distanced themselves from their works and presented themselves as innocent technocrats who were only obeying the orders of their clients. What were these orders or ideologies?

THE IDEOLOGIES

Karl Mannheim (1985, 55) suggests that the term "ideology" can be read in two ways: "particular ideology" or "total ideology." My concern here is with the "particular" usage of the term, which "denotes that we are skeptical of the ideas and representations" advanced by the subjects (in this case King Hassan II and President Houphouët-Boigny) as justifications for their actions (building the mosque and the basilica). The ideas advanced by our subjects are considered to be deliberate "disguises of the real nature of the situations," since it would not be in their interests to explain the situations, or to reveal the true meaning(s) of their ideas to the public. Mannheim (1985, 55) continues that such disguises have a wide range: They could be "conscious lies, calculated attempts to dupe others, and self deception." Thus, we may look rather skeptically at the statements that it was the Koranic verse "the throne of God was on the water" that inspired the king to build his mosque in Casablanca. We may be similarly skeptical of the statement that "universal peace and love" inspired the president to build his basilica.

The ideologies by themselves are impotent. They become powerful only after they are realized through the skills of highly specialized intellectuals—the architects. It is here that the triangulated contests between the edifices, the leaders who built them, and the people of the respective countries are played out. Architects Pierre Fakhoury and Michel Pinseau possess the new intellectual weapons, specialized skills of urban and building design, with which to consolidate the positions of their clients over their adversaries, the people. Each architect designed an edifice to be a modern idol closely tied to the personality of his client, and each architect masked his client's real position with his religious and humanist rhetoric. According to Mannheim (1985, 61), "the idols [fetishes] are 'phantoms' or 'preconceptions,' and there are, as we know, the idols of the tribe, the cave, of the market, and of the theater." Mannheim continues that all of the various idols are sources of error that sometimes come from human nature, sometimes from the individuals, and sometimes from society and tradition.

At Casablanca, the idol has roots in Moroccan antiquity, but it is justified in a contemporary circumstance by a simple verse that says that "the throne of God was on the water." At Yamoussoukro, the idol is rooted in Akan-Baoulé chieftancy traditions, but it is justified in a contemporary circumstance by a vague concept of "universal peace and love." In both cases, the idols are "obstacles in the path to the true knowledge" (Mannheim 1985, 62) in the Moroccan and in the Ivorian societies, respectively. These two monumental objects falsely suggest to the public that the leaders have the missions of liberating humanity from suffering. But we need to evaluate their missions in light of the antiquated architectural artifacts they have replicated.

The Only Bridge to the Future

> I have read in the books by Bukhari and Moslem this Hadith by the Prophet—blessings and peace be upon him—"whoever builds a Mosque where the name of God is invoked, the Almighty will build a home for him in Paradise." That is how I got the idea of building a Mosque in Casablanca by means of subscription by all Moroccans, even though it may be one Dirham." (Excerpt from His Majesty, King Hassan II's speech, 11 July 1988)

The ideology for the mosque embedded in the checkered history of Morocco aims to consolidate the belief that, "authority passes from God to Mohammed to the political ruler [King Hassan II] in the present" (Combs-Schilling 1989, 172).

There are several justifications for replicating ancient Moroccan architecture at the mosque by highly placed officials of the kingdom, including the minister of the interior and information, Driss Basri, and the minister of cultural affairs, Allal Sinaceur.[14] Each text produced by the authorities is presented as if it were a royal directive. But the texts also imply that they contain something older than the instructions of the king, namely the authentic traditions of Morocco. This implies that the authors themselves and all the people of Morocco are executing their sacred civic responsibilities, just as ancient people of the country used to do under the guidance of their kings. Thus Moroccans will continue to obey the king, as they always have. It also implies that serving the king has historically been the most sacred duty for all Moroccans, and any deviation from that cultural norm will spell doom for the whole country. In this particular context, the authors want the people of Morocco to believe that an edifice like the mosque is a visual representation of the historical manner in which the people of Morocco have always related to God through their king.

For a staunch royalist like the powerful minister of interior and information Basri, in whom the king confided frequently and who served in his post from the 1970s until the end of 1999 when King Mohammed VI took over the throne, the construction of the mosque was one more opportunity to impose his views on the relationships between God, the king, and the people of Morocco. Closely associated with the Moroccan Royal Academy, Minister Basri always teamed up with his associates in the academy and mobilized the resources of the Ministry of Interior and Information to explain the positions of the king on major national decisions. When the mosque was being built, he was concerned with countering complaints of human rights abuses by his government and spreading propaganda on what he calls "decentralization of power" through constitutional reforms in the kingdom. He addressed each issue with numerous publications. His publications on various aspects of the Moroccan government were already in circulation by the 1970s as part of his information service to the kingdom. *Trente annies de vie constitutionnelle au Maroc* (1993), and *La Maroc et les droit de l'homme: positions, rialisations et perspectives* (1994) were targeted at critics of the king's policies on these matters. Therefore, his numerous publications in defense of the mosque should not surprise us.

Basri's *Royaume du Maroc. La Mosquée Hassan II Une Oeuvre Architecturale et Spirituelle* (1994, 3), asks the question: "pourquoi une Mosquée" (why a mosque)? His response is that every religion has the idea of a "sacred place" where its faith, spirit, and psychology can be expressed. According to Basri, the fact that abstract religious concepts and symbolism cannot always be expressed materially suggests that it is also the wish of God that sacred places and mosques should represent his omniscience and omnipresence. God abides both physically and spiritually in a place blessed by his "Divinity." This concept of sacred space inspired Abraham and Ishmael to build the "Kaâba in conformity with a divine decree."[15] The sacred place is itself the symbol of divine blessing, as well as somewhere for Moslems to adore God. It "is certainly in conformity with the above philosophy that His Majesty King Hassan II"[16] decided to build a great mosque in Casablanca, Basri maintains. Reading Basri's text carefully, one gets the feeling that the king's wish to build his mosque in Casablanca predates even Prophet Mohammed. According to the text, the king was conforming to an original act of spiritual devotion initiated by Abraham and Ishmael. It is not just the king's response to the ancient Abrahamic act of constructing holy sites that legitimized the construction of his mosque, continues Basri, but his role as the Commander of the Faithful.

For Basri, the realization of the grandiose edifice in the manner of the saints is an expression of the fervent and unshakable faith of the people of Morocco, who responded to the king's inspiration that "he who builds a Mosque where the holy name of God is proclaimed shall have a place built for him in paradise." The king is represented as someone highly knowledgeable in ancient Islamic and Moroccan architecture—a man able to deploy his wisdom and skills appropriately in the construction of his mosque. His Majesty expressed his desire to build his mosque on 11 July 1988: "I want there to be a great and beautiful achievement whereof Casablanca would be proud till the end of times. I want a Mosque to be built here alongside the sea, a magnificent temple of God, a Mosque whose high minaret would indicate the way to safety—that is, the way to Allah."[17]

Basri concluded that the mosque is the result of the "expression of the genius"[18] of the king. The implication that the king was the "genius" behind the realization of the mosque gives him a special place among the ancient kings of Morocco who built monuments such as the twelfth-century mosques of Hassan in Rabat and the Kutubiyya in Marrakech. Giving all the credits for the production of the mosque to the king is a form of ritual incantation, designed to reinvent him as an ancient monarch living in the twentieth century. Thus, Basri's text reminds us that, at the Hassan II Mosque, both the subject, the king, and the object, the mosque, are replicated artifacts that Professor Davis (1996, 1) defines as "the sequentially produced similar morphologies—made or imagined material forms that are always 'artifacts' and often images—that are substitutable for one another in specific social contexts of use." In a sense all the kings of Morocco, and all the great monuments they built, were being replicated by King Hassan II at Casablanca.

The 1993 text by the minister of cultural affairs, Mohammed-Allal Sinaceur, is even more poetic than Basri's. But its objective is the same—to reinforce the belief that the ancient kings and cultures of Morocco still exist in the person of Hassan II, since Moroccan culture is a connected and "indestructible" whole. According to Sinaceur (Ploquin and Sinaceur 1993, 5):

> You cannot possibly edify such an important monument as The Hassan II Mosque without being fascinated by the idea of perfection of forms. To reach this perfection, you will need accuracy, sensibility as well as the fertile shock of indestructible cultures, the vastness of horizons, a taste of eternity, the experience acquired through centuries and condensed in one moment, collected on the enchanting spot where the work twinkles and radiates the modes and symbols of beauty.

Sinaceur's eulogy for the (then still living) king reminded the reader that the technological applications in the mosque signified tomorrow's Morocco, and the king was the only apostle who could safely lead Morocco into the future. Therefore, the king's genius in constructing the mosque demonstrates the continuity of the traditions of Morocco, spearheaded by "Averros, the apostle of reason, as well as the tolerance of thousands of ingenious artists," who were highly learned Koranic scholars. According to Sinaceur, Averros and the "ingenious artists" did not just labor to translate and exploit the cultures and the resources of the territory. They were also committed to advancing "expressions of the royalty," and "popular determinations." Sinaceur (Ploquin and Sinaceur 1993, 5) goes on to say that the royal expressions and popular determinations embody "the mysterious and irresistible determination to be present in the world, to mould history, to receive and give, to share in a world the elements that stamped perseverance of the beings we are, dedicated to creation and to God, so infinitely small in the infinite space that is reminiscent of Him." Technology, for Sinaceur, is not only a necessary ingredient for anybody waiting to experience today's world, but also an important tool for preserving and perpetuating the past into the future. Sinaceur believes that the mosque is a testimony to the proclivity of the Moroccan people to assimilate external influences—especially adaptation to modern technology—as an effective means of preserving the past. As a result, "while remaining faithful to the traditional inspiration, the Mosque uses all the sophisticated technological gains, and thus reflects the personality of the King who is tightly attached to the spirit of contemporary civilization as well as to the teaching of Islam" (Ploquin and Sinaceur 1993, 17). The technology used in the king's mosque is both an embodiment of his beliefs and a means for preserving his ancient heritage, without which the monarchy cannot survive. The mobile roof in the gigantic prayer hall, for instance, symbolizes the king's belief in the past and the future. Contemporary technology is one of the things that Morocco needs the most in order to improve the people's standard of living. The mobile roof, located in the house of God, was a good ornamental show piece for convincing the people of Morocco that the country was achieving the skills it needed to better the people's lives.

Putting this mobile roof aside—what is Morocco's real level of technological achievement and why did the king choose a religious setting to showcase his country's progress in the twentieth century? We can view the colossal scale of the project and its technological innovations as disguises of the real nature of the situations in Morocco. The technological innovations in the roof of the mosque are strategic, symbolic representations of the king. Anyone entering the mosque will notice the roof when it opens and closes. This particular device has never been applied on the roof of any mosque. It is indeed a spectacular commodity whereby "the commodity's mechanical accumulation unleashes a limitless artificiality in face of which all living desire is disarmed. The cumulative power of this autonomous realm of artifice necessarily everywhere entails a falsification of life" (Debord 1995, 45). Here we have religious, symbolic, and material evidence of how a combination of modern icons (technology) and ancient architectural styles from the twelfth century coalesces into one spectacularly falsified entity, which still points to the belief that "the throne of God was on the waters." This combination of contemporary technology, religion, and ancient architectural styles has a targeted audience, as Sinaceur (Ploquin and Sinaceur 1993, 11) explains:

> The combination of the ancient and the modern reaches a peak of perfection in the roof of the prayer hall that is so finely, so patiently decorated and that can be automatically opened in five minutes to let the sun bathe the inner space, and make of it a replica of the large neighboring esplanade, which can accommodate up to eighty thousand faithful.

The term "faithful" is highly ambiguous in this context. Does Sinaceur mean "faithful" to God, or to the king? And can the citizens of Morocco separate both and still be right according to the law of the land? The sections dealing with the site and the architecture of the edifice will concentrate on this point. For now, we will explore contrasts between the autochthonous ideology that grounds the mosque in the genius of the king, and the Ivorian ideology driven by the search for a perfect architectural style, which, it believed, could only come out of the Greco-Roman tradition.

Designing a Mansion for God

> The edifice itself rests on a granite base, respecting the wish of the architect to conform at least symbolically to the words of Jesus: "You are Peter, and upon this rock, I will build my Church." (Mathew 16:18)[19]

Unlike the Casablanca project, where zealot followers of the monarchy have produced numerous texts justifying the construction of the edifice, the only official publications on Our Lady of Peace Basilica are *The Basilica of Our Lady of Peace-Basilique Notre-Dame de la Paix* (1990), by Our Lady of Peace International Foundation,[20] and a monograph by the architect, Pierre Fakhoury, and the conservator-in-chief of the Museum of Decorative Art, Côte d'Ivoire, Francois Mathey (1990).

Fakhoury gave what is essentially a technical solution a mythological meaning by suggesting that anchoring the church on a granite foundation was specifically intended to conform to the biblical passage: "You are Peter, and upon this rock, I will build my Church." Fakhoury's evocation of a biblical passage to justify the construction of the mosque provided the church authorities with an opportunity to advance a historical fact: The basilica was supposed to open a new page in "Church history" by reminding the people of Côte d'Ivoire of more than a hundred years of Christianity in their country. However, the history of the church in Côte d'Ivoire can stand on its own without the basilica. The myth also provided the church authorities with an opportunity to further a humanitarian idea: "this house of God [the basilica] witnesses to the desire to transmit a particular message: a message of peace and love."[21] The next item in the text is an appreciation to the benefactor of the basilica:

> This Basilica, the highest in the world, was founded by a man of faith: the President of Ivory Coast, His Excellency Félix Houphouët-Boigny. His solid and profound faith clearly

expresses itself by this masterpiece, offered to God in recognition of a particular grace: Peace. Thanks to his continued generosity, the maintenance of the Basilica is for the main part assured.[22]

One hears a kind and well-meaning voice in such expressions, but it becomes difficult to separate the myth from the actions of the donor. The ideals that inspired the construction of the basilica and the extravagance of the project were justified as a fulfillment of the biblical passage that Fakhoury evoked. The authorities of the church took Fakhoury's trajectory of thought forward by explaining the action of the benefactor with texts that projected certain social ideals and imbued the grandiose object with sacred meanings. For example, the church authorities explained that "when you enter into the Basilica, when you cross the peristyle and gardens, you are at every turn taken aback by souvenirs of different cultures and civilizations."[23]

But there is nothing to suggest that one is about to explore "souvenirs" from "different cultures and civilizations" when entering the shrine of the edifice. The primary materials that make up the church monument enunciate a specific architectural style from Greco-Roman artifacts. The text itself emphasizes that, as a monument "dominated by a Greco-Roman style architecture," the basilica "brings together the most prestigious of all that man could invent, and that which is most historically interesting, and all this accomplished by the most modern of techniques."[24] As a basilica whose design manifesto professes universal peace and love, the elevation of the architectural style that the edifice incorporates above all other styles of architecture can hardly substantiate what the text is saying.

The text suggests that we should not forget that the "Basilica is of an exceptional kind, in that it bears African characteristics, especially, from the Ivory Coast. African decorative elements are incorporated in the exterior contributions."[25] To what extent do the stones, glass, wood, and all the materials that constitute the basilica contribute to the universalization of the edifice?

If we take our cues from the press in answering this question, it will be difficult to substantiate the aims of Fakhoury and the church authorities to pass the object as a universal architectural gift to the humankind. Nobody in the press has identified the colossal object as an architecture that responds to the building contexts in the Côte d'Ivoire. And, to the eye of the pilgrim, the stones read as a well-executed example of a Renaissance-inspired monument derived from Greco-Roman antiquity. The next major materials, the stained glasses,

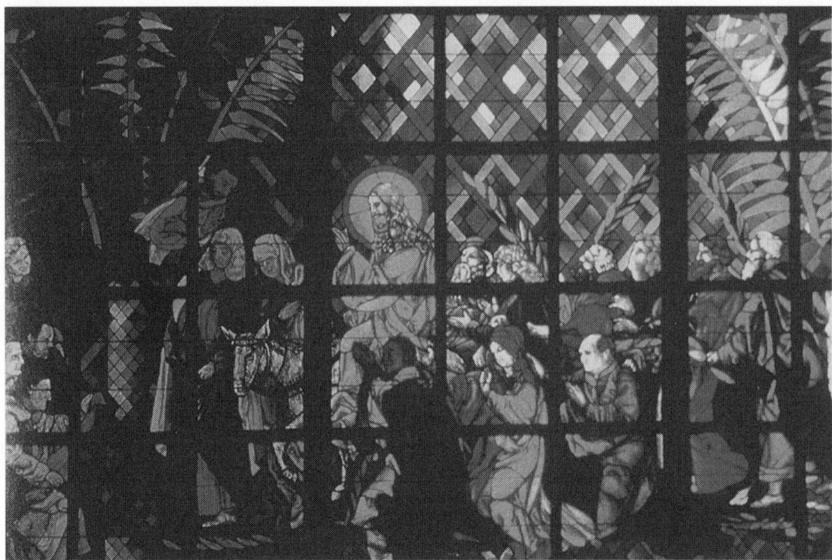

Fig. 26. A stained glass showing the president kneeling before Christ in praises among the saints as Christ rides to Jerusalem. The figure representing the president is the only African saint represented. All the others are figures looking like Europeans. Artistic director, Mr. Patrick Hautille. Manufactured by France Vitrail International. Photo by Madam de Luengas, 1999.

read like a church that is situated in Europe. The majority of the saintly figures represented on the stained glasses are Europeans, except for one black-looking figure who is kneeling before a figure of Jesus Christ (Fig. 26) and who has a distinct resemblance to President Félix Houphouët-Boigny himself. The 7,400 square meters of stained glass include no cultural elements from Judaism, nor are there any Native Americans or Pacific peoples. And there are no Africans except for the single figure who looks very much like the president. The concept of "universal peace and love" is gravely undermined by the narrow choice of art decor made by Fakhoury and his art director, Mr. Patrick d' Hautuille. The iroko wood *Madonna and the Child,* made in prison by a political prisoner whom the president freed following pressure from the Vatican, seems like an afterthought. In fact, the *Madonna and the Child* was a gift to the pope from the prisoner, who was asking the pope to help free him. The pope sent the sculpture back to Yamoussoukro and insisted that it should be kept in the shrine, perhaps as a rebuke to the president for his intolerance of political opponents.

The secret to locating the architect's intentions lies in the repeated emphasis on themes of universal peace and love in the basilica's design program:

> An immense curved colonnade marks the boundaries of the central area which covers three hectares and symbolizes the maternal grandeur of the Catholic Church embracing all populations in her love. This love of divine origin is represented by the Holy Spirit in the form of a dove, the soul of the church, which spreads its wings on the ground in the middle of the bright esplanade.[26]

It is clear that, although the design agenda advocates universal love and peace, Fakhoury had already made up his mind whence the aesthetic values that would convey these concepts would come. Fakhoury's choice was not made because it was the necessary architectural design for a basilica in the Côte d'Ivoire. It was based on the rationale that, out of all the cultures of the world, the "most prestigious of all that man could invent and that which is most historically interesting"[27] can only come out of a Renaissance-inspired Greco-Roman architectural artifact. Above all, this most "prestigious" and most "interesting" architecture is not available in Africa, Arabia, Asia, North and South American cultures, or in the native cultures of the Pacific Ocean. The hidden implication is that neither Africa nor any other part of the world, outside of Greco-Roman antiquity, has an architecture worthy to house a God that is based in Rome. In Fakhoury's own words, "Catholic Church is Roman, and [I] had to design an architecture which expresses the Roman architecture, but adapted to the circumstances at Yamoussoukro."[28] Here adaptation is conflated with exotic decorations. Fakhoury continued that his project is a "faithful translation of the ideological values of the President."

Our Lady of Peace Basilica is a celebration of the roles the president assumed at the beginning of his political career: an African chief, a farmer, a landowner, a Catholic, and above all an anti-communist. As I have indicated in my introduction, the president aligned himself with a conservative, international elite who looked out for him, and he identified that elite as his "metropolitan fraternal" colleagues. It is therefore not surprising that the president went to the metropolis, to the people he admired the most, to select an architectural style for his basilica.

Fakhoury's design failed to take into account African architectural precedents because the audience for which the basilica was intended compelled the president and his architect not to pay any attention to them. If Fakhoury had done some research on African architecture, he would have discovered that the people of Côte d'Ivoire and people in West Africa as a whole already had ways of representing columns, portals, windows, roofs, and all the architectonic elements that constitute buildings. The design outcome of the Yamoussoukro basilica would have been considerably different if it had been intended for an *African audience.* This point becomes obvious upon visiting the second-largest church building on the African continent, also in the Côte d'Ivoire, the Cathedral of St. Paul, Abidjan, by the Italian architect Aldo Spirito. It was completed and inaugurated by Pope John Paul II on 10 August 1985, on the same trip that he laid the foundation stone for Our Lady of Peace Basilica.

Although the Cathedral of St. Paul, Abidjan, cost about one-sixth the estimated price tag of the Yamoussoukro basilica, it is obvious from the design that, unlike the Yamoussoukro project, its primary audience is the people of Côte d'Ivoire.

Looking across the Bay of Cocody, toward Plateau, the hub of business activities in Abidjan, of Côte d'Ivoire, one can see an anthropomorphic, white concrete column glowing on a sunny day (Fig. 27). With one end of a set of seven cables anchored at the back of its spread arms and shoulder, and the other end of the cables pinned to a gigantic triangular structure, the object appears as if it is being tugged into the adjacent lagoon. The structure is made of concrete, steel, travertine, stones, and sheets of stained glasses. It covers a surface area of 4,500 square meters (about 14,625 square feet), with a seating capacity of 3,500 people, and standing room for additional 1,500. The modernist form of the cathedral gives it one major advantage: It could be situated on any continent and in any city in the world, and it would fit in contextually.

An official publication by the authorities of the cathedral, *La Cathédral d' Abidjan* (1989, 3), gives several symbolic meanings—"Christ with his arms spread out like the famous Christ of Rio; Jesus drawing its church towards the future; the trinity"—to the triangular form of the church and its anthropomorphic cross. There is something else about the design of this cathedral to suggest that the architect focused on the people of Côte d'Ivoire as its principal audience. Unlike the Yamoussoukro stained glasses, the ones at St. Paul's Cathedral contain two kinds of narratives: biblical narratives and narratives that tie the lives of Ivorian Catholics to the faith. Directly behind the altar, the stained glass shows the conversion of St. Paul on the road to Damascus. On the left wall of the church, facing the altar, the giant stained glass depicts various events in the

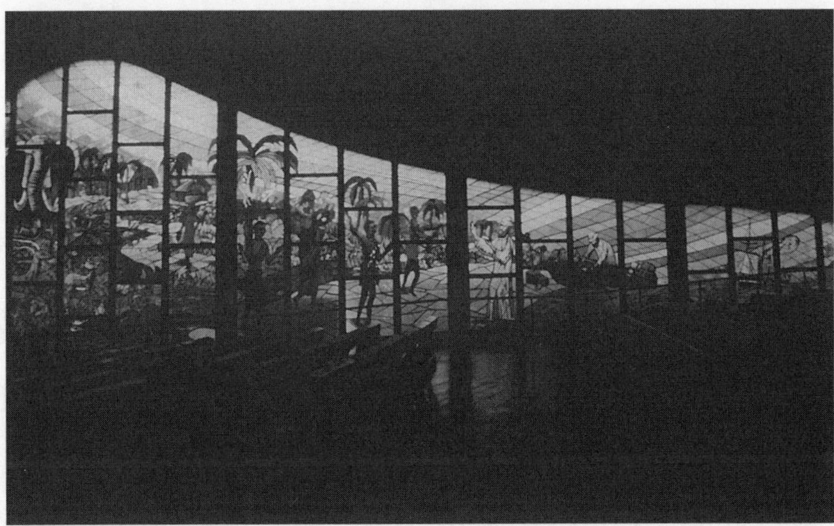

Fig. 27. A stained glass narrating the encounter between European missionaries and Ivorians in Grand Bassam in the 1880s. From left to right: the image of an African village by the ocean; a large elephant, the national symbol of Côte d'Ivoire, is in the foreground. The image also shows villagers welcoming the European missionaries as they disembark from their boat, while the missionaries also reach out to the villagers with courtesy. By the Italian artist Roberto Franzosi 1980–85.

life of St. Paul. To the left of the stained glass, St. Paul is depicted writing letters to various communities. His journey to Rome to be judged is represented in the middle, while the bottom right shows him preaching to different communities. On the right wall of the church, facing the alter, a stained glass, the same size as the one on the left wall of the church, shows the earliest encounters between the people of Grand Bassam, Côte d'Ivoire, and European missionaries on 28 October 1895 (Fig. 27).

In the latter stained glass, the background is a village setting next to the beach. At the left-hand corner, a large elephant, the coat of arms of the country, is depicted facing the viewer. Other wildlife follow, as well as the villagers who carry baskets of fruits and other gifts for their visitors. From the right, a European missionary wearing a white robe and a bowler hat spreads his arms toward the approaching villagers. Surely it is a welcoming arm reciprocating to the goodwill of the villagers. His partner is still on the boat offloading supplies. The sail of the vessel that brought them across the ocean can be seen in the distance in the right-hand corner. The encounter represents both a cultural meeting and a religious initiation. This work tells the people of Côte d'Ivoire about their lives and their relationships to the Church in Rome. The mosaics, paintings, and other stained glasses in the church also suggest that the church was built for all Christians regardless of their cultural and ethnic heritage. It would be difficult for architect Pierre Fakhoury to convince anyone who has visited St. Paul's Cathedral, Abidjan, and Our Lady of Peace Basilica, Yamoussoukro, that the latter edifice was built for the people of Côte d'Ivoire, considering that the two buildings are contemporaries, just five years apart. It was the target audience, and not architectural considerations, that drove the ideology of the basilica and gave it visual representations.

THE STYLES OF ARCHITECTURE

Hassanian Architectural Style

> One must not forget, however, that Hassanian architecture begins mainly with the edification of the Mohammed V Mausoleum and of a set of great projects that enabled the refurbishing of royal palaces in Fez, in Marrakesh, in Rabat, in Casablanca as well as the construction of new royal palaces in Agadir and Nador. (Ploquin and Sinaceur 1993, 17)

This section focuses specifically on the use of multiple architectonic elements from Moroccan building traditions, and from famous Islamic monuments around the world, to formulate what is now called "Hassanian architecture"[29] by the Moroccan minister of cultural affairs, Sinaceur (Ploquin and Sinaceur 1993, 17).

Hassanian architecture, as exemplified by the Hassan II Mosque, is essentially a form of cultural harvest.[30] It is a ritual replication of architectonic "artifacts" that contain centuries of memories of the Moroccan people, memories that represent the king as the only possible glue that can bind together the society's past, present, and future. Every replication, writes Whitney Davis (1996, 3–4), "each individual artifact or image, must be seen as the intersection of many different chains of replications." It is therefore possible to treat replicated images and artifacts as "fossilized evidence of cognition and, in narrower cases, of human consciousness." The ritual of replicating architectonic forms to formulate a Hassanian architecture is confirmed by Combs-Schilling (1989, 31), who asserts that "great orienting rituals" can equal great battles and other important historical events in the building of collective life. Combs-Schilling goes on to say that "rituals are staged cultural expressions that at their best appear neither staged nor cultural, but rather evoke life as it exists in its essence." In the context of the Hassanian architecture, the ritual is performed primarily by means of chronological erasures of the evolutionary stages of Moroccan architecture. The process necessitates the compression of all elegant ancient Moroccan architectonic artifacts into the present, and according all credits for past architectural glories of the kingdom to the king.

The architectonic elements at the Hassan II Mosque are assembled from some of the most sacred ancient shrines and monuments of Morocco, such as the twelfth-century mosques of Hassan in Rabat and the Kutubiyya in Marrakech. Another important source is the ancient Roman fortress site that now houses the tomb of King Mohammed V in Rabat. The broken, overweight minaret, the Tour Hassan, is located on the end of the site overlooking the sea, and the tomb of Muhammad V is located on the opposite end. Wedged between the two structures, slightly nearer to the broken minaret, is the Moroccan Tomb of the Unknown Soldiers. Several broken round columns still stand in linear order throughout the site—remnants of the Tour Hassan. The site in Rabat had a great influence on the architectural design of the Hassan II mosque in Casablanca. By taking the architectonic elements from the ancient site to his mosque in Casablanca, the king was able to demonstrate that he was continuing the ancient tradition of the country, and more important, he was able to do so on a grander scale and more extravagantly than his father or any king who had ruled Morocco before himself. Essentially, the principles of Hassanian architecture are rooted in a competition between the king, his father, and his father's predecessors.

The advocates for Hassanian architecture (Basri et al. 1993; Ploquin and Sinaceur 1993, 17) clearly recognized the nebulous problem of reducing several prominent distinct Islamic and Moroccan architecture styles into one periodic episode. To deal with the problem of clarity and procedure, the promoters of the concept decided to coin a selective historical narrative, which elucidates the origins of certain "artifacts" or "forms" from ancient Islamic landmarks that have been replicated at the Casablanca mosque. Giving all the credit for the application of the "artifacts" or "forms" in the new mosque to the divine wisdom and genius of the king, they grounded the design of the mosque in an evolutionary chain leading back to the Dome of the Rock (also called Qubbat al Sakhra, A.D. 688–692) in Jerusalem, the Great Mosque of Medina (A.D. 705–710), the Great Mosque of Damascus (A.D. 705–715), the Kairouan Mosque in Tunisia (A.D. 663), and the Great Mosque of Cordoba (A.D. 785–786), which was rebuilt and expanded by many succeeding Moslem leaders. Other ancient mosques from which the Hassan II Mosque claimed lineage are the Qarawiyyin Mosque (956 and 1135) of Morocco, the Great Mosque of Tlemecen (1136), and the Great Mosque of Algiers (1096).[31] According to Sinaceur (Ploquin and Sinaceur 1993, 13), "the Hassan II Mosque is part of the tradition of religious monuments, in the phases of their history, in the quest of the architectural art it consecrates by bringing it to the heights of fame, by renewing it, by adapting it to the means that enable it to get free from the impact and stamp of the city of another age."

In his text, Driss Basri (1993) adds that the Hassan II Mosque is the second-largest mosque in the world after the Al Haramayn Acharifayn, the Holy Mosque in Mecca. Nevertheless, the Hassan II Mosque surpasses the Blue Mosque in Istanbul, the Giralda in Sebilla, the Al-Azhar Mosque in Cairo, and the Ommayyed Mosque in Damascus.[32] The location of the Hassan II Mosque within this tradition shows the "capacity" of the Moroccan people to absorb external influences in order to enrich local craftsmanship. Sinaceur's narrative highlights the artistic traditions from the Almoravid Dynasty, through the influences of the Andalousian monarchs, the Merinides, and concludes: "the Hassan II Mosque undeniably marks the continuity of a modernized ancestral art" (Ploquin and Sinaceur 1993, 17). It bears the sign both of technical innovations and fertile exploration of new aesthetic possibilities.

The genealogies of Allal Sinaceur and Driss Basri do not, for instance, help us to understand why the Hassan II Mosque adopted the the basilical floor plan, instead of the usual T-shaped floor plan that is common in North African mosques. The basic plans of most mosques have the *qibla* walls parallel to the naves. On the other hand, in the basilical plan, the nave of the mosque is usually perpendicular to the *qibla* wall. The basilical plan of the Hassan II Mosque encouraged Holod and Khan (1997, 61) to comment that it is "an unconventional layout, given that it is customary for the rows of worshippers facing Mecca to be as wide as possible rather than extend further back."

Sinaceur (Ploquin and Sinaceur 1993, 13) justifies his unconventional choice by presenting it to the audience as part of the natural genealogical evolution of a specific mosque prototype, which has been incorporated in several ancient mosques, naming the Great Mosque of Kairouan and Tunisia as examples. According to Sinaceur (Ploquin and Sinaceur 1993, 13), "the layout of the naves directed in depth, perpendicular to the qibla wall, a layout called 'Basilical' and already adopted by the al-Aqsâ Mosque [in Jerusalem], will be reproduced and perpetuated in the Mosque of Ifriqiya [the present Tunisia], Spain and other parts of the Maghreb."

The floor plans of the mosques that Sinaceur used as examples had specific reasons for adopting the basilical plan, but they still managed to respond to the custom of having the widest row of people facing toward Mecca during prayers. The al-Aqsâ might be one of the earliest mosques in the Islamic world to orient its *qibla* wall to the nave at a right angle, because the builders wanted to "orient the mihrab aisle upon the south entrance of the Dome of the Rock" (Hoag 1977, 22), one of the most holy places of Islam. Hoag (1977, 22) also explains that this orientation of the nave in the al-Aqsâ Mosque enabled al-Walid I (A.D. 709–715) to reinforce the sanctity of the site. By doing so, al-Walid was able to equate the mosque with "Constantine's Basilica, which had a similar relation to the Anastasis" and with the "Church of the Nativity at Bethlehem, which has the same orientation towards Christ's birthplace." The plan of the al-Aqsâ is the typical T-shaped plan that is also the basic plan of the Kairouan Mosque, Tunisia. The Kairouan Mosque is said to have defined the major characteristics of all the mosques in the Maghreb, Egypt, and western Islamic mosques.[33] In Spain, particularly at the Great Mosque of Cordoba, the T-shaped plan originally built by Abd er-Rahman 786/76 took centuries of expansions under different leaders before the aisle perpendicular to the *qibla* wall became deep enough to give the mosque a basilical plan.

It is my position that the Hassan II Mosque adopted the basilical floor plan because of the commercial intentions of the mosque. The application of the basilical plan at the Hassan II Mosque is an inevitable result of the conflict between King Hassan II the ancient aristocrat and King Hassan II the contemporary leader who must develop commerce and industry in order to meet the needs of his country. If commerce and industry could influence the Moroccan monarch to take a theological verse that suggests that "the throne of God is on the waters" to this extent, it calls to mind Marshall Berman's (1982, 15) following observations:

> To be modern is to live a life of paradox and contradiction. It is to be overpowered by the immense bureaucratic organizations that have the power to control and often to destroy all communities, values; and yet to be undeterred in our determination to face

these forces, to fight to change their world and make it our own. It is to be both revolutionary and conservative: alive to new possibilities for experience and adventure, frightened by the nihilistic depths to which so many modern adventures lead, longing to create and to hold on to something real even as everything melts. We might even say that to be fully modern is to be anti-modern.

The justification of the basilical plan of the Hassan II Mosque as a natural evolution from the al-Aqsâ Mosque, the Great Mosque of Kairouan, and the Mosque of Cordoba not only is tenuous but also masks the underlying intention to facilitate an urban design that would engender the most intensive, capitalist urban renewal project that the city of Casablanca has ever seen. However, to say so would have driven the point home that "all that is solid melts into air, all that is holy is profaned, and men at last are forced to face with sober senses the real conditions of their relations with their fellow men."[34]

At the Hassan II Mosque, when reading the composition of the floor plans, the minaret, the superstructure, the ornamentation, and the surrounding landscape, it is futile to look for a chronological order or any sort of systematic order in which the architectonic elements from the past are replicated in the present, despite the genealogical chain that has been presented to us by the promoters of the Hassanian style. Instead, the style expands the ideology of the constancy of Moroccan culture as embodied in the person of the king. Hassanian architectural style aspires to become an achievement of unsurpassed visual harmony through the process of incremental juxtapositions of unrelated architectonic artifacts from different Islamic building traditions. The aim is to achieve a "total theater" that can serve as another icon for the king.

The predominant columns, horseshoe arches, tympanums of the major portals, and the maze of *murqarnas* that decorate the ceilings, domes, arches, and walls can be located both in ancient monuments and in recent monuments such as the Mohammed V Mausoleum in Rabat.[35] André Piccard (1980, 21) recalls in his two-volume set, *Traditional Islamic Craft in Moroccan Architecture,* that "Morocco had just lost the well-beloved Mohammed V, achiever of its independence, when Hassan II issued his call to the elite artisans to erect a mausoleum that would reflect the fervor and veneration with which this illustrious man was regarded." Exaggerated or not, Piccard's view accurately depicts the moment when Hassanian architecture started in the country. It did not begin solely to edify the late monarch; it developed because it was discovered early that the monuments could be a major source of revenue for the country whose third-largest foreign exchange earner was tourism. As Piccard indicates, since 1970, when the Mohammed V mausoleum was completed, "in every town, innumerable work projects were begun to renovate royal palaces, Mosques, medersas, mausoleums, public buildings, and bring the most varied crafts back into use." Such renovations were intricately interwoven with the political agenda of the Moroccan monarchy. For, as the renovations took on cultural meanings, they also became conduits of the cultural legacies of the monarchy. "In Marrakesh for example, some 3,000 artisans were employed to restore the Royal Palace. The king wanted this palace to be more than an adornment. He wanted it to be a spectacular affirmation of national identity" (Piccard 1980, 21).

If the Hassanian style of architecture is not chronological, and it is essentially dependent on the renovation and preservation of ancient monuments, what is special about it? At the Hassan II Mosque, although the style of architecture in the edifice is not new, the technological innovation is. What is unique is the inclusion of *hammams* (Moroccan bathhouses) in the edifice. The *hammams*, which also function as powder rooms in the mosque, are deliberately conflated with the ablution fountains, which are primarily places for cleansing the body before one goes to prayers, while the powder rooms are places where people go to beautify themselves for the vanities of the world. The proximity in the social meanings of the swimming pools, the *hammams*, and the ablution fountains makes a new cultural statement by unifying the worldly with the sacred. Perhaps it is to further the well-known fact that Islam is emphatic on cleanliness, but its secular undertone cannot be ignored. This point is new in the history of mosque designs.

But any originality in Hassanian architectural style is an inconclusive kind, raising more questions than answers as it indiscriminately mixes the old and the new. Keeping in mind that the visual artifacts of Hassanian architecture are all derived from antiquity, the question is: how far would the king have gone to consolidate Hassanian archiecture? Can he consolidate a Hassanian style of architecture without bringing major changes to the Moroccan polity, cultural body, women's aspirations, and especially to the monarchy? This question will be addressed in the context of the urban design agenda of the Hassanian architecture at Casablanca, which I have identified as a "total theater," where major commercial activities that are ultimately performances of the king take place. The concept of Hassanian architecture in Casablanca is considerably different from the stylistic architecture that is adopted at the Yamoussoukro's edifice, primarily because of the different audiences that were intended for the monument.

Designing a Repressed Consciousness and Cognition

> Notre-Dame de la paix n'est pas Saint-Pierre.
> (Our Lady of Peace is not Saint Peter's.)
>
> Fakhoury 1990, 18

Feeling besieged by the media coverage of Our Lady of Peace Basilica as a copy of St. Peter's Basilica in Rome, on Monday, 11 September 1990, one day after the consecration of the edifice by the Pope John Paul II, architect Pierre Fakhoury was on the national newspaper of Côte d'Ivoire, crying out loudly that, "Our Lady of Peace is not St. Peter's." Who is telling us the architectural facts that we need to know about Our Lady of Peace? The media or Fakhoury? Our first answer comes from the designer's own writings about his church.

Fakhoury (1990) wrote that he was ordered to design a "Mansion for God Almighty." The order was an act of grace, and of exceptional will, by an individual who aimed to create a palace for the renaissance of Christendom. Fakhoury's text confirmed that he was ordered specifically to design a Roman Catholic Church. He had no choice but to carry out the orders in an architectural "repertoire" that would speak to the time and the circumstances surrounding the creation of the church. He had to create a "dome" (a duomo) in the tradition of ancient temples, but he maintained emphatically that his duomo was a direct translation of the values of the president. According to Fakhoury, he had to go to the original "Latin Plan"—Latin artifact—to retrieve the values that the president desired in his basilica. He expressed that it was difficult working with the "Latin Plan" because it could only be realized by the numerical perfection of its proportions, and any error could make a folly of the entire design. He added that the basilica has "risen up from Ivorian soil, for it is the rose colored sand of Yamoussoukro, the essential component of the structural concrete used, 'stone of our time,' which gives to the whole, its color and appearance as though it is cut stone."[36] What Fakhoury refers to as rose-colored sand is a mixture of laterite, red soil, and concrete, which produces a purple shade on the cast concrete. Most of the exterior columns and the superstructure of the edifice were clad in this particular material. Fakhoury interprets this cosmetic, technical solution, as the contribution of the African culture to the edifice. He emphasized in addition that the "wildlife and flowers of Africa"[37] had been applied to decorate the Virgin Mary, Jesus Christ, and the saints.

Guided by the teachings of the *Bénedictins of Saint-Benoît-Sur Loire,* he was able to design the drawings of the triptych as shown in all the stained glasses, to reflect the Scriptures and also to give it some African coloring. Fakhoury made it clear that his objective was to create a space for assembly and worship. He indicated that he was also concerned about the comments of critics about the cost of the project. Fakhoury's stance was that the cost of the basilica could not be excessive as it was a project for a great continent, Africa. Fakhoury also adamantly maintained that, despite its evocation of St. Peter's Basilica in Rome, Yamoussoukro's basilica was entirely unique. He concluded that the basilica is a most beautiful gift from a man (the president) to his fellow men.

The essence of Fakhoury's plan for the basilica had to be retrieved from ancient artifact, the Latin Plan, but he had to exoticize it, to fit it into the African context. Whitney Davis has succinctly expressed how we might go about reading objects that are part of many different chains of replications: According to Davis (1996, 4), "some of these chains are situated in human persons," for example, in "intrapsychic 'fetishism'"; some of them manifest "intersubjectively in a person's social relations with others," (as is the case with relations that involve the exchange of artifacts and images); while some chains of replication "coordinate the practices of large social groups." Moreover, "every replication potentially inaugurates other chains of replication—no one of which it determines." Davis elucidates further that the meaning of an "image or an artifact" for the people who produce and use them resides in the reality of its "actual or possible replication." If we use Professor Davis's concept of replication as a tool for reading the floor plan of Our Lady of Peace Basilica, we will be better able to reconcile the form of the plan with its idealistic motives. Above all, we will be able to explore the meanings of the plan as European cultural "artifacts" that have been "replicated" in the African continent. In the Yamoussoukro situation, the plan of the edifice and its associate elements were replicated because of the president's "intersubjective relationship" with a select group of people.

Fundamentally speaking, the floor plan of Our Lady of Peace Basilica is a hybridization of St. Peter's Basilica floor plan and the Pantheon floor plan, both in Rome (see Fig. 12, page 43). At St. Peter's in Rome, the circular floor plan of the Pantheon is superimposed onto the Greek Cross–inspired plan by Bramante-Michelangelo.[38] This floor plan is primarily characterized by "a single square with four apsidal bodies forming the cross" (Argan and Contardi

1993, 273). At Yamoussoukro, the extension of the northern arm (main façade) of the Greek Cross plan to about three times the length of the other three arms enables the floor plan to retain a structure that is similar to the fundamental plan of St. Peter's in Rome. It has the advantage of defining the stairs forming the plinth that raises the entire edifice above the surrounding ground, giving it the appropriate image of an ancient Greco-Roman temple. The Doric columns that follow the outline of the Greek Cross plan also help reinforce the image of the ancient temple. Superimposing the floor plan of the Pantheon onto the St. Peter's–inspired floor plan gave the superstructure of the Yamoussoukro edifice the architectonic advantages of both plans. For example, the interior of the shrine was cleared of all supporting structures like columns in the middle, making it an open space to be furnished as the architect wished. Most important, it allowed for the transition space from the parvis to the interior of the shrine, and it is the main source of the Ambulatory of the Twelve Apostles that is anchored to the base of the tambour of the dome. As in the Pantheon, it is also the main source of the design repertoire that inspired the location of shrines in niches in the Ambulatory of the Twelve Apostles. All the apostles, from St. Peter to Mathias, are represented in stained glasses lavishly decorated with tropical leaves and framed by double Corinthian pilasters.

One cannot wander through the Ambulatory of the Apostles at Yamoussoukro without being reminded of the Pantheon in Rome. The seven planetary pagan Roman gods housed in the seven major niches of the Pantheon are reincarnated in the Twelve Apostles windows at the basilica of Our Lady of Peace. These are now presented in exquisitely finished thirteen-by-eight-meter window prisms, which wash the interior of the shrine with cascades of light. At the Yamoussoukro basilica, the double rows of columns that form the transition space from the parvis to the interior of the shrine echo the heavy walls of the Pantheon. The stained glass of the "Holy Spirit" that surmounts the canopy of the dome of Our Lady of Peace Basilica is clearly inspired by the oculus of the Pantheon. The tambour of the dome of Our Lady of Peace Basilica is, without doubt, inspired by the tambour of the dome of St. Peter's. At Yamoussoukro, the windows of the tambour do not have the gables that are present in Michelangelo's windows at St. Peter's, and there is a much bigger stylized blind wall separating one window from the other. However, the principal relationship lies in the treatment of the double Corinthian columns, the bases, and the realm of the tambour. These three elements are unified in similar ways in both basilicas.

The dome of Our Lady of Peace Basilica is essentially inspired by the Michelangelo dome of St. Peter's in Rome, but the dome of the Yamoussoukro basilica is two times taller and wider. The most significant relationships lie in the curvatures of the two domes and the delineation of the major vertical ribs. However, instead of the gabled leaflike windows of the St. Peter's dome, Our Lady of Peace Basilica windows have round oculi similar to Brunelleschi's windows in the dome of the basilica in Florence. Instead of Gianlorenzo Bernini's sickle-shaped colonnades in St. Peter's Piazza in Rome, Fakhoury's colonnade at Yamoussoukro is formed by only a pair of semicircular arms (Figs. 1 and 16). Finally, the canopy in Fakhoury's basilica is inspired by the 1624–27 Giovanni Lorenzo Bernini's baldachin at St. Peter's (Fig. 20). Whereas these are not the only component elements of the basilica at Yamoussoukro that have been modeled after St. Peter's Basilica in Rome, they are the most visible aspects of the superstructure that can remind one of St. Peter's.

If we treat the major replicated elements at Yamoussoukro as Professor Davis (1996, 4) has suggested—that is, as images and artifacts that are "fossilized evidence of cognition and, in narrower cases, of human consciousness"—the implication of the style of architecture that is adopted at the Yamoussoukro basilica will begin to dawn on us. In the description of the plan, Our Lady of Peace Foundation's text (1990, 19) began with the statement that the circle is an ideal figure that "reflects the divine nature," and it is in this image Our Lady of Peace Basilica is crafted. Moreover, the interior architecture of Our Lady of Peace Basilica "wishes to be associated with a tradition which dates back to the Middle Ages, continues throughout the Renaissance and which links the central plan to Marian devotion." The text also confirms that the dome is a form of architecture that "dates to antiquity and reminds us of the Roman Pantheon," which was appropriated by Christian architecture from the "very beginning"—first at "Saint Sophia in Constantinople from [A.D.] 532, and during the Renaissance at Saint Peter's in Rome, and more recently here at Yamoussoukro." This text is grafting the Yamoussoukro edifice onto a specific, ancient, architectural replicatory chain in order to legitimize it. The religious messages conveyed by the artistic ensemble of the ancient buildings permeated all of society. At the Yamoussoukro basilica, the message is conveyed by the stained glasses that once served to educate "[European] illiterates in the Middle Ages."

Unfortunately instead of using the stained glasses for educational purposes as in medieval Europe, at Yamoussoukro this form of art is only "associated with the African taste for color" (Our Lady of Peace Foundation 1990, 33), mainly for reasons of exoticism. The problem arises not because all the saintly figures represented on the stained glasses are people of European origin, but because the architect and his decorators failed to apply historical events drawn from their day-to-day experiences with Christianity that would tie the people of Côte d'Ivoire to the Church. If the messages contained in the stained glasses were educational, the opportunity to fully incorporate Ivorians into church history was regretfully neglected. Worse, the theme of "universal peace and love" was also neglected by the absence of people in the windows from the Americas or Asia.

As John Onians (1988, 3) observes in the *Bearers of Meaning:* "Buildings are as useful to our minds as they are to our bodies. Indeed, those elements which have the most important physical roles are also often the most important psychologically." According to Onians, elements like the posts, pillars, and columns serve both as structural functions and as an aid to people in resolving certain anxieties. Classical orders are not just "elegant solutions to structural" design problems Onians (1988, 3) says:

> Before they were commended as Classical and before they were defined with legal precision as orders, the columns, capitals, and moldings which we know as Tuscan, Doric, Ionic, Corinthian, and Composite were a material means of expression for communities, groups, and individuals. Between their appearance in ancient Greece and their eventual codification in Renaissance Italy, these forms were striking features of the buildings in which people in Western Europe formulated and developed their relationships to the gods, to each other, and to themselves; and it was often through their use that these relationships were articulated.

The edifice produced at Yamoussoukro has successfully awakened a religious consciousness, but it is also a false consciousness, a cognition that does not see any architectural history and precedent that it can consider as worthy of emulation and perpetuation in Africa's contemporary buildings. It forgets that, although contemporary Christianity in sub-Saharan Africa comes from late nineteenth-century European missionaries, the idea of Christianity is not new to Africa. This is one of the major fallacies of the Yamoussoukro monument: It identifies itself with the European Middle Ages and Renaissance, but it wants nothing to do with African history beyond its "wildlife and color." In this regard, and based on Onians's insights on the role of architectural elements in society, the architectural style of the basilica represses African Christian historical consciousness.

URBAN DESIGN AMBITIONS OF THE MONUMENTS

The Hassan II Mosque at Casablanca and the Our Lady of Peace Basilica at Yamoussoukro are the culmination of two independent, long-range urban design goals of the two leaders. The mosque caps the king's goal of building as many palaces as possible in all Moroccan cities, a program he started when he assumed power in 1961 after the death of his father. And the Yamoussoukro project began with the notion of moving the capital of the country from Abidjan to Yamoussoukro. The urban design ambitions of the monuments represent the faith of these two leaders in the capitalist enterprise, and their allegiances to specific interest groups both within and outside their respective countries.

For the king, it meant constantly representing himself as the embodiment of the Moroccan culture without appearing to be setting the country backward in a high-tech age. For the president, it meant preparing a Versailles-like environment where he could showcase his political and ideological successes to his friends in the metropole (Paris, London, Washington), whenever they visited him in Africa. The results of the two urban design projects are different visually, but they both embody what I have called the "total theater."[39] In the Casablanca "total theater," the king is the only performer, but in Yamoussoukro, the people who worship in the edifice are the performers—not so much recognized participants but exotic objects who inflate the egos of their observers—and their presence was only for the purpose of entertaining the class of people for whom the president designed the town of Yamoussoukro and the edifice.

The "total theater" aspires to achieve the absolute, and it "must be with its diversified interweaving of light, space, form, movement, sound, man—with all the possibilities of variation and combination of these elements in turn—an artistic configuration: an ORGANISM."[40] The "organism," that is, the Hassan II Mosque in Casablanca, erases all social boundaries between the king and the people of Morocco. It dominates the people with the weight of the monarchy by presenting itself as the giver of life, peace, protection, prosperity, and religion. As Tafuri (1978, 104) suggests, "this type of total theater no longer has anything in common with Wagner's *Gesamtkunstwerk*. It relies on the primary means of the various instruments of communication; its intent is to give life to a 'great dynamic-rhythmic formal event, which gathers together, in a form reduced to the elementary, the most extensive heap of means, ricocheting off one another.'" The strategy is diagrammatic and effective to the extent that, when confronted with the inevitable loss of the authentic, "in the name of the ludic and of the marvelous, the theater can still occupy the entire popular domain that lies between the religious cult and naïve popular entertainment, marking precisely the borders of legitimate meanings" (Tafuri 1978, 105).

In the Yamoussoukro design, the strategy is less sophisticated: It was the conversion of the old village of Yamoussoukro into a seemingly modern city, whose center stage was not modern capitalism but an ancient Greco-Roman artifact, Our Lady of Peace Basilica. I find Fredric Jameson's (1995) text on postmodern culture a useful tool for exploring these two forms of urban design. According to Jameson (1995, x):

> In postmodern culture, "culture" has become a product in its own right; the market has become a substitute for itself and fully as much a commodity as any of the items it includes within itself: modernism was still minimally and tendentially the critique of the commodity and the effort to make it transcend itself. Postmodernism is the consumption of sheer commodification as a process. The life-style of the superstate therefore stands in relationship to Marx's "fetishism" of commodities as the most advanced monotheism to primitive animism or the most rudimentary idol worship; indeed, any sophisticated theory of the postmodern ought to bear something of the same relationship to Horkheimer and Adorno's old "culture Industry" concept as MTV or fractal ads bear to fifties television series.

What are commodified in the two urban designs are, indeed, ancient architectural vocabularies that, under the auspices of religion, serve far more than nostalgic functions. They legitimize ancient aristocratic privileges for the people who commissioned the objects. These legitimizations are achieved in both cases by modern technology, thereby concretizing Debord's (1995, 99) suggestions that "monotheistic religions were a compromise between myth and history, between the cynical time which still dominated the sphere of production and the irreversible time which was the theater of conflicts and realignments between peoples."

Here, the leaders conceive "human circulation as something to be consumed—tourism—a by-product of the circulation of commodities . . . a chance to go and see what has been made trite" (Debord 1995, 120). In both cases, the experiences are reduced to spectacles, which Debord (1995, 17) defines as conditions that are "immune from human activity, inaccessible to any projected review or correction." The streets around these edifices assumed an "independent existence" (Debord 1995, 17), taking on roles outside their traditional architectural contexts, where they are supposed to "give form to traditional values, and consolidate urban morphology" (Tafuri 1976, 42) into understandable cues and images. Thus, instead of giving one the feeling of a processional religious pilgrimage, the scenes evoke a feeling of "vision," a process that "turns the material life of every one into a universe of speculation" (Debord 1995, 17), a distortion of reality.

Replicating Colonial Urban Design Ambitions

If the urban design of the Hassan II Mosque is a total theater, what kind of performance takes place in it?

The performance is a cultural contest between the people and the monarchy, a contest staged by the manipulation of architectonic urban design motifs that rewrite the history and cultural memory of the site on which the Hassan II Mosque is built. Rewriting history in this context implies the reconfiguration of the existing social memory of the site by superimposing a new history, with the king at its center. In a speech on 8 July 1988, the king declared the following:

> After our beloved father's death, His Majesty King Mohammed V (God's holy mercy be upon him)—I decided to build his Mausoleum in the City of Casablanca. But a few weeks later I thought that his tomb will be far away from me and my family. Many Heads of Sate who would like to meditate on his grave would have to go to Casablanca for that purpose. To its inhabitants [Casablanca] I then owe a compensation of which I thought the very day I decided to build Mohamed V's Mausoleum in Rabat. I thought of this great Mosque which is presently being built near the sea and which will make of Casablanca a city unique in its kind with this great Mosque I wanted to erect over the water.

The king's implication is that the planning for his mosque in Casablanca began upon the death of his father in 1961. But we do not have evidence of this intention earlier than 1988 when he gave his speech. Several urban studies of Moroccan cities and architecture have been conducted in recent years, but none of those studies gives any hint that the king was intending to build a colossal mosque in Casablanca.[41] Two of these studies, Abu-Lughod (1980) and Cohen and Eleb (1998), concerned the urban designs and growth of Rabat and Casablanca, but neither contains any mention of such intentions.

Cohen and Eleb's (1998) detailed history of the development of the town from 1900 through the 1950s reached the conclusion that the city grew primarily because of its seaport and commercial adventurism from the turn of the nineteenth century. A substitute narrative—specifically, "Casablanca, now known as the City of Hassan II Mosque, achieves the deep-rooted aspiration of imperial cities, in Morocco and elsewhere, to tell about the Islam whose memory will live on forever in human memory" (Ploquin and Sinaceur 1993, 5)—is a ploy by the royalists to graft their man as an important cultural factor into the history of the city. Sinaceur's narrative is driven more by the politics of consolidating the domination of the king throughout the country than by historical facts about the development of the city. When Sinaceur (Ploquin and Sinaceur 1993, 11) writes that "Casablanca, megalopolis of the Kingdom was in an urgent need to have a famous monument," he brings it to our attention that the city of Casablanca was being contested between the king and the people, and the king had decided to implant his mosque as a winning strategy under the auspices of the Moslem religion. It is apparent that the king's narrative, supposedly dating back to the death of his father, is primarily interested in glossing over the history of the site by locating himself at its center.

To this end, the urban design of the mosque is intended to mediate between the monarchy and the people's wishes. Physically, the urban design opens up a new expansive boulevard with four express lanes on one side, two local lanes on the other, and expansive sidewalks on both sides, in order to facilitate shopping. This ten-lane boulevard begins from the southern façade of the mosque and terminates at the Palace Oued el Makhazine, near the center of the city (Figs. 3 and 28). The main purpose of the boulevard is to create a shopping avenue beyond anything that Morocco has ever seen, giving in the process a focal point that terminates at the Hassan II Mosque.

The basilical plan of the mosque was adopted purely for this purpose. The plan initiated the beginning of the boulevard from the southern façade of the mosque, which is lavishly finished. Most important, the gigantic minaret, with its laser beam, forms a visual alignment along the proposed boulevard and beyond into the sea. The vast avenue suggests that the king and his advisors, especially Michel Pinseau, were conscious of the fact that the king had to give something to the people in order for him to retain his position. It is obvious from the design that religion alone was not enough to pacify the people. It had to be coupled with something: commercialism, the primary fetish of the modern world (Fig. 28).

As commercially minded as the urban design of the mosque is, it is a cultural success because the essential visual elements of the mosque and the portals of the shops are derived from existing traditional Moroccan architecture motifs. The visual elements exist in all major cities of Morocco and are readily understandable by the people. For example, one of the most expensive and

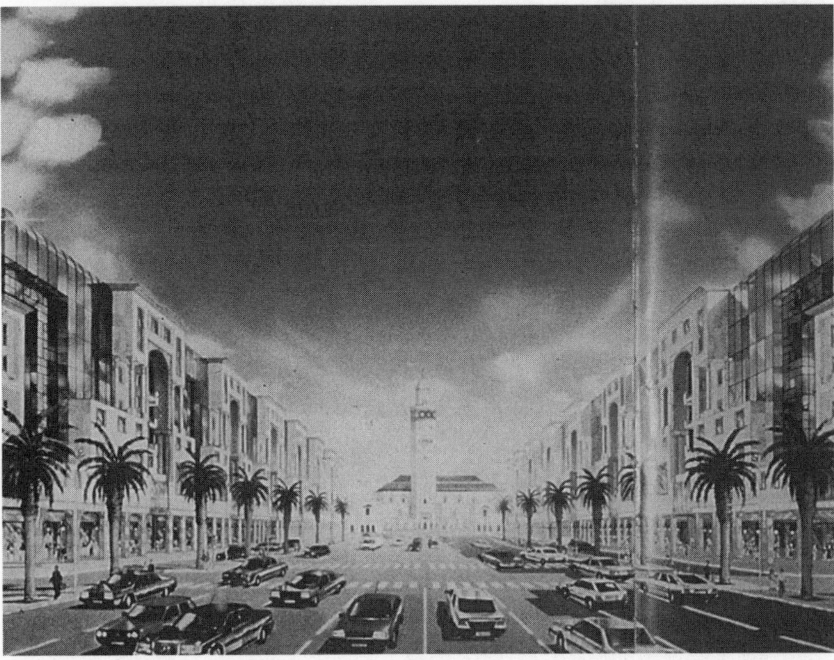

Fig. 28. View of the planned expansive boulevard leading from the Hassan II Mosque to the Place Oued el Makhazine, Casablanca. Notice how Hassan II Mosque forms the terminus of the boulevard. Compare with Fig. 29.

busy commercial avenues in Morocco, Avenue Mohammed V, is in Rabat. Planned during the colonial times, the royal palace, the administrative centers, and the central business district precincts were marked out using ruins of twelfth-century Almohad Wall, the Bab er Rouah (Fig. 29). The colonials juxtaposed and marked out their administrative centers, the central business district, and the royal palace from Avenue Moulay Hassan through Avenue Mohammed V, where it terminates on the twelfth-century Almohad Hassan Mosque. Avenue Mohammed V continues as the main business artery of Rabat all the way beyond the ancient Andalusian wall, and into the medina (village/town) where one meanders through a labyrinthine souk. One of the immediate ambitions of Pinseau was to re-create at Casablanca the same effect that the twelfth-century Almohad Hassan Mosque has on Avenue Mohammed V in Rabat (Figs. 28 and 29) by using the new mosque as a terminus and a focal point. In the souk where Avenue Mohammed V terminates, one can see fa-

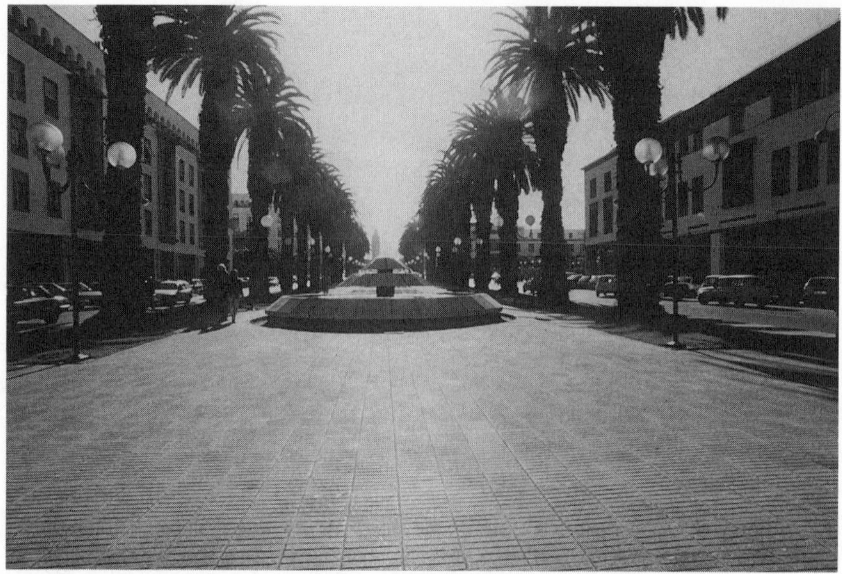

Fig. 29. Avenue Mohammed V, Rabat, Morocco. The avenue was built during the colonial times, but it is the main inspiration for Pinseau's proposed avenue in Casablanca. Notice how the twelfth-century mosque of Hassan forms the terminus of the avenue in the distant background. Photo by Nnamdi Elleh, 1998.

miliar traditional Moroccan architectural elements, such as fountains and portals. Most of the decorative motifs found in the carved stones of the portals of the Bank Al-Maghrib and the post office along Avenue Mohammed V in Rabat are also evident on the portals of private houses and shops in the medina and the souk. What comes across as one recognizes these elements is the continuity of the building culture of the people, both in the private and in the public buildings. The numerous ancient architectonic motifs in the mosque begin to make sense when one sees that they are visual quotations from the streets, buildings, mosques, and neighborhood squares of the country. One can also see quotations of colonial urban design schemes like the Avenue Mohammed V that was done by Henri Prost under the resident governor Lyautey between 1917 and 1923 (Fig. 29).

If Pinseau's urban design is executed as planned, it would be the most ambitious urban design scheme that Morocco has ever undertaken since independence. It can only be achieved by bulldozing thousands of apartments on the edge of the ancient medina of Casablanca, in order to create a focal point that would begin at the Hassan II Mosque, go through Place Oued el Makhazine, and possibly terminate at the Place League Arab and Place Mohammed V (Fig. 3). Can Pinseau create this vast commercial avenue without recouping the elements of colonial urbanism and without justifying the critiques of colonial urbanism in Morocco?

How different is the king's urban ambition from the colonial urban ambitions? Any answer to this question needs to be sensitive to people's domiciles and human rights. Completing the mosque to the urban design specifications of its blueprint would probably cost far more than the building actually did. It would also require the deployment of police power to evict the people whose homes, businesses, and cultural facilities are located on the path of the intended avenue. Fredric Jameson (1995, 103) suggests that when the old is mixed with the new in this way, the result is a sort of wrapping. And what is "perpetuated by the strategy of the wrapper and the wrapped is the suggestion . . . that none of the parts are new, and it is repetition rather than radical renovation that is henceforth at stake."

If we locate the construction of the mosque in the social setting of the mid-1980s, through the period it was completed, we will be reminded that the process of construction was a staged phenomena with a royal performance agenda. It was a period when the Moroccan economy was still in severe recession. The people employed in the project were engaging in practical economic measures designed to reduce economic hardship and minimize social unrest in the country. Sinaceur (Ploquin and Sinaceur 1993) and Basri (1992, 1) both cite the speech (11 August 1988) in which the king boasted that "the mobilization and sustained effort of a Reaf human potential consisting of thirty thousand technicians, masons, craftsmen and workers, give an idea of the enormity of the task."[42] One of the obvious outcomes of such a grand effort is the stimulation of the economy and the pacification of the society during years of economic hardship. The performative aspect of the project is also illustrated by the promotion of the mosque as a great achievement of the king.

I have also indicated how Driss Basri and his staff compared the new mosque with all the major Islamic monuments of the world in order to demonstrate that the mosque is the largest religious monument on the face of the earth (Fig. 30). Tactfully, the first comparisons omitted three of the most sacred places of Islam on the earth—the Dome of the Rock, Jerusalem, and the Holy Mosques of Mecca and Medina—from the list. King Hassan II would have appeared impious in the eyes of Moslems around the world if he had compared his mosque,

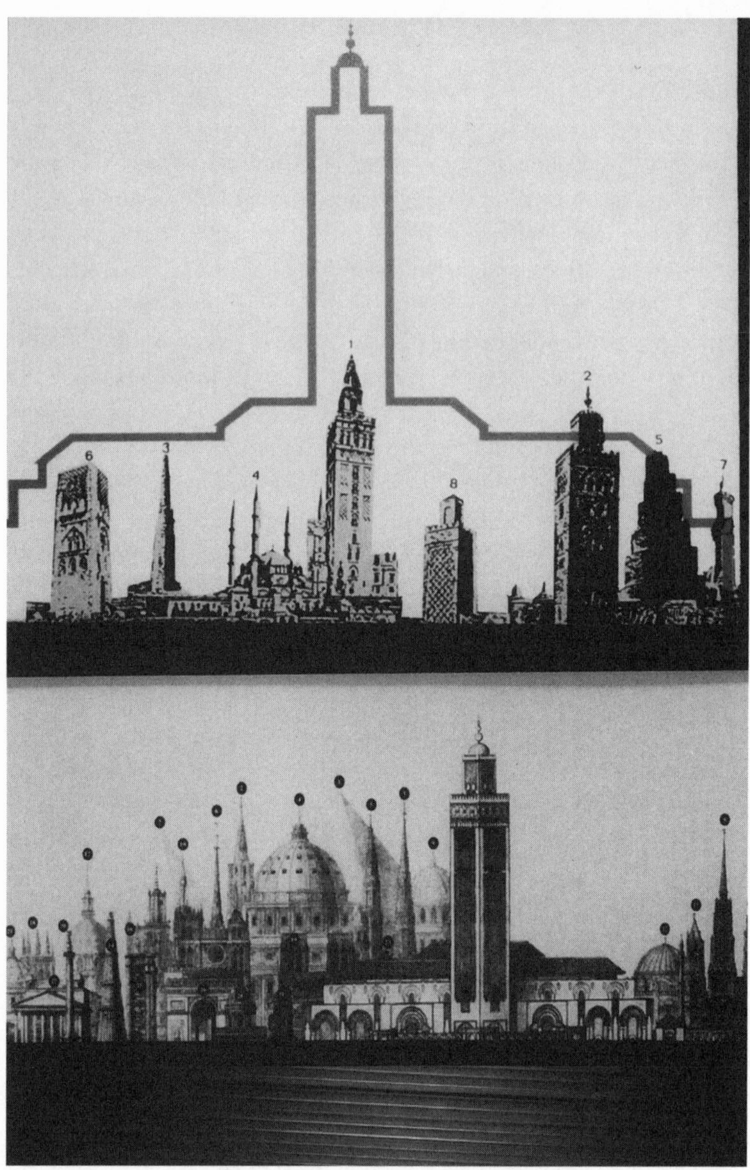

Fig. 30. *Above:* Architect's sketch of how the Hassan II Mosque dwarfs all the major ancient Islamic monuments. The authors of the sketches did not include the two great mosques of Mecca and Medina in Saudi Arabia, knowing very well that the Hassan II Mosque is taller than Islam's most sacred shrines. (1) The Giralda, the tower of the great Mosque of Seville, Spain; (2) the tower of the twelfth-century great mosque, the Kutubbiya, Marrakech, Morocco; (3) the tower of the twelfth-century mosque, Dajjam, Afghanistan; (4) the tower of Sul-

which is definitely the most ostentatious and the tallest, with the most sacred shrines of Islam. Regardless, everybody knows that his mosque has the tallest minaret and is probably the most lavishly decorated in the world. It now remains for us to see how the mosque, the king, and the people actually relate to one other.

Yamoussoukro: A Twentieth-Century Versailles in Africa

Although Yamoussoukro was officially declared the political capital of the country in 1983, Abidjan is still the undisputed cultural, economic, and political link between the government of Côte d'Ivoire, the people, and the rest of the world. To get to Yamoussoukro from the outside world, one is likely to begin the journey from Abidjan, a city at the lagoon, surrounded by the typical mangrove forests and evergreen wildlife of tropical Africa. The journey from Abidjan to Yamoussoukro takes approximately four hours on a well-paved dual carriage highway, except for the last 60 kilometers (37.2 miles). Besides driving through a few villages that are gradually being transformed into small towns, the 250-kilometer (155-mile) journey from Abidjan to Yamoussoukro lies mostly through an evergreen forest, which gradually turns to a less dense wooded savanna forest, as one moves from the Atlantic Coast and goes further toward the north. Like many newly created capital cities around the world, Yamoussoukro is an isolated place.

The president had already begun immense urban development projects in the village where he was born, long before the Ivorian Parliament declared Yamoussoukro the capital of the country in March 1983. Thus, the development

---

tan Salim Mosque, Turkey; (5) the tower of the eleventh-century mosque the Malowiya, Iraq; (6) the tower of the twelfth-century Hassan Mosque, Rabat, Morocco; (7) tower of the fifteenth-century mosque Al-Azhar, Cairo, Egypt; (8) tower of the Al Mansoura, Tlemecen, Algeria; (9) and the tower of the ninth-century mosque Kairouan (Karawan or Qarouan) in Tunisia. *Below:* Architect's sketch of how the Hassan II Mosque compares with the major monuments of the world. It dominates (1) the Pyramid of Cheops, (2) Strasbourg Tower, (3) the Steeple of St. Etienne of Vienna, (4) the dome of St. Peter's Basilica in Rome, (5) the steeple of Antwerp Cathedral, (6) the Cathedral of Amiens Flèche, (7) Cephrenne's Pyramid, (8) the steeple of Rouen's Cathedral, (9) the dome of St. Paul's Cathedral in London, and many others.

of Yamoussoukro brings a new dimension to the debate on postcolonial relocation of capital cities in Africa, which usually upheld the belief that the peripheral location of colonial capital cities like Lagos in Nigeria, Dar Es Salaam in Tanzania, and Abidjan in Côte d'Ivoire was primarily to facilitate the export of raw materials to the metropole (London, Paris, Amsterdam) at the expense of developing the interiors of the colonized countries.[43] Such texts justified the relocation of coastal capitals to the interiors as a way to develop, unify, and form a new national identity for the former colonies.

But, unlike the development-driven narratives that justified the transfer of the capital of Tanzania from Dar es Salaam to Dodoma, or from Lagos to Abuja, the narrative of the transfer of the capital of Côte d'Ivoire from Abidjan to Yamoussoukro in 1983 is primarily concerned with the origin of the head of state, President Félix Houphouët-Boigny.[44] So far, it is Pierre Cheynier (1978) who has written about the construction of Yamoussoukro. Although certain economic arguments were put forward regarding the centrality of the site and its suitability for locating the capital of the country, the book makes clear at the beginning that it is intended as a homage to "His Excellency, Le Président de la Républic, Monsieur Félix-Houphouët-Boigny."[45]

Cheynier's text (1978), the text produced by Our Lady of Peace International Foundation, Yamoussoukro (1990), and the text written by architect Pierre Fakhoury and Francois Mathey (1990) on the design and production of the basilica fail to indicate the importance of public debate on the construction of the town of Yamoussoukro and the basilica. Instead, they present their materials as the outcome of the genius of the president, whose guidance and benevolence toward the Ivorian people resulted in the realizations of the town and the edifice. In fact, Cheynier (1978) was not interested in Yamoussoukro as a national capital of Côte d'Ivoire. Instead, he was interested in the town as an autochthonous land from which the man who would shape its destiny was born. Later in the text he discusses the colonial period of Yamoussoukro.[46] However, he makes little attempt to explain why it is a convenient center for the new national capital city of Côte d'Ivoire. One would expect that a discourse on the history of the national capital of a country would be focused on the history of the entire people of the Côte d'Ivoire—especially on why it was necessary for the multiethnic society to seek a center of unity and an axis for stimulating the development of the interior of their country.

Cheynier's text impacts the way one reads the master plan of the town of Yamoussoukro, which was prepared by the Tunisian-born Olivier-Clément

Cacoub. Cheynier grounds his reading of Yamoussoukro's master plan on the personal action of the president, "the great builder" of his birth hometown, and the plan refers to the president's respect for the traditional village of Yamoussoukro and, above all, for the spirits of his ancestors.[47] Cheynier was also the first person to admit that it is difficult to read the Yamoussoukro master plan because it neither meets the requirements of the word *urban* in the Latin sense nor meets those of *village* in the real village sense. Instead, it is a plan that is driven by the desire to harmonize a great city and a village. Cheynier (1978, 63) concluded that the word that best describes the urban design of Yamoussoukro for him is the "'villa', le domaine rural des Romains." Cheynier's conclusion is unambiguous about the aristocratic intentions of the Yamoussoukro master plan, and it cannot be confused with the will of a nation to start over, as far as building developmental infrastructure is concerned.

According to Cheynier (1978, 69), Olivier-Clément Cacoub, the most active architect in Yamoussoukro, was introduced to the president by the late Tunisian president Habib Bourguiba during an official visit of the Ivorian president to Tunisia in 1968. The architect and the president had kept in touch since 1968, and it is possible that Yamoussoukro was conceived as a personal project by the president from the time he met Cacoub. The experience that Cacoub brought to the urban design of Yamoussoukro in the 1970s and early 1980s demonstrates that he was familiar with the design and construction of exclusive palaces for a limited audience, despite the fact that he had done some public projects like universities in France (Grenoble and Orleans campuses).

Cacoub was educated at the École des Beaux-Arts, Paris. He won the competition for the Grand Prix de Rome in 1957. For four years, he was part of the French Academy in Rome (Villa Medici) and in Athens, the last place he served before moving back to Tunisia.[48] As President Habib Bourguiba's chief architect since 1957, he was also the chief architect of the federation and was responsible for constructing numerous palaces and towns in Tunisia. His major projects are the Palace of Carthage, the hometown of President Bourguiba, Monastir, which he rebuilt, and the Monastir Palace of Congress. His experience from the previous projects coalesced at Yamoussoukro in the form of a new town made up of a collection of modern villas.

Here, one cannot help it but wonder whether, like the late Tunisian president Habib Bourguiba, who favored the development of his birthplace, Monastir, over many Tunisian towns, President Houphouët-Boigny was following a similar example by favoring the development of his birthplace over all other towns in the Côte d'Ivoire. The two leaders were repeating the kind of political nepotism that late President Kamazu Banda practiced in Malawi when he relocated the capital of his country from Blantyre and Zomba to Lilongwi shortly after independence in 1964. Perhaps the president's practice of nepotism helps explain the reasons why he personalized the master plan of the town. Keeping the capital of his country in his birthplace was one way for him and the people of his ethnic group to control the country while marginalizing the majority of the people who belong in the remaining fifty-nine ethnic groups that constitute Côte d'Ivoire.

The Yamoussoukro master plan has one major landmark, an island in the middle that is wedged between two branches of an artificially flooded lake. From the island, the town spreads out in all directions (Fig. 12). The road that crosses the island from the southeast corner, toward the western fringes of the town, forms the major axis. The center of the town with all the major offices and buildings is situated in the southeast half of the major road that runs from Abidjan. Although in plan the island suggests that the major arteries of the town emanate from there, the town has no real focal point. This is because it is intended to be a village made up of a collection of villas, which are separated by broad streets that echo the size of the major buildings in the town. This explains why the town is difficult to experience as one walks through it. There is no way of forming a coherent image of the town because the buildings are extremely isolated from one another. Our Lady of Peace Basilica in the southwest corner of the town is designed to be isolated from the center of the town and from all major objects in the town (Fig. 12).

There is a big contrast between the Yamoussoukro and the Casablanca urban designs. The Casablanca project aims at using the mosque to create a grand avenue for capitalism, but the Yamoussoukro project is designed as a place where the aristocrat can escape from the boisterous capitalist activities of Abidjan. I have argued earlier that the Yamoussoukro project is not intended for the people of Côte d'Ivoire. The majority of the people have yet to experience the benefits of capitalism. So how could they be in a hurry to escape from it? The golf courses of Yamoussoukro are made for a select few—the middle class can hardly afford the pleasure. Escape to Yamoussoukro was intended as a privilege for a few metropolitan elite who are in touch with the president and people of his inner circle. This thesis is confirmed by the fact that between 11 and 15 January 1978, President Valéry Giscard d'Estaing and his wife were received as the official guests of Côte d'Ivoire at Yamoussoukro. That was five years before Yamoussoukro was officially declared the political capital of the country by the Ivorian National Assembly. However, by then, the L'hôtel President, demian l'hôtel du Golf, du Golf Course, résidence du Chef de l'État, Palais Boigny, or résidence des Hôtes (all realized by architect Olivier Cacoub, except du Golf-Course), as well as the broad streets, were already in place. The president continued to receive guests at Yamoussoukro from then until he died in December 1993.

All the government departments of Côte d'Ivoire are still housed in Abidjan, despite the location of monumental educational facilities such as Félix Houphouët-Boigny's Institute National Supérieur D'Enseignment Technique and L'École National Supérieur Des Travaux Publics, by architects Henry Potteir, Phillippe Godin, Jacques Rechesteiner, and Télesphore Kouamé. Also situated in Abidjan are the Political Headquarters of PDIC by Cacoub; and other social amenities such as La Fondation Houphouët-Boigny, La Mairie de Yamoussoukro, and La Maison l'Artisanat, also by Cacoub. The location of these infrastructures actually enforces the villa-like ambience of the town as they are spread out and separated from one another by wooded lands that enhance the milieu of countryside, despite the broad, paved, empty streets.

We leave this chapter with the understanding that the urban design intentions of the mosque in Casablanca, and the basilica at Yamoussoukro, are aristocratic and commercial intensive projects, though directed toward different audiences. The former is targeted at the masses in order for the king to be able to control them and secure his position, while the latter is targeted at a select international elite with whom the president identified himself ideologically and socially. Both are projects that cap years of architectural designs and building ambitions by two contemporary leaders who had unlimited power in their respective countries. Like its counterpart in Casablanca, the Yamoussoukro monument commemorates the personal achievements of the president—not as a creator of jobs for the people in times of economic hardship, but as a man who built one of the most significant religious monuments of the twentieth century. It is along these lines that I will explore the relationships between the leaders, the monuments, and the people of Côte d'Ivoire and Morocco in Chapter 3.

NOTES

1. These were the last statements by Fakhoury in Fakhoury (1990, 12).
2. See Kpatindé (1999, 78).
3. *The Economist* Intelligence Unit, no. 3, 1986, p. 13, and no. 2, 1990, p. 12, estimated the population of the Lebanese community in Côte d'Ivoire at 100,000 and 120,000, respectively.
4. Ibid.
5. See Bistoury (1989, 1329).
6. Ibid.
7. See *The Economist* Intelligence Unit no. 4, 1989, 8.
8. See Kpatindé (1999, 78).
9. See Aye (1990) for more information on how Fakhoury describes his basilica.
10. For commentaries on Antoine Cesareo and DCGT, see Placca (1990, 44–47). Also see Kerdellant (1989, 18–20); Whiteman (1989, 2418–2419); and N'Guessan (1987).
11. Mohammed Mohammed, a doctoral student in the Department of History, Northwestern University, 1999, translated Michel Pinseau's statements from the 1993 Arabic edition of *Mosquée Hassan II* (Masjid al-Hasan al-Thānī. Casablanca: Lāk Interñasīyūnāl) for me.
12. The most recent and most extensive historical study of the urbanization and urbanism of Casablanca is the latest work by Jean-Louis Cohen and Monique Eleb, *Casablanca Myth et Figure d' Une Aventure Urbaine* (1998).
13. Driss Basri is one of the principal authors and has a number of articles on the Hassan II Mosque in different books, the most important one being *Mosquée Hassan II*, by Basri, Abow Kakr Kadiri, and Michel Pinseau (1993). This book also has editions in French and Arabic (Masjid al-Hasan al-Thānī. Casablanca: Lāk Internāsīyūnāl), all the editions by Lak International, Casablanca. Also, two other articles by Driss Basri are "Hassan II Mosque, a token of tolerance in Islam," in *Hassan II Mosque Casablanca*. Casablanca, Morocco: Agence Urbaine Casablanca, 18, Boulevard Rachidi, 1992, and *Royaume du Maroc. La Mosquée Hassan II une Oeuvre Architecturale et Spirituelle*. Rabat: Ministère de l'Information. 1994. Also see Ploquin and Sinaceur (1993).
14. See Basri (1994), *Royaume du Maroc. La Mosquée Hassan II une Oeuvre archi-Aecturale et Spirituelle*, p. 3.
15. Ibid.
16. Excerpt from the speech of King Hassan II, 11 July 1988, and also see above note, p. 4.
17. Ibid.
18. See Basri (1994).
19. The quote from the Holy Bible is a mystification of a technical solution that has to do with the building's foundation. See Our Lady of Peace International Foundation (1990), pp. 7 and 10. Our Lady of Peace International Foundation was supposedly created

by the Vatican, where its legal headquarters is situated, although its administrative headquarters, the publishers of the text quoted here, is at Yamoussoukro.

20. Our Lady of Peace International Foundation (1990, 6).

21. Ibid., 7.

22. Ibid., 13.

23. Ibid.

24. Ibid.

25. See Our Lady of Peace International Foundation (1990, 13).

26. Ibid.

27. Ibid.

28. See Fakhoury (1990).

29. A lot has been published on Islamic architecture in Africa (Creswell 1969, 1978; Briggs 1974; Piccard 1980; Hoag 1977; Hutt 1977; Prussin 1986; Frishman and Khan 1994; Holod and Khan 1997) over the years, but the term *Hassanian architecture* was never part of the lexicon. It was invented by the advocates for Hassan II Mosque.

30. The historical narrative in which Sinaceur (Ploquin and Sinaceur 1993) grafted the Hassan II Mosque can be read in detail on pp. 13–17 of *La Mosquée Hassan II* and Basri's (1994) *Royaume du Maroc. La Mosqueé Hassan II une Oeuvre Architecturale et Spirituelle*, p. 5.

31. See Basri (1992).

32. See Hoag (1977) and Frishman and Khan (1994).

33. See Hoag (1977, 77–93) for a chronology of the expansions of the Cordoba Mosque.

34. I am drawing this quote from Berman (1982/1988, 89).

35. So far, I find André Piccard's (1980) monumental two-volume set of *Traditional Islamic Craft in Moroccan Architecture* the most comprehensive in detailing the history, the application, and the technical processes of constructing Moroccan buildings and ornaments.

36. See Fakhoury (1990).

37. Ibid.

38. My objective here is not to discuss the evolution of the St. Peter's floor plan, which can be traced to the reign of Emperor Constantine, who granted Christians the right of worship in A.D. 313 and founded the first basilica in A.D. 324, or even earlier when Christians used the site for burial. Such a discussion would involve major archeological study of the evolution of the floor plans from the earliest Christian tombs through the series of the architects who worked on the St. Peter's before and after Michelangelo. Several studies have been published on the subject. I am interested here in investigating how the floor plan of the Yamoussoukro basilica is consciously grounded in the traditions of the institution of St. Peter's of which the floor plan is only one symbolic aspect. See Argan and Contardi (1993, 272–372); Onians (1988, 207–246); Gardner (1980, 215–218); Janson (1986, 199–201); and Bergere (1966).

39. See Kostof (1985, 217–223); Silver (1993, 75–78); and Janson (1986, 164–166).

40. This quote originally by Moholy-Nagy is taken from Tafuri (1978, 104).

41. Other studies about Casablanca include Abu-Lughod (1980), Piccard (1980), Wright (1991), Robinow (1989), and Culot and Thiveaud et al. (1992). There was no mention of the king's plan to build a grand mosque in Casablanca by any scholar mentioned here.

42. The "Reaf" is a part of Morocco where stones and other building materials were obtained for the construction of the mosque.

43. Joe Doherty's article "II Mode of Production and Third World Urbanization" (1977) makes a strong argument about the relationship between colonial capitals and the metropole, but Cheynier's book (1978) is focused on Yamoussoukro.

44. See Cheynier (1978).

45. Ibid., 149.

46. Ibid., 17.

47. Ibid., 63.

48. My biography of Cacoub is based on Cheynier's 1978 text, pp. 69–74.

REFERENCES

Abu-Lughod, Janet. 1980. "Origins of Urban Apartheid." In *Rabat, Urban Apartheid in Morocco,* 131–149. Princeton, N.J.: Princeton University Press.

Argan, Carlo Guilio, and Bruno Contardi. 1993. *Michelangelo Architect.* London: Thames and Hudson.

Aye, Jeb-Pierre. 11 September 1990. "M. Pierre Fakhoury, Architect de la basilique: Notre-Dame de la paix n'est pas Saint-Pierre." *Fraternité Matin.* Abidjan, Côte d'Ivoire, 18.

Basri, Driss. 1992. "Hassan II Mosque, a Token of Tolerance in Islam." In *Hassan II Mosque Casablanca.* Casablanca: Agence Urbaine Casablanca, 18, boulevard Rachidi, Morocco.

———. 1993. *Trente annies de vie constitutionnelle au Maroc.* Paris: Libr. Ginirale de droit et de jurisprudence.

———. 1994. *La dicentralisation au Maro:: de la commune la rigion.* Paris: Natime than.

———. 1994. *La Maroc et les droit de l'homme: positions, rialisations et perspectives.* Paris: L'Harmattan.

———. 1994. *Royaume du Maroc. La Mosquée Hassan II Une Oeuvre Architecturale et Spirituelle.* Rabat: Ministère de l'Information.

Basri, Driss, Abow Kakr Kadiri, and Michel Pinseau. 1993. *Mosquée Hassan II.* Casablanca: Editions Lak International.

Bergere, Thea, and Richard Bergere. 1966. *The Story of Saint Peter's.* New York: Dodd, Mead.

Berman, Marshall. 1982/1988. *All That Is Solid Melts into Air: The Experience of Modernity.* New York: Penguin Books.

Bistoury, Nicholas. 14–20 August 1989. "Lebanese Presence." *West Africa,* no. 3756: 1329.

Briggs, Martin. 1974. *Muhammadan Architecture in Egypt and Palestine.* New York: Da Capo Press.

Cheynier, Pierre. 1978. *Yamoussoukro, Cœur de la Cotê d'Ivoire.* Abidjan: Fraternit-Hebdomadaire.

Cohen, Jean-Louis, and Monique Eleb. 1998. *Casablanca Myth et Figure d'une Aventure Urbaine.* Casablanca: Éditions Hazan.

Combs-Schilling, M. E. 1989. *Sacred Performances. Islam, Sexuality and Sacrifice.* New York: Columbia University Press.

Creswell, K. A. C. 1969. *Early Muslim Architecture,* 2d ed. Oxford: Clarendon Press.

———. 1978. *The Muslim Architecture of Egypt.* New York: Hacker Art Books.

Culot, Maurice, and Jean-Marie Thiveaud, et al. 1992. *Outre-Mer. Architecture Francais.* Institute Francais d'Architecuture. Paris: Mardaga.

Davis, Whitney. 1996. *Replications Archeology Art History Psychoanalysis.* With the editorial assistance of Richard W. Quinn. University Park: Pennsylvania State University Press.

Debord, Guy. 1995. *The Society of the Spectacle,* trans. Donald Nicholson-Smith. New York: Zone Books.

Doherty, Joe. 1977. "II Mode of Production and Third World Urbanization." *Antipode, A Radical Journal of Geography* 9, no. 3 (December): 32–42.

Fakhoury, Pierre. 1990. *La Basilic Notre-Dame de la Paix.* Paris: Margada, 12.

Frishman, Marin, and Hassan-Uddin Khan. 1994. *The Mosque, Architecture, Development & Regional Diversity.* London: Thames and Hudson.

Gardner, Louis. 1980. *Art through the Ages.* New York: Harcourt Brace Jovanovich.

Hall, Edward Twitchell. 1969. *The Hidden Dimension.* Garden City, N.Y.: Doubleday.

Hoag, John D. 1963. *Western Islamic Architecture.* New York: George Braziller.

———. 1977. *Islamic Architecture.* New York: Harry N. Abrams.

Holod, Renata, and Hassan-Uddin Khan. 1997. *The Mosque and the Modern World.* London: Thames and Hudson.

Hutt, Antony. 1977. *North Africa.* London: Scorpion Publications.

Jameson, Fredric. 1995. *Postmodernism or the Cultural Logic of Late Capitalism.* Durham, N.C.: Duke University Press.

Janson, H. W. 1986. *History of Art,* Vol. 1. Englewood Cliffs, N.J.: Prentice Hall.

Kerdellant, Christine. 11 December 1989. "Côte d'Ivoire: La Chute de l'empereur des grands travaux." *Jeune Afrique,* no. 1510: 18–20.

King Hassan II. 11 July 1988. Extract from a speech. Washington, D.C.: Embassy of Morocco.

Kostof, Spiro. 1985. *A History of Architecture, Settings and Ritual.* Oxford: Oxford University Press.

Kpatindé, Francis. 24 May 1999. "Que Sont Devenues les Hommes d'Houphouët? Pierre Fakhoury un bâtisseur pour l'éternité." *Jeune Afrique* no. 2000–2001: 72–78.

La Cathédral d'Abidjan. 1989. Edited by the Parish of Abidjan, and photos by Pierre Trichet. Printed by Saint-Paul, 38 bd Raymond-Poincaré, 5500 Bar le Duc.

Mannheim, Karl. 1985. *Ideology and Utopia: An Introduction to the Sociology of Knowledge.* New York: Harcourt Brace.

N'Guessan, Raphael. 13 May 1987. "La Chef de l' État hier á la Directiondes Gands Travaux." *Fraternité Martin,* Abidjan.

Onians, John. *1988. Bearers of Meaning.* Princeton, N.J.: Princeton University Press.

Our Lady of Peace International Foundation. 1990. *The Basilica of Our Lady of Peace (Basilique Notre-Dame de la Paix).* B.P. 1888 Yamoussoukro, Côte-d'Ivoire.

Piccard, André. 1980. *Traditional Islamic Craft in Moroccan Architecture,* trans, Mary Guggenheim. Saint-Jorioz, France: Editions Ateliers 74, vol. 1.

Placca, Jean-Baptiste. 26 February 1990. "Côte d'Ivoire L'héritage de 'César'." *Jeune Afrique,* no. 1521: 44–47.

Ploquin, Philippe, and Mohammed-Allal Sinaceur. 1993. *La Mosquée Hassan II* (*The Hassan II Mosque*). Photographiée par Philippe Ploquin et Francis Peuriot; textes de Mohammed-Allal Sinaceur; assisté par Mustapha Kasri, Ali Amahane, Houceïne Kasri. Drémil-Lafage: Editions D. Briand.

Prussin, Labelle. 1986. *Hatumere: Islamic Design in West Africa.* Berkeley: University of California Press.

Rapoport, Amos. 1969. *House Form and Culture.* Englewood Cliffs, N.J.: Prentice Hall.

———. *The Meaning of the Built Environment: A Nonverbal Communication Approach.* Beverly Hills, Calif.: Sage Publications.

Robinow, Paul. 1989. "Techno-Cosmopolitanism." In *French Modern,* 277–319. Cambridge, Mass.: MIT Press.

Tafuri, Manfredo. 1976. *Architecture and Utopia. Design and Capitalist Development.* Cambridge, Mass.: MIT Press.

———. 1978. "The Stage as a 'Virtual City': From Fuchs to the Totaltheater." In *The Sphere and the Labyrinth.* Cambridge, Mass.: MIT Press.

The Economist Intelligence Unit. 1986. *Country Profile, Côte d'Ivoire.* London: *The Economist* Intelligent Unit, no. 3, p. 13.

———. *Country Profile, Côte d'Ivoire,* no. 4, 1989. London: *The Economist* Intelligence Unit, 8.

———. *Country Profile, Côte d'Ivoire,* no. 2, 1990. London: *The Economist* Intelligence Unit, 12.

Whiteman, Kay. 1989. "Houphouët's Promise." *West Africa,* no. 3724 (26 December 1988–8 January 1989): 2418–2419.

Wright, Gwendolyn, 1991. "Introduction." In *The Politics of Design in French Colonial Urbanism.* Chicago: University of Chicago Press.

Chapter 3

The Leaders, the Monuments, and the Peoples

UNDERSTANDING THE MONUMENTS

Understanding the triangular relationships that the press sketched among the leaders, the monuments, and the peoples of the countries in which the objects are located calls for the knowledge of the specific contexts of use, while keeping in mind that both objects are replicated artifacts that are currently being substituted for earlier ones. Context is important because visual motifs that enhance the articulation of the surfaces, for example, portals, arcades, domes, and columns, are not the only elements that help people to give meanings to buildings. People also give meanings to buildings according to the social contexts of use.

In other words, while these leaders were busy making ostentatious presents to God, how were they relating to their fellow citizens? I pursue these questions with the hope of exploring how the objects might or might not serve as "public spheres" where the citizens of the respective countries might engage in political activities and deliberate on issues that concern their personal lives,[1] as the leaders who commissioned the edifices would like us to believe. My specific interests here are in the manner in which the peoples of the respective countries give meanings to the monuments: How do they know the objects, how do they utilize the schemata in order to structure these monumental environments in their minds, and how do these schemata affect their behavioral patterns in the particular environments? There is abundant literature on how people construct spatial, temporal, and social cognitive schemata.[2] Some of the literature explores mutual interactions between subjects and objects in the visual arts and the built environments, from the points of view of perception, creativity, personality, existing artistic conventions, and the beholder's expectations. I am particularly interested here in how the president and the king categorized the edifices they constructed in the "public spheres" of their respective countries as a domain for the worship of God, and a domain for the preservation of peace and universal love.

THE PEOPLES AND THE MONUMENTS

Consolidating "Official Islam"

> The Center is emphasized in Islam, and this emphasis is reflected in Islamic cities, all of which are regarded as holy cities. The city functions as a constant reminder of the sacred dimension through the calls to prayer which issue five times each day from the Mosque at the city's center. The market place also functions as a reminder, in which the relationship between buyer and seller, the labor which created articles to be sold, and the need for food for nourishment from outside the individual all possess sacred meaning. Islam does not regard the sacred as a realm apart from the secular, but as the ultimate significant of all aspects of life. (Eaton 1993, 48)

What does it mean when we hear that King Hassan II is the *Amir al-mu'minim*—"Commander of the Faithful" or "Prince of the Faithful"? Was he the commander of those who are faithful to God Almighty, or was he the commander of those who were faithful to his rule? When Liz Nickson (1989, 47) commented on the king's mosque in *Life* magazine, the title was: "Mega Mosque: Allah Be Praised and Hassan II." Nickson (1989, 47) translated the title to mean "Allah's Deputy on Earth." In recent years, deliberate use of the title in a conflated term was one of the powerful tools for the king and his followers to institutionalize an "official version of Islam," regardless of the fact that such a title does not exists anywhere in the Holy Koran.

I am defining "official version of Islam" here as a contested political leadership that uses religion to consolidate itself whenever it is convenient. Many Islamic groups in Morocco did not acknowledge the title and were willing to do away with it. Thus, I locate the king, his mosque, and his people in the social context where Islamic leadership was being contested in his country. In addition, I also review the mosque comprehensively within the king's building endeavors throughout his country.

Historically speaking, Morocco has only four imperial cities: Fèz, Marrakech, Meknès, and Rabat-Salé. The history of these cities has been well documented, some accounts covering events since the times of the Carthaginians and the Romans (Pickens 1995; Ploquin and Sinaceur 1993; Sijelmassi 1986). The imperial cities of Morocco were characterized by the locations of royal palaces, mosques, royal necropolises, and other secular and religious civic centers that served the interests of the ruling dynasties. However, King Hassan II's building program has by far extended beyond the historical royal cities to urban centers where the ancient royalties of Morocco had little or absolutely no residential presence. While maintaining three palaces in Rabat, the king also had palaces in Meknès, Fèz, Marrakech, Casablanca, Tangiers, and Ifrane. The most recent one was completed at Agadir at the cost of US$360 million on 3 March 1990. "It is decorated with carved cedar-wood, gold leaf, marble and mosaic. One room contains an eleven-ton Venetian crystal chandelier. Within the palace grounds lie three golf courses (one has only nine holes)."[3] And, of course, the architect was Michel Pinseau, as I have indicated in the previous chapter. The king's eleventh and twelfth palaces were being planned at the ancestral home of his Aloute dynasty, the Saharan Oasis of Tafilalt, and at the Mediterranean coastal town of Nador, respectively. *The Economist* sarcastically repeated after a Moroccan official that the king has to have so many palaces because he rules the kingdom "from the saddle," and "wants to be seen ruling from every part of his Kingdom. The royal entourage is several hundred strong." As a result, huge palaces are needed to accommodate all of them.

The chain of palaces that the king built throughout his country suggests a new form of internal colonization by an autochthonous elite, although we cannot immediately say if it is worse or better than the kind of colonialism that was perpetuated by the French. The mechanism for constructing the palaces appears to involve the same approach that colonialists adopted, and it echoes the mistakes of European urbanists in Morocco under the direction of resident Governor General Lyautey. This topic constitutes the primary subject of the Moroccan colonial urban works mentioned earlier in the introduction, where I cited the works of Abu-Lughod (1980), Paul Robinow (1989), Gwendolyn Wright (1991), and Zeynep Çelik (1997), who discussed the same subject with regard to Algiers and the French urban policy. Lawrence Vale (1992, 9) indicates that postcolonial use of architecture to legitimize the government, promote democracy, and form national unity and identity often "reproduce existing hierarchies of dominance and submission," similar to the colonial power hierarchy. As *The Economist* reports,[4] the king's building program has not gone unnoticed, nor unchallenged, although the majority of Moroccans do not have the liberty to publicly criticize the regime.

> Only the Islamic fundamentalists have objected outright.[5] Some years ago Sheikh Abdesalam Yassine, leader of the outlawed Al-Adl wal Ihsaan "Justice and Welfare" party, attacked the King's extravagance in a 104-page open letter. Sheikh Yassine is under house arrest in the town of Sale. In January his party was dissolved. Last month 21 of his supporters were jailed.

The social milieu presented here does not suggest that the relationship between the king and the people of his country, particularly Islamic groups, was a good one. Consider the fact that certain leaders of Islamic groups, for whom he was supposedly building the great mosque, were criticizing his extravagance, and, in return, he was busy sending them to jail. These events were taking place when the mosque was under construction. Thus, it is valid to say that the king was building his mosque for reasons other than devotion to Islam.

It does not appear that the king was having such a great relationship with the Islamic community to the extent that he wanted to indulge them with an extravagant gift. Something else must have inspired him to build his mosque. According to one school of thought, the king had already revealed that the "Mosque will, on his death, serve as his mausoleum,"[6] in order to outshine the monument that he built for his father, King Mohammed V, in Rabat. This is unlikely, considering that the king died on Friday, 23 July 1999, and the funeral was planned in Rabat on Sunday, 25 September 1999. Nevertheless, a later school of thought sees the king as a megalomaniac who is full of self-aggrandizement. Such an idea is not implausible, but something more cogent might have inspired the monumental edifice.

The king's "Mega-Mosque," as the press has dubbed it, partly originates from events that took place in the Persian Gulf, particularly the Iranian revolution of 1979. It is elucidated in *Jeune Afrique* that the king might not have "petroleum nor money,"[7] like his contemporary leaders in the Persian Gulf, but he has the "ideas," especially the premonition: "That is, the King was anti Khomeiny. He was the champion of sunnism, and anti shiism." *Jeune Afrique* explains further that King Hassan's unshakable pro-Sunni and strong anti-Shiite stance is in consonance with the ideology of "anti-Soviets." We gain two insights from the *Jeune Afrique* (1980) article. First, the king's opposition to any possible Shiite influence in the politics of his country was primarily from the standpoint of protecting his aristocratic position. It confirms the premise of this book that the mosque represents a specific economic alignment between an emergent postcolonial African elite, and a powerful international elite, who control the capitals and the major business interests of the world. In other words, what was being contested between the followers of Sheikh Abdesalam Yassine and the royalists has less to do with religion and more to do with how the economic resources of Morocco should be managed. However, the nature of the prejudices that exist within the international alignment makes it very easy to put people who take the stance of the sheikh and his followers into a slot that classifies them as "Islamic fundamentalists." It is definitely not a neutral terminology.

We gain a second insight from the *Jeune Afrique* (1980) article. The king was already contemplating the containment of Islamic activists in his country, long before the crisis that resulted after the cancellation of the Algerian elections that could have brought the Front du Salut Islamique (FIS) to power. The FIS would have come to power in Algeria had the national elections (1990) not been canceled by the army, following the overwhelming success of the movement in local and regional contests.[8] It is appropriate to suggest that the events that took place in Algeria before and after the elections inevitably added to the urgency to construct the edifice on time, and at the most extravagant scale. The king was so concerned that he commented after the Algerian elections that nobody should judge the FIS until they had demonstrated their policy. The king's comments came in the wake of a total bureaucratic meltdown in Algeria: President Chadli Benjadid had resigned on 10 January 1990; the second round of the parliamentary elections had been canceled on 16 January 1990; the army had seized power and declared a state of emergency; and massive violence had erupted between the FIS, the army, the civilians at large, and the police forces. "In Morocco, however, there have been scores of arrests over the past few months of members of the clandestine Islamic association, Al-Adl Wal Ihsaan, and many of those arrested have been held incommunicado for long periods and charged under broadly worded legislation with membership of an unauthorized association and offences against public order."[9]

According to *The Economist* Intelligence Unit (1991/1992, 6), "the growing isolation of the political parties from public opinion led to the growth of extra-legal opposition movements during the 1970s and 1980s." Moreover, although most of the outlawed movements were almost totally dismantled by the 1980s, new movements that enjoyed popular support continued to emerge.

One of the king's antidotes to the emergent Islamic movements in his country was his grand mosque, which was intended to camouflage his heavy-handed policy toward the largest group, the Al-Adl Wal Ihsaan, (Justice and Charity). The leader of the Al-Adl Wal Ihsaan, Sheikh Abdesalam Yassine, was kept under house arrest beginning in 1989 while his followers were sent to prison. The most militant Islamist group was the Abdelkarim Mottai's Islamic Youth Society and the Mujahedin movement of Abdesalam Naamani. "The government considers these groups to constitute a significant threat, and since August 1985, when 26 members of the Islamic Youth movement were charged with plotting to overthrow the monarchy and establish an Islamic state, many activists have been sentenced to long prison terms or to death for their political actions" (*The Economist* Intelligence Unit 1991/1992, 6; Bidwell 1993, 702–703). It is also reported that many individuals belonging to both secular and Islamist groups have been in prisons under harsh conditions since 1984.

From 1990 through 1993, the year in which the mosque was inaugurated, Islamic activists, trade union leaders, student union leaders, and all other kinds of political opposition to the leadership were increasingly sent to prison mostly for voicing their opinions. For example, Nabir Amaoui, the secretary general of the Confédération Démocratique du Travail (CDT), was sent to prison for two years in April "for an article he wrote for the Spanish daily El Pais,"[10] while two students were sentenced to seven- and ten-year prison terms, respectively, "for their parts in campus clashes in Fez, Kenitra, and Oujda, in October 1991."[11] Moreover, evidence suggests that the mosque was constructed during the period that the king had the worst record with the organization Amnesty International, and with the Moroccan people, who shared political beliefs that did not agree with the orthodox version that was endorsed by the government.[12] It is along this line of argument that I suggest that the king's inspiration for his mosque was motivated primarily by his desire to create an official version of Islam of which he would be the sole leader. The official version of Islam that the king intended for his country was in tandem with his style of administration.[13]

It is ironic that most of the people who had a problem with the king's desire for an official Islam were those who would have been more likely to use the mosque more often, had the political atmosphere been tolerant of their beliefs.

From this point of view, the dissent segment of the Moroccan population, that called "fundamentalist," derived negative meanings from the edifice. Being among the most zealous in the country, it appears that they would have been more likely to utilize the mosque had the situation been safe for them. The meanings people derive from the edifice cannot be separated from the social context of production because issues such as how the funds were raised also influence people's feelings about the mosque. Professor Vale elucidates that if there is perception of any kind of threat in the social milieu in which the edifice was built:

> The buildings themselves can appear to be part of that threat. "The scale of the structure reminds the mass of political spectators that they enter the precincts of power as clients or as supplicants, susceptible to arbitrary rebuffs and favors, and that they are subject to remote authorities they only dimly know or understand." Moreover, this monumentality may reciprocally reinforce the self perceptions of those government officials who identify this exalted territory as their own. In this way, existing hierarchies can be legitimized at all levels, and extremes of power and impotence intensified. (Vale 1992, 8; also see Hillier and Hanson 1984, 27)

Thus, there is a large segment of the Moroccan population that has a difficult time accepting the edifice as a public sphere, where they can express their political opinions. The mosque has become suspect in their minds, regardless of the fact that its design incorporates motifs that are traditional Moroccan architectural artifacts.

A Site for Domestication and Surveillance

> Fundamentalist elements of Islam gain popular support when the state fails to meet the needs of its citizens. Opposition to the state assumes a religious character because all secular political opposition has been eliminated in countries such as Iran and Egypt. Though Islam is portrayed in Western media as a monolithic entity threatening rational politics, it is a varied phenomenon. Properly understood, it serves less to explain political developments than to justify certain political stances that are motivated more by social factors, such as class, than by theological concerns. (Sampson 1993, 60)

Perhaps we can clarify this subject further by looking at how the people of Morocco are utilizing the mosque compared with how they see the roles that mosques play in their respective communities. The premises of the mosque are physically accessible to the citizens of Morocco, and one can say that it is well utilized on an informal basis. To me, the most impressive aspect of the mosque is that people go on strolls there, sit on the embankments, and sometimes picnic. This happens around the clock. Couples holding hands, families with their young children, friends, and tourists can all go there to relax in the evenings, especially after the sun has gone down. To me that is one of the most successful aspects of the mosque—the fact that its premises are open to the public, and the visitor does not have to go through any gate before getting to it. Granted, the presence of several security officials both in uniform and in civilian clothing is bound to make people uncomfortable on the premises. Nevertheless, people still sit on the expansive layers of arcades to relax and meditate. It also appeared to me that people were utilizing the hammams (heated swimming pools) during the day at scheduled hours, when the administrators of the complex were not giving tours, and when the prayers were not in session. One can actually imagine how successful this site would be as a park in the future, when the expansive avenue is created, and the site becomes the terminus of the busiest commercial avenue in the country.

Based on these observations, one can suggest that the basilical plan of the mosque, its architectural motifs, and its commercial intentions were realized. However, the architectural motifs and the role that the mosque was playing in the city of Casablanca were under heavy contest between the monarchy and the zealot groups. What was more disturbing to the resistance movement was the fact that the architectural repertoires of the mosque invoke the characteristics of what Gai Eaton (1993, 48) calls "the ideal Islamic city"—a center of "remembrance"—the primary reason why Prophet Mohammed was sent to the earth. In the "ideal Islamic city," the mosque symbolically and spiritually holds the position of the most important landmark in the city. Any secular house or building for secular uses that is taller than it commits a sacrilege. There is no doubt that the mosque meets all these requirements in Casablanca, due to its scale and the lavishness of its finish, making it a potent mnemonic device for the king to deploy against his people. According to Eaton (1993, 48), "what is referred to again and again as '"remembrance'" in the Koran is at the very heart of the religion of Islam," and the major reason why Prophet Mohammed was sent to us was "not to introduce an innovation in human faith, but, precisely, to 'remind' us of the meaning of our existence."

Therefore, as a mnemonic device, the mosque reminds the opposition that their existence on earth is dependent not on God but on the king. As a holy place for worship, the mosque calls people to prayers five times a day, reminding the people to take moments away from the problems and activities of existence, and to turn to God, and to the king, for guidance and nourishment. Eaton (1993, 48) also notes that "the call to prayer, made from the top of the minaret (an Arabic term that also means 'lighthouse'), echoes over the city and pierces through the hubbub of daily life. It is a repeated 'reminder' of who we are and where we are and, indeed why we are." However, at the Casablanca mosque, the people of Morocco are called to prayers, and are reminded of who they are, where they are, and why they are—all because of the king. Eaton's (1993) observations confirm what Professors Rapoport (1982, 82) and Duncan (1990, 19) have said: When architectural landscapes are deployed as mnemonic devices on quotidian bases, and in situations where the architectural cues are legible to the people who are supposed to decode them, "in effect, one can routinize many behaviors and make them habitual." An architectural landscape can be as "unwittingly read as it is unwittingly written," once it becomes part of the quotidian experience.

By deploying ancient Moroccan architectural techniques and vocabularies, the mosque attempts to domesticate Moroccan people into believing the political narratives that the king was advancing. It serves as a center of surveillance by attracting Islamic groups who might be lulled into believing that it is truly a center for the worship of God. By so doing, it institutionalizes an official version of Islam that the king wishes to advance. In addition, the Islamic members who refuse to accept the ideological propositions coming from the king and his ministers can be easily identified as enemies of the state, the Moroccan monarchy, and they can be punished accordingly. On the other hand, those who accept the messages propagated through the mosque and go there to worship regularly will also be under constant surveillance. In fact, that was actually what the king wanted: to bring all the oppositions under one common roof where he could keep an eye on them.

The mosque is currently not available as a public sphere where the people of Morocco can come to debate issues relating to their lives. It is, instead, a center of government domestication of the masses, and a center for the surveillance of possible dissent against the king's wishes. It is the changing role of the mosque as a public sphere for the expression of social concerns and group identities that made it an attractive center for surveillance by the Moroccan regime.[14] According to this view, countries like Egypt, Iran, Iraq, Saudi Arabia, and several countries with large Moslem populations around the world are using mosques as pacification centers for their populations, who are often politically deprived of the democratic process.[15] Elissa Sampson (1993, 60) put it succinctly: "Islamic forces are ascending today because the secular option has been defeated, and the authoritarian regimes that exist in the name of secularism have made the secular option bad. Who wants to live under authoritarian rule?"

In an article titled "King Hassan's Strategy of Political Dualism," Denoeux and Maghraoui (1998) explored how the king maneuvered political situations in his country. The article began with the premise that political clientelism, a patronage system in which the king used to buy off his opposition, was no longer effective. Besides, it was becoming too costly for the king to maintain the system. Hence, the king adopted a dualistic approach, one that gives the appearance of concessions from the throne, but also a heavy-handedness that cannot be misread. According to Denoeux and Maghraoui (1998, 4), the method adopted by the king draws from the monarch's "religious authority and role as a symbol of national identity and historical continuity." Moreover "Hassan II still relies heavily on a practice, royal arbitration, that reaches deep into Morocco's past. Which side of his strategy of political dualism the King emphasizes depended in part on the situation" (Denoeux and Maghraoui 1998, 4), whether he was dealing with friends or with foes.

The Virgin and Queen Poku

Two narratives were aggressively promoted by the president and his men about Our Lady of Peace Basilica at Yamoussoukro. Both narratives were cited in Chapter 1, but we will revisit them here so that we can understand how the people of Côte d'Ivoire responded to the president and his church. The narratives will also help us understand why the president was devoted to the "Virgin," and why he dedicated his edifice to her.

The first narrative is about the myth of the origins of the Baoulé ethnic group from the ancient Ashante kingdom: the ultimate sacrifice was made by Queen Aura Poku, who threw her only son into the river, so that the tide would subside and the monsters would make way for her people to pass. According to the legend, Queen Aura Poku could only say, "ba-o-li," meaning "the child is dead," while holding back tears after she had sacrificed her child in the river. Ba-o-li is now elided to Baoulé. "From this experience, claim the

Baoulé, they derive not only their name and consciousness as a distinct group, but also the importance of matrilineal descent" (Guerry 1975, 13). The second narrative describes the president as a native who had converted to the Catholic faith and was well educated by the most "civilized culture on earth," the French.

These two narratives have a common base. First, Queen Poku was ancestor goddess to the late president. Second, conversion to Catholicism brought him closer to the Virgin Mary. Both narratives are about two women who sacrificed their children for higher objectives. Above all, the first narrative inculcated a matrilineal culture into the president.

It is not difficult to see how these two distinct female deities could be conflated into parallel religious practices that profess reincarnation, ritual sacrifice, and mystical imageries that are tied to deep-rooted fetish beliefs. Conflating Queen Poku and the Virgin is not a new phenomena in Africa; traces of such practices can be found in *Vodun, Orisa, Mami-water,* and several estranged ancestor and Christian rituals in sub-Saharan Africa.[16] Jan Vansina (1984, 46) suggests that "artistically, the taste of social classes could differ very much within a given society. In Kongo, in the sixteenth and seventeenth centuries, the upper class was Christian and adopted Christian imagery and indigenized variants of Renaissance styles, whereas most of the population remained faithful to its own art objects and their styles." Similarly, at Yamoussoukro, the president showed the elite behavior that Professor Vansina described. It is therefore not surprising that the two narratives were equally architecturally delineated by the president: the former at his private residence at Yamoussoukro, and the latter manifested as Our Lady of Peace Basilica.

In reading the president's basilica, the people of Côte d'Ivoire take their cues from how he represented himself as the chief of the Baoulé people and his relationship to Queen Poku. Popular perception is based on how he represented his chieftancy totem at a shrine that he built at his private residence at Yamoussoukro. To those who are not familiar with Western African settlement patterns, the ancestor and shrines of the deities are located in the compounds, particularly those of the Ashante, Baoulé, Hausa, Igbo, Senufo, and Yoruba compounds. The giant shrine that the president built in front of his expansive private palace might probably pass for a large pool of water for keeping his dangerous and exotic pet crocodiles. However, scholars (Blier 1987; Fassassi 1978; Moughtin 1985; Swithenbank 1969) who have studied West African settlement patterns mostly agree that certain protective shrines are often sited near the entrances of compounds, in order to keep away evil spirits, enemies, and misfortune, while at the same time facilitating good luck.

Keeping in mind that Our Lady of Peace Basilica reflected the president's Roman Catholic convictions, where does the ancestors' shrine enter in, for whom was it intended, and can one be a worshiper of the ancestors and, at the same time, a devotee of Christianity? According to Jean-Noël Loucou (1989, 34), the great pool in front of the president's residence represented the reunion of the three sacred rivers: Akundekamin, Babla, and Kangabla. And the deities it contains protect the occupants of the compound, as well as ensuring the fertility of the women. I must add that sacred ponds of that scale usually belong to the whole community and are often placed at the outskirts of the village. Rarely would one find a shrine to the ancestors on that scale in any private compound. The president's shrine reveals his ability to combine African religious traditions and European traditions into exotic artifacts that concealed his true religious choices.

The president was seen by Ivorians as being like most contemporary African leaders, who go to their ancestors for protection, prosperity, and spiritual guidance in their quotidian existence. These leaders erect shrines for the ancestors, where they offer sacrifices according to the prescriptions of the oracles (Apter 1987; Ayisi 1980; Metuh 1981; Opkarocha 1976) because there cannot be ancestor worship without offerings. At Yamoussoukro, offerings of several chickens are made to the deities, the crocodiles in his shrine, usually at midday. V. S. Naipaul (1984, 52–119) correctly identified the feeding of the president's crocodiles as a "ritual sacrifice" in his article "The Crocodiles of Yamoussoukro." According to Naipaul, "there is the Presidential palace, with its artificial lake. Outside the blank walls that hide the President's ancestral village and the palaver tree from the common view, the President's totemic crocodiles are fed with fresh meat every day. People can go and watch."

There is something more revealing. The president indulged in such practices beginning in 1953, when the crocodiles where taken from the region of Aboisso and placed in the pool when they were very little. It was the period when the president was beginning his political career. It was quite natural for him to seek the protection of his ancestors early in his career. We also learn that the president's ancestral shrine was already at the site of his mansion before he employed architect Olivier Cacoub to build the mansion in 1977. It is also likely that the pool was expanded and fenced off, following the completion of the president's private mansion. Keep in mind that the president cannot just choose his totemic animal arbitrarily; he must first consult with oracles and diviners, who make the prescriptions and determine the totemic animal, as well as the nature of the shrine to be erected (Apter 1987; Ayisi 1980; Metuh 1981; Opkarocha 1976). It implies that an oracle might have been consulted once Houphouët-Boigny decided to participate in politics. Thus, one can suggest that the president had always been attached to his ancestors regardless of his conversion to Catholicism.

Therefore, the sacred pond, which from now on I will call the "shrine" of the president, is not just an exotic pool for keeping his dangerous crocodile pets. It is the traditionally evolved totem based on oracles and diviners' prescriptions. The diviners prescribe animals that they feel are the ideal spiritual guardians of the patient. The patient begins to exhibit behaviors symbolic of their totems. Jeane Maddox Toungara (1990, 31) reminds us that "the elimination of opponents by means of human sacrifice and indiscriminate decapitation was a familiar tactic used by Ashante princes and the Ahantene. The kind of political decapitation carried out by Houphouët throughout his rise and consolidation of power might be compared to those ancient practices, in that several ambitious men were silenced by his tight-fisted manipulation of local political activities." Loucou has mentioned that the crocodiles are for the protection of the inhabitants of the compounds. Naipual (1984, 112) also has suggested that "there are three symbols of Kingship. On the savanna, the panther. In the forest, the elephant. In water, the crocodile. The crocodile is the strongest creature in the water. With one blow of that tail, it can kill a man."

The practice of adopting totemic animals and consulting ancestral oracles and gods for protection in political office is common practice in Africa. Such practices were carried to a higher extreme by several postindependence African leaders who generally had one leadership model in common: They ruled their respective countries like kings who were accountable to nobody, but the whole nation was always accountable to them. For example, Emperor Haile Selassie of Ethiopia was known as the "Lion of Judah," and he kept several lion pets. Late President Mobutu Sesseseko of Zaire, now the Democratic Republic of Congo, saw himself as the powerful African leopard, and he always wore his leopard skin hat and shirt. Emperor Jean Bodel Bokassa sat in an oversized eagle throne decorated in gold. And, finally, General Aguiyi J. Y. U. Ironsi, one-time Nigerian head of state, 1966–67, walked around with a small carved wooden *aguiyi*—crocodile—in his hand. At least, he gave that impression by carrying his carved crocodile around. Literally, the Igbo word *agu-iyi* translates to "leopard of the water." In this case Ironsi was patterning himself after his totemic animal and family name. It is therefore not surprising when Naipaul (1984, 58) wrote that in the Côte d'Ivoire, "success became an expression of the nonideological personality of the ruler, the man of an established ruling family; this rested on an African idea of authority. And at the bottom of it all was magic." The latter point has been articulated in the introduction by Murphy (1998, 566).

The president's action shortly after the consecration of his basilica gives credence to the characterization that he behaved like a crocodile whenever he wanted to destroy his political enemies. His unsubstantiated accusation of the opposition parties involvement in the alleged attempt to kill the pope, just one month before a national election, was clearly described as an attempt to drown the opposition by the archbishop of Abidjan, Mgr. Yago Sennen Andriamirado (1990, 21) also suggests that the Vatican was skeptical about the accusation against the opposition. According to Andriamirado (1990, 21): "who would want to kill the Pope anyway in the Ivory Coast?" The president's accusing fingers pointed at his nemesis, Laurent Gbagbo. Gbagbo was a major thorn in the president's flesh for not playing according to politics as usual. He mobilized trade unions and student demonstrations, and finally he forced the PDIC to allow multiparty elections in the country in 1990, the year of the consecration of the basilica.

The ongoing discussion suggests that the people of Côte d'Ivoire saw two sides of the president. They saw the side that they feared, the crocodile personality, and they also saw the side that they admired, the Our Lady of Peace personality. Moreover, to the citizens of his country, he was the powerful man who single-handedly ruled their country for thirty-two years. Thus, when the people of Côte d'Ivoire think about the edifice that the president built, they are reminded of the economic situation under which the edifice was realized, as well as his ambivalent personalities: the ancestor worshiper and the devoted Catholic. Keeping in mind what Professors Rapoport (1982) and Duncan (1990) have said about how environmental cues influence our behaviors in different settings, one might ask which Houphouët-Boigny the people of Côte d'Ivoire believe.

A Site for Social Differentiation and Performances

Many years ago several
Of you here present planted a champion yam.

> Well, that yam you sowed several seasons gone by
> Has now grown beyond arm's span. (Johnson Pepper Clark, 1959)

> What does it mean in the African context then to claim and live out the dignity of being God's children today? It means getting rid of the misconceptions inculcated in us that we are inferior and that ours is a "dark continent." (Muita 1998, 147)

The great fence around the compound of Our Lady of Peace Basilica has drawn a powerful line that differentiates the Versailles-like gardens from the untamed bushes in the premises beyond the compound (Fig. 15). Most important, it has determined when people can go to the premises and when they cannot. This control of access to the premises undermines anything I know about church compounds in West Africa. Generally speaking, the church compounds were called missions, due to their colonial missionary origins. The missions were always open for people to wander through and lounge under the shades of the trees. This was particularly true in the villages, where there were few churches. The experience of the mission compound as a place for people to wander and meditate under the shades cannot be realized at the compound of the basilica. It is controlled: One has to enter when it is open for tourists, and leave when it is closed, except on Sundays or for special Christian events. Admittedly, the premises must be maintained and the money collected goes for that, but the president also left a vast endowment for that purpose.

On Christmas Eve 1998, I was expecting Yamoussoukro to be a crowded place, with pilgrims rushing to the edifice and preparing for services or engaging in some Catholic religious activity or another. To my disappointment, only a handful of tourists were at the basilica on that day. Like the empty broad streets, empty golf courses, empty complex of Houphouët-Boigny Peace Foundation, empty PDIC headquarters, underoccupied seven-star hotels, underenrolled universities, and underutilized amenities in the town of Yamoussoukro, Our Lady of Peace Basilica was empty. Admittedly, *Jeune Afrique* published recently that up to 100,000 people visited the shrine in 1998. That is a start. The fact still remains: The people of Yamoussoukro and the edifice are far apart from each other.

Inside the church, around the choir, can be found band instruments and drums, which the church plays during worship, reminiscent of African music. A traditional harvest festival, which often followed the cycles of the seasons, involved rituals and masquerade festivities. Offerings of sacrifices to the ancestors and different deities that occupied the various pantheons of agriculture for different ethnic groups were easily appropriated to the celebrations of Christmas by the early European missionaries who visited sub-Saharan Africa. It was easy for their converts to adapt the old traditions to the new religion because they believed in giving thanks to God or gods and deities for their crops, the seasons of the year, and the cycles of life. Whereas such performances can be enacted on occasions at the basilica, they also have to be represented visually in order to tie them to the quotidian existence of the worshipers. Making such images permanent would fossilize them in the consciousness of the worshipers, as suggested by Davies (1996, 4).

Such performances dramatize farmers, old and young, mothers with babies on their backs, children carrying firewood, cooking containers, and utensils for carrying water. Fishermen, hunters, and people in all agricultural and different crafts that support village life are often represented, including the elders of the village who are the priests to the shrines of the ancestors and the deities. Usually, the dramas are accompanied by throbbing rhythmic music from the talking drum that invokes the traditional village scene. However, in recent times, the lyrics of the music have been Christianized. When properly staged, the dramas can be moving experiences. I must emphasize again that the Italian architect, Aldo Spirito, acknowledged the existence of such traditions in African ritual practices at his Abidjan Cathedral of St. Paul.

On the other hand, the reality of the architecture of the basilica does not reflect any aspect of this indigenous African performance. According to Victor Turner (1986, 23), cultural performances such as these are "cultural media"—modes of communication that include not only spoken language but such nonlinguistic media as "song, dance, acting out, and graphic and plastic arts," which can be combined in different ways to express the contents of a culture.[17] Turner also wrote that "cultural performance" such as this is a mode of symbolic action, a mode of communication that constitutes the "peculiar relationship between the mundane, everyday sociocultural processes (domestic, economic, political, legal and the like)" that can be found in different societies: tribal, feudal, socialist, and capitalist. Turner elucidates further that the performative genres do more than "reflect" or "express" the social system or cultural configuration. Instead, they are also "reflexive" and direct or indirect critiques of the social order it "grows out of, an evaluation (with lively possibilities of rejection of) of the way societies handles history."

The implication of the disconnection between the performances and the architecture of the basilica goes beyond the quotidian experiences of the people of

Côte d'Ivoire. It reinforces a historical narrative that does not acknowledge the role of African culture and history in the Church. In an essay titled "Beyond the Discontinuity Paradigm: Towards a Pan-African Church History," R. Joseph Hoffmann (1997, 136) discusses the problems of teaching Christianity in Africa from a model of a discontinuous past grounded on the falsity that Christianity was to be spread in Africa in terms of "export and import," or in terms of early north African and later south African dissemination history. Calling it the "discontinuity paradigm," Hoffmann asserts that it posits a historical approach based on the notion that "a dark age beset the church in Africa between the rise of Islam and the missionary counter-offensive in sub-Saharan Africa, the brief, sporadic and largely unsuccessful interlude provided by Portuguese missionaries in coastal Africa being sometimes cited as a partial exception." On the contrary, Hoffmann (1997, 136) proposes a regional-based church history of Africa, which must repatriate intellectual works produced by figures like "Tertullian, Cyprian, Origen and Augustine, names long since regarded by Western thinkers as the paradigmatic figures of early theological construction." Such an approach would eliminate what he considers an intellectual apartheid, which sometimes appropriated even the Ethiopian Church into European church history, leaving African Christians isolated from their own religious roots. W. H. C. Frend's study on the Donatist movement of North Africa in the fourth century A.D. also espouses similar views as Hoffmann. The most ambitious and recent works along this line celebrating Africa's church history is by Adrian Hasting (1994), *The Church in Africa: 1450–1950.* Hasting discusses the history of the African church during the 1400s, with the Ethiopian Church as its point of departure.

My point is, Africa's church experience and history should have been dramatized visually on the stained glasses of the basilica in a manner similar to those of Aldo Spirito's cathedral, so that the illustrations can serve as educational tools for the worshipers in the church, as well as histories empowering the people to advocate for their rights and orient their self-identity. As it stands, the music played in the church and the cultural values encoded on the stained glasses of the basilica are not in harmony. They are too far apart. Whereas the musical performances during worship delineate African cultures, the visual messages all around such performers do not make any effort to include African people within the Christian narrative, as Aldo Spirito has demonstrated.

Consequently, the Yamoussoukro basilica recoups every repressive cultural policy that had been practiced by the colonialists in Africa. As a matter of fact, it exceeds all built, colonial-inspired chauvinist projects on the continent. It falls within the category of the discourse that Jean-Paul Sartre described as "anti-racist's racism." Here, the anticolonialist, antiracial segregationist, and peace-loving leader is himself the segregationist. His segregation is based purely on social hierarchy and educational enculturation. His basilica is primarily a façade designed to demonstrate the extent to which the president was able to accept his former colonizers' culture. In doing so, he also recouped the colonial practice of subjugating his own African heritage. His choice regrettably primitivizes the African continent by incorporating only the exotic aspects of the continent into the basilica, the decorative leaves and the red soil, as the architect has indicated. Incorporating Africa's wildlife into the basilica is inconsonant with the worldviews of the elite with whom the president aligned himself. To "reject the exoticization of Africa is to destroy an entire worldview carefully and painstakingly fabricated over several centuries" (Oguibe 1998, 322). Pierre Fakhoury understood this worldview properly, and he demonstrated it in his design. By so doing, the ideology recoups all the colonial argument that Africa is a continent that has neither civilization nor history, and it confirms what Sartre has said about the "antiracist racism." Moreover, the basilica at Yamoussoukro dramatizes the historical condition that "incarnates three overlapping powers: the colonial state, science, and Christianity" (Mudimbe 1991, 4) for the purposes of grounding three arenas of conversion as follows: first, the colonial administrators' "transmutation of 'savage-spaces' into civilized settings"; second, the domain of anthropological research that classified "humans, institutions, and beliefs by their particularity," based on a functional model; finally, the role of the Christian missionaries who believed that they have made "self-sacrifice among 'primitives' in the struggle between the true-light and the local tradition."

One of the points that needs to be mentioned is this: At Yamoussoukro, we are also dealing with problems that are inherently tied to multiple personalities and identity crises, an issue that also relates to the French colonial policy of assimilation that I mentioned in the introduction. The Yamoussoukro case is not new. It differentiates the architectural taste, cultural orientation, and social affiliation of a president who felt that he was fully assimilated into the French culture from those who have not been fully assimilated. Such practices and mechanisms of differentiation have been observed for a long time by scholars who study postcolonial leaders of Africa. For example, Frantz Fanon's *The Wretched of the Earth* (1961) and *Black Skin, White Masks* (1952/1967) and

Ali Mazrui's (1986) *The African: A Triple Heritage* all elucidate the identity crisis that confronts the elite and the intellectuals of African postcolonial states, despite the fact that they have deep knowledge of their native cultures and history. Anthony Appiah (1992, 68) acknowledges that third world intellectuals are a contradiction because they are a product of a "particular social formation" that originates from a "historical encounter with the West."

CONCLUSION: A CRITIQUE OF UTOPIAN ART IN AFRICA, 1960–2000

I began this project on the premise that Our Lady of Peace Basilica and the Hassan II Mosque are products of ideological alignments that are tied to the colonial times and the independence eras in Africa. Using the term "ideology" along similar lines as Mannheim (1985, 40), I suggested that in "certain situations," like postindependent Côte d'Ivoire and Morocco, in the 1960s and later, where there were ongoing social conflicts, "the collective unconscious of certain groups obscured the real condition of society both to itself and to others and thereby stabilized it."

Based on a selected list of monuments and nationally inspired cultural programs from across the continent, I am going to conclude by expanding my usage of Mannheim's thesis beyond the borders of Côte d'Ivoire and Morocco. I hope to emphasize that, if Africa's nationalist art and architecture ideologies are located in the colonial and the postcolonial times, we will discover that they incorporate certain elements of "utopian mentality." In such a mentality, an indigenous elite that felt marginalized by the colonial authorities is intellectually motivated to replace the status quo to the extent that it "unwittingly sees only those elements in the society that tend to negate its" objective. Here, the belief of the principal actors, the marginalized African elite, is "never a diagnosis of the situation; it can be used only as a direction for action" (Mannheim 1985, 40), which results in monumental urban "wishful representations" like Our Lady of Peace Basilica and the Hassan II Mosque.

I must also emphasize that each project needs to be evaluated within the fluctuating economic, political, and social setting in which it is produced. For example, the particular ideologies adopted by the president and the king favored Western models of production of material life. However, the two leaders combined the models with their aristocratic heritage, which mostly favored themselves and their immediate supporters in their respective governments. As a result, several social boundaries between the leaders, the states, and the citizens of the respective countries were dissolved. There is a strong irony in each project. The builders of the programs truly believed that they were the antithesis of colonial legacies. However, in the processes of realizing the programs, they recouped all the characteristics of colonial-inspired projects. The reason is this: The projects were designed to function as tools for reforming the collective memories of the citizens in order to suit the exigencies of the leaders, just as the colonialists were invested in transforming the memories of the people whom they colonized from free citizens into colonial subjects.

There are several methods of cleansing the collective memories of communities. Architecture is one of the most powerful methods by virtue of its visibility, stability, multiple functions, history, and of course, visual representations. It is therefore not surprising that, at Casablanca and Yamoussoukro, architecture has been deployed as the core for collective rituals: (1) for cleansing the present of past memories; (2) for strengthening and constructing a desired future; and (3) for idealizing and representing the present as if it is perfect. This was too much to ask of architecture. In both cases, the demands that the leaders made upon architecture and its visual representations undermined all the ideals of the projects. In the Côte d'Ivoire, Houphouët-Boigny would not be the last leader to exploit architecture for political gains.

In December 1998, when I was in Abidjan around the luxury Quartier Ambassades, part of the exclusive Cocody neighborhood, I observed construction activities in a fenced premise that used to be the state house for President Houphouët-Boigny. The old residence had been demolished, and the construction of a new a complex was in progress. There were security men all over the premises.

The question occurred to me: Why would the government of Côte d'Ivoire build a new presidential complex at Abidjan when it is planning to move to its luxury capital city, Yamoussoukro? To me, the construction of a new presidential complex at Abidjan, on the very site where President Houphouët-Boigny used to reside and rule the country for thirty-two years, was an indicator of self-assertion by the new president, Konan Bedie, who has since been overthrown, in December 1999. I also knew that President Bedie was cleansing the quarters, erasing the memories of his predecessor, but he barely made a dent before he was deposed in a military coup.

President Konan Bedie's cleansing activities in Abidjan were not new. Such programs have been going on in Africa for a long time. Often, they were aimed at reformulating the memories of the citizens, through the consolidation of certain historical and mythical narratives. Also, they incorporated certain ideologies that have to do with social hierarchy, the production of material life, social space, and the senses of belonging and exclusion. Of all the most exclusionary monuments built in Africa, the Vootrekker monument in Pretoria, Republic of South Africa, is the most prominent and ideologically oppressive. Constructed to commemorate what Afrikaners considered as their "covenant" with God for giving them the land, not to mention vanquishing the majority of their fellow citizens, the project was driven by the ideology of apartheid, the horrors of which we need not retell here.

When President Robert Mugabe of Zimbabwe came to power in 1979, one of the first urban policies he implemented was the removal of the colossal monument of Cecil Rhodes from its location at Jameson's Square, Harare. Mugabe's primary reason for this action involved the fact that the monument reminded him too much of apartheid, and he wanted to get rid of it. Mugabe's decision, surely, had to do with the aims of reconstructing the national memory and identity of the people of Zimbabwe. The social setting in which the object was produced was definitely not the most memorable one for the Zimbabweans. The application of toponomy after independence, changing the name of the country from Rhodesia to Zimbabwe, and the name of the capital city from Salisbury to Harare, is part of the memory reformulation ritual.

Ghana is the first sub-Saharan African country to gain independence. The occasion has long been memorialized in Accra. President Kwame Nkrumah's independence arch is one of the most self-contradictory monuments in postcolonial Africa. The arch, finished in beautiful stonework with inscriptions of "Freedom and Justice," could be standing in Berlin, London, Paris, Rome, or any other Western capital. It is clearly an adaptation of the concept of the Roman triumphal arch for the celebration of Ghana's freedom from the British. Is the adoption of a Roman-based iconography for the celebration of an African victory an oversight or a deliberate act, and how can one ignore the identity and memory crisis that results from such an oversight or deliberate decision? The whole of the Western Sudan, most of West Africa, particularly northern Ghana, Mali, and Hausa in northern Nigeria, are full of different kinds of architectonic precedents of entry pylons and plazas. In ancient cities like Kano, Nigeria; Zaria, Nigeria; and Jenne in Mali, the plazas usually served as the meeting places between the leaders and their citizens. They often constituted the major nodes for cultural celebrations because the markets, mosques, civic buildings, and royal palaces were the major structures that encircled the main plaza and facilitated its unique characteristics. Often, each building or structure elegantly displayed its own pylon. Some of them adopted visual forms that replicated faces of ancestor masks, and columns, which represented the sacred processes of reproduction and the continuity of the cultures. Also, they represented the solidity of the structures and the protection of the ancestors. How does one explain Nkrumah's far-fetched triumphal arch?

It was in Ethiopia, during the socialist regime of Mengistu Haile-Mariam, that the exploitation of art and architecture to reformulate national memories reached its peak in the recent history of Africa. The ideologies of socialism determined the construction of the Tiglachin, the Karl Marx, and the Lenin monuments. The structures were designed to commemorate the tenth anniversary (12 September 1984) of the overthrow of Emperor Haile-Selassie on 12 September 1974. The Mengistu regime was inspired to act and produce these objects as a symbolic replacement for the imperial regime of Selassie, with its Lion of Judah symbols. This is the point that Mannheim elucidated clearly in his definition of utopia mentality. "Our Struggle" is the English translation of "Tiglachin" from the official language of Ethiopia, Amharic. The Tiglachin memorial is a 50-meter-tall triangular column, which was located in a 30,000-square-meter park in front of the Black Lion Hospital, Addis Ababa. It has three parts: (1) a central column with a highly decorated twenty-ton base, showing a relief of the soldiers who fought for the Ethiopian revolution. The visual message of the relief paints a picture of Ethiopia before and after the 1974 revolution, and it suggests that the people of Ethiopia were better off after the revolution. "To the left and right of the central column are flag-shaped tableaux with profiles of Comrade Chairman Mengistu—and a cross-section of the Ethiopian people" (12 September 1984). The narrative propagated by the Tiglachin was designed to announce the miseries and sufferings of the Ethiopian people before the revolution. On the right are depicted the efforts of the working people of Ethiopia, their dedication to building a material and technical foundation for a brighter future through the guidance of ideologies of socialism. (2) The median part of the column, at the height of thirty meters, is decorated by Ethiopia's highest national award for heroes. The Heroes Medallion weighs 700 kilograms and has a diameter of 2.7 meters. (3) Finally, the apex of the column is topped with a large star, one of the emblems of socialism, at the height of fifty meters. The monuments of Karl Marx and Lenin were simultaneously produced and inaugurated for the same anniversary, an event that took place when Ethiopia was going through one of its worse droughts in recent history. Tens of millions of dollars that could have been used for feeding the needy were being diverted for the monuments and the celebrations.

One of the greatest errors committed by the erection of these expensive socialist-inspired monuments was the attempt to completely erase all aspects of Ethiopian visual culture. Columns (stelae or obelisks) have been in Ethiopia since the ancient times, particularly the period of Aksum, which scholars date between 100 B.C. and 300 B.C. (Selassie 1972, 61). What inspired Colonel Mengistu to believe that he could erase that history? The Ethiopian culture endured, while the Megistu government collapsed in 1992.

In the Central African Republic (CAR), the deposed Emperor Jean Bedel Bokassa spent tens of millions of dollars earned from the nation's diamond riches to purchase from France an imperial crown and a gigantic throne that were lavishly decorated with gold and diamonds for the personal hubris of crowning himself the emperor of CAR. In Alexandria, Egypt, a new national library was constructed (clearly an evocation of the legendary library of ancient Alexandria, which was supposedly burned down), and the people of Egypt now aspire to utilize the new center as an instrument for elevating the intellectual profile of the city and the country as a whole, as a center of knowledge among the nations of the world. In Abuja, Nigeria, tens of billions of dollars have been spent in the construction and inauguration of a new federal capital. These projects have often mirrored the ideologies of the elite who commissioned them, and they often recreated all the evils of colonialism that they set out to erase.

One day, these edifices will truly be the people's forums. That will be in the distant future, which will inevitably come. Hope tells me so.

NOTES

1. I am using the concept of "public sphere" here along the lines of Jürgen Habermas, which Diane Ghirardo (1996, 43) has explored very well in her book *Architecture after Modernism.*

2. See Gombrich (1969, 242–287), Rapoport (1977, 111), Hatcher (1985, 85), Duncan (1990, 17), and Schapiro (1994, 32).

3. *The Economist* 315, no. 7650 (14 April 1990): 52.

4. Ibid.

5. One must be careful and conscious of the use of the words "Islamic fundamentalism." It is definitely not a neutral terminology, and it has been invented by the Western press as a tool for demonizing those whose religious philosophies they disagree with. It functions in a similar way that a racial stereotype might function against any ethnic group around the world, but it is often taken for granted because it is applied to religion. Perhaps, an appropriate term might be religious activists, and each group must be evaluated based on its social philosophy and platform.

6. See Nehme (1993, 7) and Nickson (1989, 47).

7. See *Jeune Afrique*, no. 999 (27 February 1980): 45.

8. Omar Bendourou (1990, 133–163) gives a good history about the reinstatement of democratic elections in Algeria since 1962 in his article "Les Reformes Democratique en Algérie."

9. *Morocco Country Report*, no. 2, 1990, London: *The Economist* Intelligence Unit, pp. 8–9. Also see no. 3, 1990, pp. 10 and 6; no. 1, 1992, pp. 7, 11, and 12; and no. 2, 1992, p. 10.

10. *Morocco Country Report*, no. 2, 1992, London: *The Economist* Intelligence Unit, p. 10.

11. Ibid.

12. See Soudan (1990, 4–5) for the piece on human rights and the rights of the state.

13. It should also be kept in focus that the social unrest was worsened by severe economic condition due to an IMF-prescribed structural adjustment program. See Santucci (1986, 749–755); "Morocco: Watching for Trouble," *Africa Confidential* 31, no. 8 (20 April 1990): 5–6; and Bussink (1991, 465–474).

14. Numerous articles in recent years adopted Elissa Sampson's (1993) views in "Islam Politicized: In the Middle East, Is the Mosque the Only Resort for Change?" Some of these essays believe that many countries in the Islamic part with large Islamic populations are also trying to use religion to sway the opinions of the masses to believe in their governments. See Harrison (1994, 35) and Engel (1998, 38). There are scholars who espouse the view that the search for self and group identity in addition to political participation might have instigated the Ayodhaya Mosque incident in India on 6 December 1992 following the destruction of Holy Moslem shrine by Hindu militants. See Tilly (1998, 491).

15. See *The Economist* 344, no. 8027 (26 July 1997): 6 and 346, no. 8053 (31 January 1998): 47; and Nehme (1993, 7).

16. The Blier (1995) study of Vodun is a good source for familiarizing one's self with the multiple links between several religious rituals in West Africa.

17. Victor Turner (1986) wrote this passage in relation to the 1972 work of Milton Singer, *When a Great Civilization Modernizes*, which discussed Indian culture. The application here is my own adaptation of the thesis that I believe applies.

REFERENCES

Andriamirado, Sennen. 10–16 October 1990. "Mai Qui Voulait Donc Tuer la Pape?" *Jeune Afrique,* no. 1554: 20–21.

Appiah, Anthony. 1992. *In My Father's House.* New York: Oxford University Press.

Apter, Herman Andrew. 1987. "Rituals of Power: The Politics of Orisa Worship in Yoruba Society." Ph.D. diss., Yale University.

Ayisi, Eric, O. 1980. *An Introduction to the Study of African Culture.* London: Heinemann.

Bendourou, Omar. 1990. "Les Réformes Démocratique en Algérie." *Maghreb Review* 15, no. 3–4: 133–163.

Bidwell, Robin. 1993. "History." In *The Middle East and North Africa,* 39th ed., 702. London: Europa Publications.

Blier, Suzanne Preston. 1987. *The Anatomy of Architecture: The Ontology and Metaphor in Batammaliba Architectural Expression.* Chicago: University of Chicago Press.

———. 1995. *African Vodun: Art, Psychology, and Power.* Chicago: University of Chicago Press.

Bussink, Norbert, 1991. "La Presse d'Opposition Marocaine et la Guerre du Golfe; l'Impact d'un Événement Extérieur Sur la Politique Intérieure." In *Annuaire de L'Afrique du Nord,* vol. 30, 465–474. Paris: Édition du Centre National de la Recherche Scientifique.

Clark, Johnson Pepper. 1959/1970. "Champion Yam." *Journal of the New African Literature and the Arts* 2, no. 4.

Davis, Whitney. 1996. *Replications Archeology Art History Psychoanalysis.* With the editorial assistance of Richard W. Quinn. University Park: Pennsylvania State University Press.

Denoeux, Guilain, and Maghraoui Abdeslam. 1998. "King Hassan's Strategy of Political Dualism." *Middle East Policy* 5, no. 4: 104–131.

Duncan, James. 1990. *The City as a Text: The Politics of Landscape Interpretation in the Kandyan Kingdom.* Cambridge: Cambridge University Press.

Eaton, Gail. 1993. "Light from the Center." *Parabola* 48, no. 4: 48–52.

Engel, Richard. 17 August 1998. "Modernizing the Mosque: Moslem Leaders Disagree on How to Modernize Islam." *Insight on the News* 14, no. 30: 38.

Fanon, Frantz. 1952. "The Negro and Language." In *Black Skin, White Masks,* trans. Charles Lam Markmann, 17–40. New York: Grove Press, 1967.

———. 1961. "Concerning Violence." In *The Wretched of the Earth,* trans. Constance Farrington, preface by Jean-Paul Sartre, 35–106. New York: Grove Press.

Fassassi, Masudi Alabi. 1978. *L'architecture en Afrique Noire: Cosmoarchitecture.* Paris: F. Maspero.

Ghirardo, Diane. 1996. *Architecture after Modernism* London: Thames and Hudson.

Gombrich, Ernst Hans. 1969. *Art and Illusion: A Study in the Psychology of Pictorial Representation.* 2d ed. Princeton, N.J.: Princeton University Press.

Guerry, Vincent. 1975. *Life with the Baoulé,* trans. Nora Hodges. Washington: Three Continents Press.

Harrison, Drew. 1994. "Restoration of Holy Shrine." *Middle East,* no. 235 (June): 35.

Hasting, Adrian. 1994. *The Church in Africa: 1450–1950.* Oxford: Clarendon Press

Hatcher, Evelyn Payne. 1985. *Art as Culture: An Introduction to the Anthropology of Art,* introduction by E. Adamson Hoebel. Lanham, Md.: University Press of America.

Hillier, Bill, and Julienne Hanson. 1984. *The Social Logic of Space.* New York: Cambridge University Press.

Hoffmann, R. Joseph. 1997. "Beyond the Discontinuity Paradigm: Towards a Pan-African Church History." *Journal of Religious History* 21, no. 2: 136–159.

Jeune Afrique. 27 February 1980. No. 999: 45.

Loucou, Jean-Noël. 1989. *Yamoussoukro; Guide Pratique.* Abidjan: Ministère de l'Information de Côte d'Ivoire.

Mannheim, Karl. 1936/1985. *Ideology and Utopia, an Introduction to the Sociology of Knowledge.* New York: Harcourt Brace & Company.

Mazrui, Ali Al' Amin. 1986. *The Africans: A Triple Heritage.* London: BBC Publications.

Metuh, Emefie Ikenga. 1981. *God and Man in African Religion.* London: Geoffrey Chapman Book and Cassell.

Morocco Country Report, no. 2, 1990, London: *The Economist* Intelligence Unit, pp. 8–9.

———, no. 3, 1990, pp. 10 and 6.

———, no. 4, 1991/1992, p. 6.

———, no. 1, 1992, pp. 7, 11, 12.

———, no. 2, 1992, p. 10.

———, no. 1, 1993, pp. 8, 9.

———, no. 3, 1993, pp. 8, 9.

———, no. 4, 1993, pp. 10, 11.

"Morocco: Watching for Trouble." 20 April 1990. *Africa Confidential* 31, no. 8: 5–6.

Moughtin, J. Cliff. 1985. *Hausa Architecture.* London: Ethnographica in association with Institute of Planning Studies, University of Nottingham.

Mudimbe, V. Y. 1991. *Parables and Fables. Exegesis, Texuality, and Politics in Central Africa.* Madison: University of Wisconsin Press.

Muita, Isreal. 1998. "Turning to God: Claiming Our Identity and Responsibility as God's Children." *International Reviews of Missions* 87, no. 347: 485–492.

Naipaul, V. S. 1984. "The Crocodiles of Yamoussoukro." *New Yorker* 60 (14 May): 52–119.

Nehme, Michel G. 1993. "Saudi Arabia 1950–80: Between Nationalism and Religion." *Middle East,* no. 227 (October): 7.

Nickson, Liz. 1989. "Mega Mosque: Allah Be Praised and Hassan II." *Life* 12, no. 10 (September): 47.

Oguibe, Olu. 1998. "In the 'Heart of Darkness.' " In *Art History and Its Methods: A Critical Anthology,* 314–322. London: Phaidon.

Okparocha, John. 1976. *Mbari Art as Sacrifice.* Ibadan, Nigeria: Daystar Press.

Pickens, Samuel 1995. *Maroc: Les Cités Impériales: Fès, Marrakech, Meknès, Rabat-Salé.* Texte de Samuel Pickens; photographies de Françoise Peuriot et Philippe Ploquin. Courbevoie, Paris: ACR Edition.

Ploquin, Philippe, and Mohammed-Allal Sinaceur. 1993. *La Mosquée Hassan II* (*The Hassan II Mosque*). Photographiée par Philippe Ploquin et Francis Peuriot; textes de Mohammed-Allal Sinaceur; assisté par Mustapha Kasri, Ali Amahane, Houceïne Kasri. Drémil-Lafage: Editions D. Briand.

Rapoport, Amos. 1977. *Human Aspects of Urban Form. Towards a Man-Environment Approach to Urban Form and Design.* New York: Pergamon Press.

———. 1982. *The Meaning of the Built Environment.* London: Sage.

Sampson, Elissa. 1 March 1993. "Islam Politicized: In the Middle East, Is the Mosque the Only Resort for Change?" *Christianity and Crisis* 53, no. 3: 60.

Santucci, J. C. 1986. "Turbulence Diplomatiques et remous politiques internes." In *Annuaire de L'Afrique du Nord,* vol. 25, 749–755. Paris: Édition du Centre National de la Recherche Scientifique.

Schapiro, Meyre. 1994. *Theory and Philosophy of Art: Style, Artist, and Society. Selected Papers.* New York: George Braziller.

Selassie, Sergre Hable. 1972. *Ancient and Medieval Ethiopian History to 1270.* Addis Ababa, Ethiopia.

Sijilmassi, Mohammed. 1986. *Les Arts Traditionnels au Maroc.* Préf. de Jean Duvignaud. Paris: ACR Edition Internationale, Vilo.

Soudan, Francois. 21 May 1990. "Maroc: des droits del l'État à l'État de droit." *Jeune Afrique,* no. 1533: 4–5.

Swithenbank, Michael. 1969. *Ashanti Fetish Houses.* Accra, Ghana: Ghana Universities Press.

The Economist 315, no. 7650 (14 April 1990): 52.

——— 344, no. 8027 (26 July 1997): 6.

——— 346, no. 8053 (31 January 1998): 47.

——— 326, no. 7802 (13 March 1993): 49–50.

Tilly, Charles. 1998. "Contentious Conversation." *Social Research* 65, no. 3 (Fall): 491.

Toungara, Jeanne Maddox. 1990. "The Apotheosis of Côte d'Ivoire's Nana Houphouët-Boigny." *Journal of Modern African Studies* 28, no. 1: 23–54.

Turner, Victor. 1986. *The Anthropology of Performance.* New York: PAJ Publications.

Vale, Lawrence. 1992. *Architecture, Power and National Identity.* New Haven, Conn.: Yale University Press.

Vansina, Jan C. 1984. *Art History in Africa: An Introduction to Method.* New York: Longman.

Glossary of Select Architectural Terms

Aisle: A part of a church alongside the nave, choir, or transept, arranged by rows of columns or piers.
Ambulatory: A passageway surrounding the apse of a church or a shrine.
Arcade: A series of arches supported by columns.
Architectonic: Relating to technical architectural principles or practice.
Balcony: A projecting platform on a building, sometimes supported from below, sometimes cantilevered. Often balconies are decorated and enclosed with railings or balustrades.
Basilica: A Roman palace of justice, court, or auditorium. It often had a high central space, the nave, and was lit by a clerestory; sometimes it had a lower aisle all around the central nave. Early Christian churches adopted the plan and the form of the Roman basilica.
Basilical plan: See basilica.
Capital: The topmost member of a column.
Citadel: A fortification; a fortified place or city.
Clerestory: An upper zone or a wall mounted with windows to allow natural light into the center of a tall room.
Cloister: A covered walk surrounding a court usually linking a church to other buildings.
Clustered column: Columns that are grouped together, sometimes physically connected to function as one structural member.
Column: A pillar serving as support to a building or a structure.
Corinthian: The most ornate of the three Greek orders of architecture. It is characterized by the distinguishing features of its bell-shaped capital adorned with rows of simplified acanthus leaves.
Dome: A vaulted roof of circular, polygonal, or elliptical plan formed with hemispherical curvature.

Doric: The oldest and simplest of the three Greek orders of architecture.

Façade: The face of a structure or a building. The exterior sides of a building or a structure. Also known as the elevation.

Finial: An ornament that terminates the points of a spire, pinnacle, cross, etc.

Flute: A groove or channel used for decorating columns.

Frieze: A continuous piece of painted or sculptured decoration. In a classical building, the part of the entablature between the architrave and the cornice.

Labyrinth: A structure or plan with intricate and multiple passages.

Lintel: A horizontal structural member (a beam) spanning over an opening and carrying the weight of the masonry above it.

Madassa: A theological school that provides Moslem students with lodging, prayer hall, and sometimes with classrooms.

Mausoleum: Tombs or funerary monuments.

Mezzanine: A low-ceilinged story or balcony usually constructed near the ground floor.

Mihrab: The small niche that indicates the *qibla* wall of a mosque showing the direction of Mecca.

Minaret: A tower with balconies from which Muslims are summoned to prayer. They also functioned as defensive watch stations.

Mouqarnas: A decorative design on columns, walls, domes, and other parts of buildings. It often involves multiple combinations of three-dimensional shapes corbeling.

Nave: The central aisle of a basilica.

Pier: A column designed to support a concentrated load.

Pilaster: An engaged pillar or pier with capital and base; decorated features that imitated engaged pillars but do not carry any weight; a projection of the wall often with capital, shaft, and base. Pilasters also decorated entrances, fireplaces, etc.

Portal: A monumental entrance, door, or gate.

Pylon: Monumental gateway to an Egyptian temple.

Qibla: The element that indicates the direction of Mecca in a mosque. It is marked by a *mihrab*, and Moslems face it during prayers.

Rotunda: A structure that is round both outside and inside, sometimes domed.

Sanctuary: A sacred or holy place within a building.

Souk: A bazaar; a marketplace, consisting of many narrow streets that are roofed and often interconnected with one another. They are flanked by shops on all sides.

Stalactite work: See mouqarnas.

Stucco: An exterior finish that is usually textured. It can be made out of a mixture of Portland cement, lime, and sand.

Symmetry: Similarity of form or arrangement on either side of a dividing line; balance of form on all sides.

Terrace: A paved, elevated, flat roof or platform (space) adjoining a building.

Zellij: An ornamentation on the wall, floor, ceiling of a building made with multiple colored pieces of stone in the form of a mosaic.

Index

About the Author

NNAMDI ELLEH is Assistant Professor of Architecture at the College of Design, Art, Architecture & Planning (DAAP), and was a Samuel Ittleson Fellow at the Center for Advanced Study in the Visual Arts (CASVA), National Gallery of Art, Washington, D.C.